COMMITTED TO DISILLUSION

COMMITTED TO DISILLUSION

Activist Writers in Egypt in the 1960s–1980s

DAVID F. DIMEO

The American University in Cairo Press
Cairo New York

First published in 2016 by
The American University in Cairo Press
113 Sharia Kasr el Aini, Cairo, Egypt
420 Fifth Avenue, New York, NY 10018
www.aucpress.com

Exclusive distribution outside Egypt and North America by I.B.Tauris & Co Ltd., 6 Salem Road, London, W4 2BU

Dar el Kutub No. 14557/15
ISBN 978 977 416 761 4

Dar el Kutub Cataloging-in-Publication Data

DiMeo, David
Committed to Disillusion / David DiMeo.—Cairo: The American University in Cairo Press, 2016
p. cm.
ISBN 978 977 416 761 4
1. Arabic Literature – History and Criticism
I. Title
II. 892.709

1 2 3 4 5 20 19 18 17 16

Designed by Sally Boylan
Printed in the United States of America

Contents

Note on Transliteration and Translation

In writing in English about Arabic literature and history, one always faces the difficult questions of what to translate, what to transliterate, and how. Given the myriad of transliteration systems in use, a reader can find Naguib Mahfouz's name, for example, rendered as Najib Mahfouz, Najib Mahfuz, Naguib Mahfuz, or Neguib Mahfouz in various sources. Recognizing that there is no perfect mean between consistency, ease of use, and familiarity, I have struck a balance. For those authors who have established their own preferred English transliterations of their names (such as Alaa Al Aswany and Ibrahim Abdel Meguid), or those rare historic figures known by a single transliteration in English (such as former Egyptian president Nasser), I have kept with the established rendering. For other names and terms—the vast majority—that have no consistent English transliterations, I have applied the Library of Congress transliteration system with some modifications for ease of use. Each Arabic letter is represented by a corresponding English letter or combination of letters, with the left-facing single quotation mark (') representing the Arabic *hamza* and the right-facing single quotation mark (‘) representing the Arabic *‘ayn*. No diacritical marks have been used, nor have I distinguished long and short vowels. The Arabic definite article has been written as *al-*, regardless of whether the letter *l* would be assimilated in normal pronunciation (thus, the title of Naguib Mahfouz's novel *The Beggar* is transliterated as *al-Shahhadh*, rather than *ash-Shahhat*, as it would be pronounced).

Unless otherwise noted, all translations of Arabic quotations from original sources are my own. For ease of use, I will generally refer to Arabic literary works by their English titles, although my sources are the original Arabic texts, as noted in the the bibliography. In cases where I have quoted an Arabic writer or speaker from an English-language secondary source (as noted in the citation), I have kept the English author's translation. For the numerous Russian, German, and French writers quoted, I have relied on English translations as noted in the citations.

Preface and Acknowledgments

For a movement that once claimed to "dominate" Arabic literature, the fate of committed Arabic writing *(al-adab al-multazim)* in the years after the 1952 Egyptian revolution has been little treated in literary history. This gap became particularly acute after the (unexpected) 2011 revolution, which was influenced in no small part by activist Egyptian writers. The question of what became of *al-adab al-multazim* in the years between the highs of 1952 and 2011 is of great importance to the study of Arabic literature, Egyptian society and culture, the Arabic language, and, perhaps most importantly, for the question of the power of the literature to effect real social and political change.

This book aims to fill that gap through the study of three exemplars of socially engaged writing in Egypt, but also through the comparative study of committed literature movements in a variety of different countries. In this way, I hope this study will be of value not only to students of Arabic literature but also to students of world literature or of any national literature with a trend of socially engaged writing. One need not read or speak Arabic to make use of it; all necessary terms and quotes have been translated into English. Nor need one have in-depth familiarity with Egyptian literary or political history.

I have been blessed with an incredible set of academic mentors, only a few of whom I can mention here. My interest in activist Arabic literature owes largely to my mentor and guide, Professor William Granara of Harvard University. Indeed, I little understood the pivotal role of the writer in Arab politics and society, the key position of literature in the transformation of modern Arab society, or the central importance of *al-adab al-multazim* until I studied with Professor Granara. Over a period of mentorship lasting well over a decade and continuing today, he has taught me to see the Arabic language and literature in an entirely different way. Professor Granara has been the constant source of wisdom, advice, and encouragement without whom this book would not have been possible. Everything in the book has been influenced by Professor Granara, particularly the history of *iltizam* in chapter 2. The paradigm of the tripartite relationship of the actors in *iltizam*—a critical component of the theoretical model used in this book—came directly from Professor Granara. I have had the privilege of working with him for over a decade to refine and apply this paradigm to the works discussed in this book.

My other mentor and inspiration, Professor William Mills Todd III, remains for me the epitome of the gentleman, scholar, and teacher, a man whose vast intellect is surpassed only by his genuine humility and kindness. Although he always taught us to look inside rather than outside ourselves to seek greatness, he remains for me and for countless students and graduates of Harvard the role model that we all look to as an exemplar of everything an educator should be. The section on Soviet literature is a direct result of my work with Professor Todd, but his advice and influence are present in every word herein.

Professor Christopher Johnson, a selflessly dedicated teacher and literary theorist of amazing depth and insight, was also a constant source of guidance and inspiration during my research, not least for his ability to challenge his students to think critically, dig deeper, and never stop asking the tough questions.

My greatest inspiration and support come from my two great children, Michael and Christine, always my closest companions and the source of joy in my life. Whenever I write about *al-adab al-multazim*, I am reminded of how they were fresh out of kindergarten when I began studying committed literature in Egypt and are now in college. They have changed greatly over these years, and I'm reminded of how much the world they live in has changed as well. Through it all, they continue to amaze me with their optimism and hope.

I would also like to thank the dedicated, supportive, and helpful staff at the American University in Cairo Press for all their help and guidance, in particular Neil Hewison, Nadine El-Hadi, Nadia Naqib, and Kevin Dean. Their patience, flexibility, and encouragement contributed tremendously to this work.

Lastly, this book, and my interest in Egyptian literature, is inspired by the amazingly kind and welcoming people of Egypt. For anyone who has been to Egypt, the deep love of a writer like Naguib Mahfouz for the Egyptian people needs no explanation; for one who has not been there, no explanation will suffice. This book is in large measure my attempt to understand the intense devotion, with all its disappointment and hope, of writers whose lives and passion are committed to the sons and daughters of Egypt.

Introduction

Activist or Observer?

At the heart of the project of activist writing sits a simple yet profound question: Can a writer make a difference in the struggle for social and political justice? Is he or she an instigator, leader, or contributor in the movement to shape a more just and equitable society, or merely a chronicler of that struggle? Is the author an agent of 'climate change' in the society around him or her, or merely its barometer? With pantheons of literary talents as diverse as Zola and Baudelaire, Dickens and Wilde, Poe and Beecher Stowe, literary history offers no simple answer to this question. Thoreau in his wilderness cottage influenced generations while thousands of political crusaders faded from memory. The 'Dean of Arabic Literature,' Egypt's pioneering novelist and critic Taha Hussein, even challenged whether an author's intent to target his or her work toward social change was relevant to its impact (see chapter 1 for more detail). Nonetheless, no question sparked more intense debate among writers in mid-twentieth-century Egypt than that of the role of author as activist or observer.

This question of the author's role, at its most essential level, revolves around the relationship of the writer to the two key actors in the process of social transformation: the political authority and the public. In their

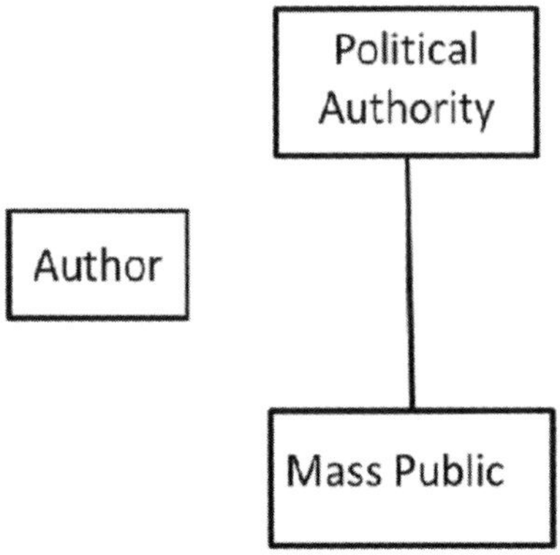

Figure 1: Author-Observer Model

starkest contrast, these two alternatives can be captured in two competing models (figures 1 and 2), which I will dub for convenience the Author-Observer Model and the Activist-Author Model.

In the former, the author stands apart from the social and political struggles of the day. In the latter, the author participates in those struggles with an active, albeit distinct role in the transformation of society. The former model draws legitimacy from traditions of artistic independence, a call encapsulated in the nineteenth-century appeal to *l'art pour l'art* embraced by Western writers like Baudelaire and Poe, writers whose introspective examinations of their own psyches were driven by their alienation from or curiosity about the society around them. In Egypt, this call was epitomized (perhaps unfairly) by Tawfiq al-Hakim's famous exhortation for authors to take to the "ivory tower." The latter model, by contrast, clearly reflects socialist thinking, in which the writer, like all other productive members of society, actively puts his or her talents in the service of social transformation. In either case, the writer's role is defined in relation to the public and the political authority, whether that relation be one of engagement or alienation.

This simple dichotomy, of course, papers over a good deal of variation. From these two extremes, there arise countless hybrids. Throughout much of early literary history, particularly in the Arab world, the author was bound closely to patrons in the political elite, but with little connection to an illiterate mass public. Popular storytelling,

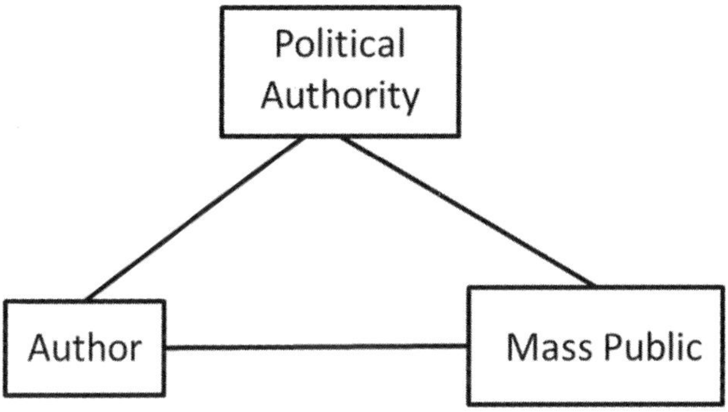

Figure 2: Activist-Author Model

such as the oral traditions that would form classics like the *Arabian Nights*, by contrast, bound the artist to the public, while mocking a distant political authority. Similarly, classic literary works could confound this simple dichotomy. Dostoevsky's Underground Man, or Kafka's Josef K were, at face value, models of total alienation from society and authority, yet they endure in popular memory as powerful expressions of social critique. As discussed in detail in chapter 2, socialist reflection theory, for its part, cast out the author's perception of his or her social position entirely, ruling that as long as the writer gave an accurate picture of society, such perceptions were superfluous. Ibn Khaldun certainly did not write for the illiterate masses, yet his conclusions spoke volumes to the bonds between the ruling authority and those masses.

Despite its weaknesses, the activist writing paradigm gained so much momentum in Egypt during the early to mid-twentieth century that its victory seemed total and permanent by the time of the 1952 revolution. 'Art for art's sake' was pilloried in literary journals; writing for, to, from, and with 'the people' was exalted, while 'the elite' became a term of derision. However simplistic the dichotomy of the committed activist and introspective artist may have been, it formed the axis of critical debate into the 1950s. Avowedly detached artists meanwhile became scarce, yet continued to loom large in the imagination as a foil for the committed writer.

Al-Adab al-Multazim: Dominance of the Activist Author

As Egypt's foreign-backed monarchy fell in 1952, the question of the author's role seemed decisively settled in favor of the Activist-Author Model. So much so, in fact, that even Tawfiq al-Hakim rushed to redefine his "ivory tower" as a symbol for political engagement (see chapter 2 for further discussion of al-Hakim's period). The 1952 revolution, however, was but the crowning moment in a movement that had been building in momentum since the turn of the twentieth century. In the decades prior to the revolution, pioneering literary minds had applied themselves to a vision of literature rooted firmly in the concept of the author as a partner in the transformation of society. Egyptian writers took their obligation to the public so seriously that by the 1940s, that responsibility had acquired an uncompromising title—*iltizam*, meaning a duty. Its associated literature—*al-adab al-multazim*—meant no less than 'bound' or 'committed' writing. *Al-adab al-multazim* was a very specific application of the Activist-Author Model. Not only did it take the bonds between the writer, public, and political authority as given, it had very definite prescriptions on the working nature of those bonds. By mid-century, to be accused within Egyptian critical circles of producing art for art's sake was so serious a charge that even novelists who wrote moving tales of the suffering of peasant farmers could find themselves called to task for insufficient commitment. The debates of the mid-twentieth century largely focused on the finer points of the model of *al-adab al-multazim* and the variants it spawned, rather than the virtue of the author as social activist—a concept firmly entrenched by that point.

After years in which Naguib Mahfouz wrote realist novels that caused readers to shout "Why, People?!" and Yusuf Idris wrote short stories that struck "like the nuclear bomb," the toppling of the British-backed monarchy in 1952 felt like the realization of a dream. Both authors were duly lauded by the revolutionary regime for their roles in exposing the social injustices of the corrupt old order. In the wake of the revolution, writers, critics, and theorists representing countless shades of activist literature—from the 'bound' to the 'targeted'—eagerly debated the finer points of a literary movement that worked in a close, but equal, partnership with the political leadership and mass public to shape a new society. That the political powers, with wide popular support, had declared their intent to eradicate so many of the social ills against which the activist writers had been writing only validated the essential, active role of the author in shaping a new society.

Alas, the 1952 revolution turned out to be a disappointment. Though they had ridden many of the same popular sentiments in the 1940s and 1950s, Egypt's revolutionary leaders and committed artists found themselves at odds as revolution turned into regime. As a consequence, the artists of the 1960s ran from the model of committed literature as eagerly as they had embraced it a decade earlier. No longer a partner, the author now saw him or herself isolated and alienated from both the political authority and the mass public. In fact, the idealism of *al-adab al-multazim* became a safe target for ridicule in the difficult decades that followed the revolution. Popular literary buzzwords like *multazim* and *iltizam* disappeared from critical discourse while the luminaries of committed literature turned inward, producing a type of dark, self-absorbed writing that would mark the output of the 1960s. Where once the author denied himself and instead elevated the noble peasant and his struggles, the writer of the 1960s often turned the lens on himself, exposing his disillusion with the public, the state, and writing altogether. There was little in the disillusioned works of the post-revolutionary period to suggest that the author felt any power to impact, shape, or guide society.

In the ensuing decades of disappointment, those who had once written so hopefully of social change turned instead to self-mockery. In the depths of the 1960s or 1980s, it could be difficult to remember the optimism that welcomed the Free Officers of 1952. When the great Mahfouz entered his 'period of silence' and the fiery Idris took to his bed with the disgusted exclamation "why write?" it seemed safe to pronounce *al-adab al-multazim* and its aspirations dead.

The Question of Disillusion

The scathing and bitter works of formerly *multazim* authors marked a definitive turning point in Egyptian writing. Yet the fundamental nature of this turn remains open to debate. Did this turn toward disillusion indicate a retreat to the Author-Observer paradigm? That is to say, having set up such a clear dichotomy of committed versus detached writers in the glory days of *al-adab al-multazim*, would the proponents of that movement have to declare the withdrawal of their exemplars necessarily an embrace of pure, detached aesthetics? Some analysts certainly saw the choice this way. When one of his most enthusiastic critics called on Idris to choose "which way now," he left no middle ground between embracing and rejecting *iltizam*. Literary criticism in general, however, has remained rather silent on what the disillusionment of the latter half of the twentieth century meant in terms of the vision that once defined committed writing.

As tempting as it may be to simply declare this period a wholesale retreat into the Author-Observer mode, such a conclusion is at odds with the nature of the works of disillusion the former *multazim* artists produced. The tripartite relationship of author, public, and political authority remained central to the writings of disillusion. That relationship was seen as dysfunctional, distorted, or inverted, something that once existed and was desired for the future, but never far from the consciousness of the pained writer. The disheartened protagonists of Mahfouz, Idris, or Sonallah Ibrahim were not absorbed with eternal questions of existence but rather the failure of their vision of activist writing.

This study will argue that during the disillusionment of the 1960s to 1980s, activist authors remained fully immersed in the Activist-Author paradigm. Their expressions of disillusion marked experimentation with that model—bending, inverting, reversing, and renegotiating it from all angles, but never losing a concern for their connection to the public and the political authority. A detailed analysis of some of their key works will demonstrate how *al-adab al-multazim* remained central to their expressions of disillusion. In fact, underlying that disillusion, a distorted vision of *al-adab al-multazim*—an inversion—can be seen. This study will examine this inversion in detail in order to show how central committed writing remained to the author's conception of his or her role during this gloomy period. The continued dialogue with committed writing explains in large part why a broad field of activist writers was ready to embrace the movement for political change that swept Egypt in the digital age.

For this reason, I have chosen to focus on one of the darkest and most challenging periods in the history of activist writing in Egypt—the decades of the 1960s to 1980s. After the enthusiastic *iltizam* of the early 1950s, but before global, electronic media and the opening of the Egyptian economy began to break the hold of the regime on communication, this marked a most disheartening period for the activist writer. The chronologically last novel to be analyzed in depth in this study, Sonallah Ibrahim's *The Committee*, fittingly ends with the hero's warning that the intrusive, controlling state apparatus that silenced his literary aspirations would be overtaken by the forces of Western capitalism that had already begun to invade Egyptian society. My focus in this study, therefore, is on the apparently dark years from the disappointment of the Nasser regime to the emergence of those forces that Sonallah Ibrahim accurately predicted would change the relationships between writer, public, and political authority. The wilderness of the disillusioned decades of the 1960s to 1980s remains a vital period in Egyptian literary history, demonstrating how the activist writer dealt with the disappointment of a fading revolution.

Activist Writing Today

A valid question emerges, however, as to whether the models of writing that developed in the previous century still have relevance in the digital age. Has the Internet consigned the pained struggles over *al-adab al-multazim* to the pages of history? In the revolution of 2011, Egypt's authors were thrust into leading roles as social spokespeople that seemed to validate, at least for a time, the transformative power of electronic media. Popular authors like Ibrahim Abdel Meguid, Ezzedine Choukri Fishere, Radwa Ashour, and Khaled al-Berry led discussions on the future of the revolution on their blogs and Facebook pages. While Western and Arab media scrambled to find opinion leaders for interviews, Egypt's most popular novelist, Alaa Al Aswany, became a most sought-after subject. A leading member of the Movement for Change, better known by the Arabic name *Kefaya* (Enough) and a precursor to the Facebook-organized protest movement, Al Aswany had in 2002 published his immensely successful novel *The Yacoubian Building*, a scathingly realistic work of fiction compared by legions of critics to the novels of Mahfouz, and had maintained an extremely popular blog since 2004. When his equally scathing, non-fiction essay collection *On the State of Egypt* came out on the eve of the 2011 revolution, it was deemed so relevant to the events unfolding in Tahrir Square that the subtitle "What Made the Revolution Inevitable" was hastily added. After the fall of the Hosni Mubarak regime, Al Aswany became an unofficial spokesman for a revolutionary movement that had no official leaders. The relationship of the author to the political authority and mass public was never more tangible than in March 2011, when Al Aswany grilled Egyptian Prime Minister Ahmed Shafik on television so aggressively that Shafik resigned the next day.

In the aftermath of the 2011 revolution, then, it was easy to proclaim the triumph of a new kind of digitally empowered writer. The electronic age offered a very different environment for the activist writer than that under which the vanguard of *al-adab al-multazim* had lived. Critics rushed to crown literary superstar Al Aswany with "the mantle worn by Naguib Mahfouz,"[1] implying a continuity with the works of *al-adab al-multazim* in the 1940s, yet the writers of the digital age possessed tools of communication of which their predecessors could only have dreamed. An instant, global communications network that the regime couldn't silence and that virtually every student and intellectual could carry in their pockets would have seemed a magic weapon to a writer like Idris back in the 1960s. Writers were now able to put a sentence, paragraph, or even a whole book in the (electronic) hands of millions at the push of a button. Moreover, that communications network was largely outside the control of the regime—witness the disastrous attempt of the Mubarak government to shut off the Internet for one day in January 2011. In the moment when Al Aswany faced down Shafik, it seemed that the painful decades of disillusion of the activist author of the past had been overcome.

Yet the euphoria of revolution gave way rather quickly once again. No doubt, the replacement of government-controlled printing presses with electronic media had profoundly changed the relationship of the writer and the public. Yet, much had stayed the same. Writers who cheered the Tahrir protest movement soon found themselves isolated by the political power again—in this case, Egypt's first democratically elected government, led by the Muslim Brotherhood. So bitter had the divide become that thirty-one leading Egyptian artists and intellectuals, including novelist Sonallah Ibrahim (discussed in depth in chapter 5), protested at the

Ministry of Culture—not with their literary works, but by staging a sit-in at the ministry in 2013. Ibrahim was one of a further one hundred fifty intellectuals who signed an appeal that the Muslim Brotherhood be declared a terrorist organization, tantamount to inviting a military coup. When the military takeover did occur, rather than serving as leading idealogues and spokespeople, Ibrahim and his colleagues were overshadowed by much larger and more violent popular demonstrations in the streets. For one who had supported the January 25 movement, Ibrahim declared that the 2011 uprising "certainly was not a revolution,"[2] consoling himself that "the military power is working on behalf of the people." Then, despite having been imprisoned by the Nasser regime for six years, he praised President Abdel-Fattah al-Sisi after the takeover as the man who "for the first time since Gamal Abdel Nasser challenged America and the West."[3]

The revolution may have filled Egyptian writers with "enthusiasm and faith in the future" and in their power "to change the course of history,"[4] but by 2015, Ibrahim declared "the only role of a writer is to entertain his readers."[5] Acknowledging his own active role in opposing the post-revolutionary government, Ibrahim was quick to caveat that this was in his capacity as a citizen rather than an artist.[6] Such pronouncements took the author far from the heyday of committed literature.

For Ibrahim, who spent the vast majority of his career in the tough decades after the 1952 revolution, the experience of writing in an era filled with disillusion may well resonate more with the challenges facing today's Egyptian writer than the high points of the revolution. Ibrahim had earlier conceded that revolutions "always passed through" two stages: the first marked by "enthusiasm and faith in the future and the ability to change the course of history," while in the second "shadows of gray begin to smudge the whiteness and the blackness."[7] The immediate future seems to promise far more of the "graying" of the second, difficult phase of revolution of which Ibrahim spoke.

Thus, both the era of *al-adab al-multazim* and the disillusioned decades after the 1952 revolution have relevance to the activist author today. Electronic media will bind the author to the public in ways that *multazim* authors felt only in their moments of greatest popularity. The political authority, as well, will be forced to acknowledge activist authors whether it wants to or not. Yet even in a democratic system, authors may find themselves so alienated from the mass of public opinion and the actions of elected authorities that they retreat into pronouncements of writing "for entertainment only."

This book, therefore, will follow the path of activist writing in Egypt from its beginnings in the early twentieth century, through its most carefully structured form mid-century, to focus on the wilderness of the latter decades of the century. In that dark period, marked by outward disillusion with the earlier model of *al-adab al-multazim*, the paradigm of activist writing remained very much alive, its key players, roles, assumptions, and relationships as vital as during the heyday of *iltizam*. The future of Egyptian society, and the role of the writer in that society, can hardly be predicted, yet in the few years since the 2011 revolution, Egypt has seen moments harkening back to the glory of the 1950s, the disillusion of the 1960s, and many that fit no pattern from the past.

The Path of Activist Writing

To sketch the path that leads through the glory days of *iltizam* to the wilderness of disillusion, this book's journey starts outside Egypt and well before the 1952 revolution. Activist writers in Egypt inherited a (largely) European tradition of writing for social justice as well as political strivings based (again largely) on European socialism. These influences were mixed with a far smaller influence from the classical Arabic literary tradition to produce the literary movement that would adopt *al-adab al-multazim* as its title. That name came from a translation of Jean-Paul Sartre's idea of *engagement*, a testament to the conscious modeling after European influences. At the same time, Egyptian writers were keen to distance themselves from some of the excesses of socialist writing programs gone awry. In this regard, the Soviet experience with socialist realism served as powerfully as a model of what was to be avoided as of what was to be imitated. Chapter 1 will look at the predecessors and influences that shaped *al-adab al-multazim*. It is by no means an attempt at a comprehensive history of committed writing but rather a focus on the models of writing that had a direct impact on the Arabic and, more specifically, Egyptian project of politically engaged literature.

It is then necessary to define the Egyptian project of politically engaged literature. As a clear definition of committed writing is essential for this study, chapter 2 is dedicated to defining and examining the model of *al-adab al-multazim* that emerged in the mid-twentieth century. When it comes to examining theory, separating Egypt's experiment with *al-adab al-multazim* from that in the rest of the Arab world would be as inadvisable as it is unfeasible. The Arabic movement of *al-adab al-multazim* was focused overwhelmingly in the dominant literary centers of Cairo and Beirut, with constant traffic between them. Therefore, chapter 2 looks at the Arabic movement as a whole, with emphasis on Egypt. The remaining chapters, however, will be exclusively focused on Egypt, as application of the theories of committed writing remains, by its very nature, heavily rooted in a local political environment. Thus, while Egyptian writers like Taha Hussein went to Beirut to engage in some of the most fruitful discussions of committed writing, their novels remained firmly rooted in the soil of Egypt.

Distilling a working definition of *al-adab al-multazim*, the ultimate aim of chapter 2, is a challenging task, not due to a lack of critical and theoretical writings, but rather their abundance. By the middle of the twentieth century, competing visions, schools, and doctrines abounded, captured in often heated debates over the true meaning of literary commitment. To be *multazim* in 1950s Egypt was much like being anti-Communist in 1950s America or anti-terrorist anywhere in the 2000s: an allegiance everyone claimed so vehemently that the only debate centered on the finer points of its definition. From the vantage point of several decades of hindsight, however, the consistencies across all models of activist writing become clearer. The model of *al-adab al-multazim* offered in chapter 2, then, is not a summary of any particular school but rather an identification of key assumptions that set *al-adab al-multazim* apart from the disillusioned writing of the following decades.

Doctrines and theories have some import to literature, but the actual literary works that make up the corpus of any movement are its meat and bones. This is especially true in the realm of committed writing, where the lofty goals of *engagement* proved maddeningly difficult to translate into practice. After all, the call for novels, plays, and stories that could illuminate systemic social injustices in such a way as to enlighten the masses without devolving into dogmatic, Soviet-style formulae was as hard to fulfill as it was easy to propose. Nonetheless, several Egyptian authors have stood the test of time as leading exemplars of writing for social change. Accordingly, chapters 3 and 4 apply the model of *al-adab al-multazim* to two exemplars of its writing—Mahfouz and Idris. I will consider two works that represent the principles of *iltizam* in action, Mahfouz's 1949 novel *A Beginning and an End* and Idris's 1954 short story "An Errand." Then, I will examine four novels by Mahfouz and five stories by Idris that exhibit the 'inversion' of *al-adab al-multazim.* Chapter 5 addresses the work of Ibrahim, a writer who fits an important chronological gap between the post-revolutionary period and the beginning of the change brought on by globalization. Few writers could be considered more committed to social justice in Egypt than Ibrahim, and the evolution from the disheartened and resigned tone of his 1966 *That Smell* to his confident declaration in 1981's *The Committee* of the coming demise of the controlling order marks the end of this long period of disillusion.

The choice of three authors was both a difficult and necessary one. As I aim to show the operation of the literary model of *iltizam* at a deep, structural level in not merely a few isolated works, depth was more important than breadth. As I further wanted to show a moving progression, an inheritance from one generation to the next, I chose three writers with prolific careers, who chronologically sit roughly a decade apart. Mahfouz's literary career effectively spans from the 1930s to the 1980s, flowering with the growth of *iltizam* and continuing on into the period of disillusion that followed. Idris's career begins at the height of *iltizam*, and by his tragic early death in 1991, he had experienced a much more profound fall into disillusion than the elder Mahfouz, who participated in the beginnings of the movement from its early antecedents. Finally, Ibrahim provides a crucial link to the present generation. Having gotten his early start in the waning of revolutionary fervor, Ibrahim became a leading chronicler of the period of disillusion and stood well into the 2000s as a towering figure of activist literature. Taken as a whole, the texts studied in depth, from Mahfouz's *A Beginning and an End* to Ibrahim's *The Committee*, trace the path of socially engaged writing from its optimistic peaks of the 1940s, through the valleys of 1960s, and to the breaking of the hold of the regime in the 1980s.

Some Notes on Terminology

Throughout this book, several terms are used, often interchangeably, to refer to the movement of politically and socially engaged writing. The somewhat loose interchange of terms is intentional, as it reflects the fluid nature of the debate among writers and critics of the movement. As will become clear in the following chapters, those theorists never achieved a consensus on what these terms meant, and the goal is not to adopt one particular school's definitions but rather to capture the entire, often uncoordinated effort of committed writing. Strictly speaking, *iltizam* is a noun, meaning a duty or commitment. Here, of course, it refers to the writer's commitment to use his or her craft for social and political justice, a usage given to it by Taha Hussein's 1947 translation of Jean-Paul Sartre's *engagement*. The word *multazim*, then, by virtue of the logic of Arabic grammar, is the participle meaning 'committed' or 'duty bound.' An artist or a critic (or anyone else) can be *multazim*, as can literature *(adab)*, and thus was born the term *al-adab al-multazim*.

As will be discussed in chapters 1 and 2, Arab writers sought to commit themselves to the cause of social justice, keeping the business of defining *iltizam* and its requirements under the purview of the artists, avoiding the horrors of state-run literary enterprises like those in Stalinist Russia. They knew well that being judged as insufficiently, or improperly, committed to Marxist social change could be fatal in the Soviet Union, a frightening prospect given how quickly standards for proper socialist writing could change. As a result, definitions of *iltizam*, and its related terminology, tended to focus on the poles: the ideals of committed writing versus the abyss of 'art for art's sake.' Marking the boundary between committed and uncommitted literature was always a thorny point that theorists of *al-adab al-multazim* avoided, lest they begin to sound like the Soviet cultural organizations they dreaded. Therefore, the model of *al-adab al-multazim* in this study accordingly focuses on the ideals: the ideal writer, political authority, and reading public, and the ideal of a shared language binding them. The inversion of *al-adab al-multazim* also focuses on the extremes: writers, a public, and a state who reject the guiding principle of cooperative social change through free, committed literature.

One of the hallmarks of *al-adab al-multazim* was realism, a term that has been subject to countless competing definitions. As with their debates over definitions of commitment, advocates of *al-adab al-multazim* were never able to settle on a single definition of realism, and the Arabic literary world is undoubtedly richer as a result. The purpose here is not to settle the argument for them. Rather, it is to show that experimentation with different approaches to realism marked one of the seismic shifts in Arabic literature during the mid-twentieth century. The fundamental debate between the Lukácsian 'school' and the Brechtian 'school' in European socialist writing provides the most illuminating framework to chart the major shift in Egyptian writing. Thus, a significant portion of chapter 1 is dedicated to the discussion of this debate before moving to the Arabic model of *al-adab al-multazim*. The competing concepts of realism offered by Brecht and Lukács capture two different spirits of realism in the service of social change, two diametrically opposed orientations that capture the dramatic changes in Egyptian writing from the 1940s and 1950s to the decades that follow.

Lastly, a period of 'disillusion' and 'works of disillusion' refer to the loosely bounded category of texts, beginning primarily in the early 1960s, that show a clear move away from the imperatives of *al-adab al-multazim*. This is not to say that the entire period was characterized by a uniform spirit of disappointment, but rather to capture a general shift in orientation among writers of socially engaged fiction. These works will be the focus of this book, as they form the 'missing link,' so to speak, between the *multazim* writing of the 1940s and 1950s and the overtly political writing leading up to the recent revolution. In all cases, my concern is not on minor doctrinal differences but the major changes in orientation that mark these periods in literary history.

It's a common trope in popular entertainment to open with a seemingly absurd and inexplicable scene and then trace through flashback the path that led to that point. For the story of *al-adab al-multazim*, that moment came in Beirut in 1955 with the most unlikely of persons defending himself against the tidal force of *iltizam*. It is to that intriguing scene that we now turn.

Chapter 1
Early Influences on Arabic Committed Literature

The high tide of committed literature in the Arab world was marked by a scene replete with ironies. That no one laughed at the absurdity then, or for years to come, spoke volumes for the momentary power of *al-adab al-multazim*, as 'committed' literature was known. At a 1955 United Nations-sponsored debate on committed writing in Beirut, the largest and most significant of the escalating exchanges on the subject throughout the 1950s, a writer took to the podium to defend the heavily loaded position "The Author Writes for the Elite" *(al-Adib yaktub li-l-khassa)*—a title starkly at odds with the spirit of the conference. Yet it was no ordinary writer assigned the difficult task of countering the assertion that "The Author Writes for the Masses" *(al-Adib yaktub li-l-kaffa)*.[1] Taha Hussein was, in fact, the man who had introduced the term for literary commitment *(iltizam)* into Arabic critical discourse, when he brought Jean-Paul Sartre's landmark works on *engagement* to the Arab world. Hussein was also arguably the most respected living figure in Arabic writing at the time, known informally as the 'dean' of Arabic writing, and one who had already authored some of the most powerful social commentary in Arabic fiction, targeting rural poverty, urban corruption, and the inefficiencies of the Egyptian education system, as in his autobiographical trilogy *The Days (al-Ayyam)*.

In truth, the title of Hussein's speech proved to be something of a misnomer—a title assigned to him by conference organizer Suhayl Idris and one which Hussein immediately disavowed upon taking the podium.[2] If attendees had come hoping to see the spectacle of the author of *The Days* reject socially conscious literature, they were to be disappointed. The man who had been rendered blind by the resident barber in his poor village, who had spent his life challenging the corrupt and antiquated educational system through which he had suffered, and who showed little reticence in taking on the political, religious, and cultural elites of his day was not one to advocate a retreat into decadent literary salons. Rather, Hussein's impeccable credentials made him one of the few who could raise concerns about overly vigorous prosecution of any program of committed writing without losing respect. In the heyday of *al-adab al-multazim*, that was as close as this gathering was going to come to an 'anti-*iltizam*' position.

Ultimately, Hussein's characteristically eloquent speech in defense of his difficult position has held up far better than that of his opponent. Hussein transcended the simple dichotomy of committed and uncommitted writers and even denied that such a dichotomy could exist. An author wrote as he or she saw best, without controlling whom he or she would impact or how. He went so far as to challenge whether literature could, in fact, be *targeted*, as his opponents claimed. Writers of past centuries had exerted great impact on the moral progress of Arab civilization and improved the lives of contemporary Arabs, he asserted, even though their reading audiences at the time represented a tiny fraction of the population. Above all, Hussein spoke for the freedom of the writer. Having effectively brought social and political injustice to light through his own writing, Hussein disdained the need for any theorist to tell him how to do so. He summarized his position with the polite yet definitive assertion, "I will be free whether it pleases you or not."[3] That the man who introduced engagement to the Arab literary world was now cautioning against the increasingly restrictive definitions of literary commitment dominating the Arabic critical discourse testified to the momentum that the movement of committed literature had gained in a short time.

The Theoretical Problem of Committed Literature

While few would have thought so at the time, the tougher side in the debate belonged not to Hussein but to his counterpart, Ra'if Khuri, an outspoken advocate of committed writing who also strongly opposed the kinds of restrictions under which authors in the Soviet Union, with its official policies of literary engagement, had been forced to operate. Khuri repeated calls familiar to the audience for writing for the masses and for using the 'language of the people.' Meanwhile, he asserted, despite Hussein's misgivings, that a writer could indeed target his or her audience with a clear message. For the attendees at this literary conference at the zenith of *al-adab al-multazim*, these mantras were quite familiar. Yet Khuri was careful to insist that the writer should remain free, safe from any external direction. For all their zeal, even the most committed Arab writers shared Khuri's aversion to repeating the Stalinist experience, particularly in the wake of the (then) recent socialist revolution in Egypt. Khuri was hard pressed to maintain his delicate balancing act between a writer's duty and freedom without lapsing into essentially the same position Hussein had argued. If the Arab literary community was not going to impose Stalinist rules on writers—enforced under threat of being labeled 'uncommitted'—then why speak of 'duties' and 'imperatives' at all? If Soviet-style production literature and the pure aesthetics of *l'art pour l'art* were the two diametrically opposed evils facing the world of committed literature, then theorists like Khuri were hard pressed to draw boundary lines separating acceptable literature from these extremes, without putting such shackles on the author. Failing that, then, they would be forced to accept Hussein's model—that of a superbly effective artist who serves the cause of social justice only because he chooses to, and thus needs no talk of an artistic 'duty.'

Khuri's challenge was nothing new. Literary commitment had always been more a process of historical reaction than a theoretical school, more certain of what it was *not* than what it was. The movement of literary commitment, for all its positive-sounding exhortations, was fundamentally one built on negative definitions. The foundational negative characterization was that committed literature could not be "art for art's sake," never better expressed than by Theodor Adorno in his assertion "that to write lyric poetry after Auschwitz is barbaric."[4] Yet Adorno's warning, like all statements of committed writing, ran into trouble from the beginning. Wasn't the dream of a committed artist a society in which one was free to pursue art for any sake he or she chose? Wasn't the opposite of Hitler's Germany a society in which one *could* write lyric poetry, as barbaric as that may be? Taha Hussein asserted his right to write for pure aesthetics "whether it pleases you or not,"[5] while in fact choosing most often not to exercise that right. He was certainly not the first socially engaged writer to do so. Artists had long bristled at the threat of imposed duties or expectations—witness Mark Twain's opening caveat to one of the most powerful works of social critique in American literature: "Persons attempting to find a motive in this narrative will be prosecuted; persons attempting to find a moral in it will be banished."[6]

Hussein and Khuri's argument was the culmination of an extended debate that centered, to a large extent, on diverging interpretations of literary history. Classical Arabic traditions, Soviet writing programs, post-war European movements of literary commitment, and many other trends influenced their visions of writing for Arab audiences at a critical juncture in history. A brief look at some of the most important influences on that debate is necessary to fully appreciate what *al-adab al-multazim* meant, and what it could not mean, to Arab audiences. No stop on the journey of committed writing left such a cautionary impression on Arab writers as the literary enterprise of socialist realism in the early Soviet Union.

The Soviet Legacy of Directed Literature

Like a newlywed couple setting up their first home, Egypt received a vast array of gifts from its Soviet benefactors following its socialist revolution. Some were broken from the start, while others hung around for years before being consigned to the dustbin. The monstrous central office building—the notorious Mugamma'—that dominates Cairo's Tahrir Square was intended to be the showpiece of a Soviet-style bureaucracy, yet for decades it merely served to inspire jokes about the hapless souls lost in its maze-like corridors. The Aswan Dam, the promised "new pyramid,"[7] was a model of Soviet engineering in all the worst ways, and only

Israeli generals were really glad that Nasser had filled his massive army with Soviet equipment. Egyptian writers, however, were determined not to be the recipients of a Soviet-style writing system, no matter what was going on in other professions.

The Soviet experience, above all, taught the importance of the relationship between the writer and the political power. Even the most vigorous proponents of committed literature, men like Khuri and Mahmud Amin al-'Alim, were strongly opposed to a state-directed writing system. They knew, however, that while the socialist realism officially imposed in the Soviet Union in the 1930s by Stalin's Cultural Commissar Andrei Zhdanov was indeed the nightmare of every *multazim* writer, nevertheless it had not developed in a vacuum. Rather, it was the result of an evolution that began with questions not far removed from those under debate by Arab writers of the 1940s and 1950s. Justly or not, successive organizations of Russian writers had been crushed when they failed to adequately answer those questions, as the Soviet political leadership grew increasingly impatient with disagreement in the literary sphere. With the Egyptian monarchy removed by a socialist revolution in 1952, and the future direction of the revolutionary state that followed it still very uncertain, *multazim* authors were quick to define their own limits of committed writing, rather than fall into the same fate as Russian writers decades earlier. A brief look at the rapid spiral of Soviet writing from an artistic program of cultural liberation into an oppressive, state-directed system helps explain the urgency that *multazim* writers felt in defining their relationship with the state.

The imposition of a restrictive model of literature with gratingly low aesthetic standards was by no means an inevitable byproduct of revolution. Indeed, Lenin and Trotsky both at times warned against such a move. How much autonomy any group of specialists could have hoped to preserve in the early Soviet Union is questionable, but the failure of committed Russian writers to come to a consensus on key questions about the nature of a truly transformational literature certainly facilitated the state takeover. Fundamental among these questions was what constituted 'writing for the people.' Since Marxist doctrine held the 'dictatorship of the proletariat' to be but a temporary phase in the movement toward a truly classless society, the need for a distinctly proletarian Soviet culture was one of the first points in that debate. Recognizing that the 1917 revolution had thrust Russia into its temporary proletarian phase of historical development, Soviet leaders hoped the seismic changes gripping Europe at the time presaged a rapid worldwide movement toward a classless society. If so, then establishing a deliberately proletarian culture, with its accompanying distinctive literature, would be both unnecessary and impractical. Both Lenin and Trotsky opposed efforts to create a proletarian culture on practical grounds, seeing that the backward condition of the masses would make such an effort slow and difficult. Lenin even saw benefit in appropriating elements of bourgeois culture to raise the standard of living of the Russian working class.[8] This was a promising sign for the freedom of the writer, as Marxist theorists had found much to commend in the works of bourgeois writers of nineteenth-century France and Germany (see the discussion of Gyorgy Lukács at the end of this chapter).

The disappointments of the aborted European revolutionary movements following World War I snuffed out any optimism for widescale, rapid social transformation and set the stage for a long proletarian phase of development. Literature would not remain outside this proletarian transformation. Founded in 1917, the leading organization in the move toward proletarian culture, the *Proletkult*, developed out of a series of conferences and initiatives prior to and during the Bolshevik takeover that aimed to provide some guidance and structure to the diverse efforts aimed at building a proletarian culture. By 1920, wildly differing estimates saw the organization's subordinate membership as including well over a thousand local groups.[9] The roots of *Proletkult* were extremely intricate and its reach grew faster than its internal efforts to achieve consensus on the myriad issues that divided its leaders. Hardly united in doctrine, the leadership sat atop an intense debate on basic principles, such as the nature of proletarian culture, the forms of acceptable art, and the proper place of pre-revolutionary classical literature. A central tenet of the organization's platform was its insistence on independence from government control, stressed particularly by its most prominent leader, Alexander Bogdanov, who had left the Communist Party and believed *Proletkult* should complement rather than serve under the party.[10] Exactly what this meant, however, remained unclear, as the political situation in Russia from 1917–20 was in tremendous flux, preventing any clear picture of how the practical relations between the emerging state and the cultural organization would have worked out in a long period of stability.

Despite its best efforts to the contrary, the organization came under party control in 1920, as *Proletkult* represented a threat to the party on several fronts. On the personal level, Bogdanov was a longtime rival of Lenin. Moreover, the group demanded creative independence, yet was dependent on state funding. On ideological and practical grounds, Lenin grew opposed to the idea of multiple, parallel organizations. He believed the Communist Party was the sole guardian of true Marxism and an all-embracing organ responsible for and to the people. Logically, all aspects of government and social development belonged under its control. In a strongly worded Politburo resolution in October 1920, exerting the doctrinal impossibility of separating the cultural organization from the party, Lenin brought an end to *Proletkult.*[11] Moreover, differences on literary approach helped open the door for *Proletkult*'s absorption into the party machinery. Like the *multazim* artists working in Arabic, Bogdanov's group believed it could balance two guiding imperatives: growing genuine proletarian artists, while allowing members to study a variety of styles, media, and approaches, free from government control. Although Lenin supported the appropriation and reworking of bourgeois culture, the danger of infiltration of foreign ideas through an independent organization like *Proletkult* concerned him so much that he specifically cited the *Proletkult*'s acceptance of foreign artistic trends like futurism when placing the organization under party control.[12]

Even before *Proletkult* had succumbed to party authority, members had split on theoretical and technical issues. Breaking from the *Proletkult* in 1919, a small group of poets had formed the Smithy *(Kuznitsa)*—so named for its principal publication—and continued to work into the 1930s. The Smithy initially wanted no part of the mass organization efforts of *Proletkult* and demanded even greater freedom for the writer than *Proletkult* had. The Smithy found itself at odds with VAPP (The All-Russian Association of Proletarian Writers), founded in 1920 for the purpose of developing strong mass cultural organizations. The Smithy further placed itself at odds with the state in expressing disappointment with Lenin's 1921 New Economic Policy, which backtracked on the earlier demands for elimination of capitalist enterprise in the Soviet Union, a move that seemed to the idealists of the Smithy as selling out the revolution.[13] The Smithy would reverse course late in the 1920s and advocate mass cultural organization, but by that time, the small group, riven with divisions, was easy prey for its rival. After suffering several internal splits, the organization's members were absorbed into RAPP (The Russian Association of Proletarian Writers), the successor to VAPP.

The Smithy nonetheless exerted a lasting influence on the style of industrial idealism that would come to characterize Soviet literature—that is to say, exactly the kind of works that Arab writers of *al-adab al-multazim* did not want to be forced to write. Smithy lyric poetry, as well as its later prose writing, glorified industrialization and machine culture and replaced the individual hero with the triumphant collective proletarian mass. The Smithy offered a fetishized vision of machinery and the workers who operated it, an approach that perhaps impressed party bosses but was unlikely to appeal to the laborers who knew what real factory conditions were like. The term "Smithy poetry" eventually became a pejorative for any kind of poor-quality propaganda ostensibly aimed at rousing barely literate factory workers.[14] It was not a poet, however, but rather one of the Smithy's novelists, Fyodor Gladkov, who would come to be the standard bearer for socialist realism, for better or worse. Gladkov's 1925 novel *Cement*, initially decried by critics of the time, later came to exemplify the dominant genre of Soviet socialist realism, the production novel.[15] Russian writers replicated the very rigid formula of Gladkov's novel during the decades of socialist realism in a manner that took to heart the assembly-line mode of production that it glorified.

The production novel not only sacrificed aesthetic quality—it very often sacrificed factual accuracy for the sake of idealism. Gladkov's novel *Power (Energiya)*, which depicted the construction of a power station, for example, was exalted by the party mouthpiece *Pravda* as one of the most realistic works of Soviet literature. Yet the engineer who actually designed the power plant Gladkov described in the novel criticized it as completely riddled with factual errors about the plant, the workers, and the construction process.[16] Officially, the party felt that Gladkov's realism lay not in the nuts and bolts of everyday detail, but in his feel for the larger progress of social change. Yet there was clearly a sense—which would have been apparent to anyone who actually worked in the kinds of factories Gladkov described—that this supposedly deeper level of realism was an excuse for whitewashing away the real problems besetting Soviet factories. No matter the reason, the 'realism' of Soviet socialist realism, then, seemed more like propaganda. Notwithstanding the fact that his well-intentioned novels came to be the emblems of committed writing gone overboard, Gladkov himself found much to worry about in the direction that socialist literature was taking in Russia.

The issue that put Gladkov on the wrong side of the rising power struggle in Soviet writing was one that would vex theorists of politically committed literature—and indeed, technicians and artists of all types—throughout the twentieth century: Did one's personal ideology matter more than one's technical skill? The havoc wreaked on the hapless populations of Communist countries by 'doctors' and 'engineers' chosen solely for their party loyalties makes the answer seem painfully obvious today, yet in the 1920s, it was a lively issue, particularly in the arts. Egyptian writers in the 1930s and 1940s also debated whether party membership was desirable, or even possible, for a free but committed writer.

Despite the dissolution of *Proletkult*, the mid-1920s did see a relative tolerance of diverging opinions on literature in the Soviet Union. A key issue under debate was that of the 'fellow travelers *(poputchiki)*,' a category Trotsky introduced for non-Communist writers, predominantly from the petite bourgeoisie. Despite their lack of party affiliation and their deviations from a proper Marxist perspective, their works nonetheless managed to capture the struggle of the proletariat. Trotsky and the leading Marxist journal writer Alexander Voronsky advocated a nurturing stance toward the fellow travelers, in order to bring them into the Soviet fold.[17] Voronsky, however, was strongly attacked by VAPP as part of a tightening of the previously tolerant policies, beginning in 1928. Voronsky would be expelled from the party and arrested in 1929, and after a brief return to grace, he was executed in 1937.

Meanwhile, RAPP, the successor to VAPP, and its leader Leopold Averbakh, now the dominant force in Soviet literature, took a hard line on the primacy of party loyalty. The emergence of a deliberate 'party-ness *(partiinost)*' in literature would become a dominant characteristic of Soviet literature. Citing comments written by Lenin as early as 1905, advocates of *partiinost* held that reality must be rendered from the viewpoint of an active ideological framework in a literary text, which required a conscious effort on the part of the artist to dedicate his or her work to the cause of socialism. While Lenin insisted on the freedom of the artist, his version of freedom differed substantially from that of the bourgeois writer. Lenin, in fact, saw "individualism" as a leading hindrance to true freedom, which depended on a conscious solidarity with the purposes of socialism.[18] This posed an obvious problem, as the great part of the world's artists, including Russia's great realists, had not written with a conscious intent to further socialism. Did Dostoevsky now belong in the trash?

The forceful Leopold Averbakh and his RAPP organization seized on the momentum of Stalin's consolidation of absolute power and the forced industrialization of the First Five-Year Plan (which began in 1928) to strengthen their hand. Playing well to Stalin's strengths, RAPP not only invited strong party control over writers, it pushed for a more active party role in cultural affairs. At the same time, RAPP attacked competing organizations and absorbed their members, while taking an unyielding approach toward 'the fellow travelers.'[19] Doctrinally, RAPP opposed the propagandistic idealism of Gladkov and the Smithy and demanded the kind of detailed realism that only true veterans of the proletariat could provide. If the Smithy represented one extreme of Soviet art in its near-comic idealism, RAPP would manifest the opposite extreme in its crude attempts to achieve realism. Many of RAPP's projects seem like sheer folly today. In 1931, RAPP issued a policy "obligatory for every proletarian writer, with no exceptions," to go to factories to write about labor heroes, granting them a mere two weeks to accomplish the task. Meanwhile, thousands of 'shock workers,' with little or no background in writing, were pulled from the labor field and pressed into service for immediate training as proletarian writers. The dismal results likely contributed to the party's dissolution of the mighty RAPP the following year.[20] Averbakh was condemned as a Fascist subversive and an "enemy of the people," on the unlikely charge of his secret collaboration with people that he long opposed, like Trotsky.[21]

Ironically, as Stalin was rounding up scapegoats in all fields and rapidly switching direction from the disastrous First Five-Year Plan, RAPP's cruel end was but the literary field's share of what was going around all of the Soviet Union. RAPP's emphasis on realism had become obsolete in light of the rise of the national glorification campaign surrounding Stalin's personality cult. Instead of emphasizing the equality of all 'little' men, literature accordingly elevated the giant of industrial accomplishment, the "positive" Soviet hero.[22] Poor state planning, second-rate technology, and unrealistic ambitions made a realistic picture of factory life an unpalatable subject for art. Meanwhile, technical failures forced workers to step up with extraordinary efforts that were better captured in literature by the idealized Soviet hero. From his temporary demise, former Smithy writer Gladkov now became a national exemplar, regardless of the technical errors in his work.[23]

Soviet writing finally came under a single, state-run Soviet Writers' Union in 1932, when all previously existing organizations were brought under one umbrella. Joseph Schull points out that many writers actually welcomed the change as bringing an end to the divisive battles of the past.[24] What followed did not live up to their hopes, but the relief that the Writers' Union brought spoke to the extreme divisiveness of the previous decade. In any case, the events left a lasting impression on all advocates of politically engaged literature: bickering within the literary community could well lead to takeover by the state.

In 1931, after much persuasion, Maxim Gorky returned to Russia, threw his support and pen behind Stalin, and became the first secretary of the Writers' Union in 1934. RAPP and all other proletarian organizations were disbanded while Andrei Zdhanov exercised party control over the culture enterprise. Gorky, whose 1907 novel *Mother (Mat')* had laid the groundwork for socialist realism, believed firmly in idealized Soviet heroes—men who were "hard as swords."[25] Zhdanov himself admitted the usefulness of romanticism in socialist realist writing in his landmark speech inaugurating the approved method.[26] A neat official history papered over the numerous doctrinal swings, purges, and conflicts to present the now-solidified socialist realism as a natural development in literary history, rather than the imposed order that it was.

The lessons of the Soviet experience impressed Arab writers with the importance of defining their relationship to the political power. Discussions of *al-adab al-multazim* necessarily included reference to the state, and *multazim* theorists were eager to define that relationship before their lack of consensus could invite the state to do it for them. Khuri, in his zeal to persuade reluctant writers to declare their "commitment" and agree what that commitment meant, was in some measure seeking to preclude such internal divisiveness. At the same time, however, consensus in *al-adab al-multazim* would prove elusive precisely because Arab theorists were loath to let their talk of 'duty' and 'responsibility' lead to a self-imposed literary dictatorship.

Sartre's Call to *Engagement* in Post-War France

While committed writing had evolved in the Arab world in the menacing shadow of Soviet socialist realism, it was Jean-Paul Sartre's vision of *engagement* that gave a name to the corresponding movement of *iltizam*. Although Arab writers had been actively applying their art toward political and social change since the turn of the twentieth century, it was the 1947 commentary on Sartre's essays in *Le Temps Modernes*, by none other than Hussein, that brought the concept of committed writing to a head.[27] Sartre had reexamined the role of the writer in a dramatically changed society—that of post-war France. Arab writers who studied Sartre were also assessing their role in view of the seismic shifts brought about by the end of colonialism. In the late 1940s, Sartre was asking—and offering some answers to—questions that were dividing Arab writers as well. Eventually collected into a single volume—*What Is Literature? (Qu'est-ce que la littérature?)*—Sartre's essays on *engagement* bore titles like: "What Is Writing?" ("Qu'est-ce qu'écrire?"), "Why Write?" ("Pourquoi écrire?"), and "For Whom Does One Write?" ("Pour qui écrit-on?"). That the latter title would serve to frame the 1955 Hussein–Khuri debates speaks to the degree to which the Arabic literary world was consciously following Sartre's lead.

Additionally, the Arab debate shared Sartre's polemical dichotomy, in which there were but two kinds of writers. In this dichotomy, a writer was either engaged, that is, using one's literary skill to expose the conditions of social injustice and encourage freedom and democracy, or else serving the forces of oppression. "The 'engaged' writer knows that words are action. He knows that to reveal is to change and that one can only reveal by planning to change."[28] This formulation recalled Adorno, who considered lyric poetry "barbaric" precisely because it didn't address issues like Auschwitz. Sartre defined the committed writer in terms of what a writer should have done in years past:

> By clarifying and supporting the claims of the proletariat, he would have attained the essence of the art of writing. . . . by trying to awaken the consciousness of the working class while giving evidence to the bourgeois of their own iniquity, his works would have reflected the entire world . . . he would have abandoned the analytical and psychological interpretation of 'human nature' for the synthetic appreciation of *conditions*.[29]

On the other hand, the ways in which a writer could become a tool of oppression were legion, and not always obvious to the writer. In fact, much of what Sartre condemned as blind servitude to injustice had often passed for great art and its practitioners had once been lauded as great social critics. In Sartre's historical moment, as in the Arab world of the 1940s, political conditions were changing rapidly and the standards applied to the writer would need to change with them.

The historical conditions in post-war France no doubt contributed to the uncompromising polemic in Sartre's writing. The effects of two world wars and the humiliating collaboration of thousands of France's greatest minds with the Nazi occupiers, not to mention the brutal turn that socialism had taken in Eastern Europe, strengthened the urgency of employing literature on behalf of the oppressed. Sartre would modify his demands significantly in his later writings and back off the uncompromising position in *What is Literature?*, but these later nuances were largely lost in the Arab world, where Sartre's (perceived) support of Israel in the 1960s discredited anything else he had to say. For better or worse, the strong polemics of 1947, captured in *What Is Literature?*, remained the dominant influence on *al-adab al-multazim* throughout the 1950s and 1960s. Sartre began by branding his opponents as the "imbecile," "hack-journalist *(folliculaire)*," and "petty mind," who wrote without asking the most basic of questions:

> since critics condemn me in the name of literature without ever saying what they mean by that, the best answer to give them is to examine the art of writing without prejudice. What is writing? Why does one write? For whom? The fact is, it seems that nobody has ever asked himself these questions.[30]

To be committed was to ask the fundamental questions that defined one's art. These were questions, of course, that Khuri had demanded answers to and to which Hussein had politely deferred. The epitome of the lost artist in Sartre's formulation was the producer of "art for art's sake," which remained the ultimate condemnation in both Sartre's world and in that of the Arab critics who emulated him.[31] Those who sought "pure" aesthetics were but dupes of the bourgeoisie. "Pure art and empty art are the same thing . . . aesthetic purism was a brilliant maneuver of the bourgeois of the last century."[32]

Yet one did not become 'committed' merely by eschewing 'pure' art. Indeed, Sartre's list of those who had been unwittingly duped into serving in the oppression of the masses in their writing was quite extensive and no doubt a surprise to many who found themselves on it. "Idealism, psychologism, determinism, [and] utilitarianism" were nothing but means for the writer to bury class distinctions from view and thus entrench class injustices.[33] Writing about eternal truths, or an ahistorical concept of a general human nature or even historical moments outside the present, were all tantamount to diverting the public from the very real problems of the current age. Even Flaubert, who pilloried the bourgeoisie in some of his writing, ultimately served the aims of that class, since he moved freely from profiling bourgeois decadence one day to the historically removed subject of "Carthaginian mercenaries" the next.[34] Worse, Flaubert's critique of the bourgeoisie centered on internal, psychological failings, such that they could continue to exploit the proletariat as long as they would "practice high thinking in private."[35] Indeed, writing about anything other than the class system was inevitably to serve the bourgeoisie.

> The bourgeois could be recognized by the fact that he denied the existence of social classes and particularly of the bourgeoisie . . . he demonstrated by analysis that all men are alike because they are invariant elements of social combinations and because each one of them, whatever his rank, completely possesses *human nature*. Hence, inequalities appeared as fortuitous and passing accidents which could not alter the permanent characteristics of the social atom. There was no proletariat, that is, no synthetic class of which each worker was a passing mode; there were only proletarians, each isolated in his human nature.[36]

Somewhat ironically, Arab theorists of *al-adab al-multazim* chose the term "existentialist" to label all the practitioners of empty, misleading metaphysical directions. Nonetheless, like Sartre, they believed that to pursue any of those trends was to shirk one's *iltizam*.

Not surprisingly, Sartre felt that the majority of leading artists throughout history were unwitting servants of the established order. Medieval writers focused on eternal religious truths, while writers of the Enlightenment fixed their sights on the equally unchanging scientific and psychological principles of the universal man. Yet in both cases, writers were inadvertently using their craft to distract the masses from the true social injustices around them. By the nineteenth century, the bourgeoisie had taken over from the nobility in the exploitation of the masses. Literature, once the property of the nobility, passed during the nineteenth century into the hands of Marx's 'rising class': the bourgeoisie. That rising class did allow writers to expose the injustice of the social order just long enough to mount a revolution and seize power, Sartre conceded, but once in the driver's seat, the bourgeoisie again turned writers away from the mission of exposing society's flaws.[37]

Eternal questions of human nature were mere distractions, Sartre believed, because the truly committed work must recognize its situation within a particular historical context. "It wins itself in an historical situation; each book proposes a concrete liberation on the basis of a particular alienation." An effective work of literature, therefore, may have a very limited shelf life and address only a limited, particular audience. Sartre applauded Vercors's *The Silence of the Sea (Le Silence de la Mer)* for addressing the situation of the French people living under the Nazi occupation. The text lost its effectiveness, however, when the political situation began to change.[38]

Sartre further believed that those writers who concentrated on aesthetic technique and innovation cut themselves off from the masses, by making their works inaccessible to the general public. The writer who innovated shut out the masses:

> as the masses had no culture or leisure, any would-be literary revolution, by refining its technique, put the works it inspired out of their range and served the interests of social conservatism.
>
> Thus, he had to revert to the bourgeois public . . . he lived in a state of contradiction and dishonesty since he both knew and did not want to know *for whom* he was writing. He was fond of speaking of his *solitude*, and rather than assume responsibility for the public which he had slyly chosen, he concocted the notion that one writes for oneself alone or for God.[39]

Among these guilty innovators, none ranked as low as the pure artist, who occupied a special level in Sartre's (very large) abyss of failed artists. The surrealist "squandered literary traditions" and the astheticist had "no greater concern than that of establishing his irresponsibility." In his attempts to show off his impenetrable artistic skills, such an artist was guilty of no less than "setting up the rights of genius which replaced the divine right of the authoritarian monarchy."[40] Indeed, advocates of *l'art pour l'art* were quite comfortable with both the divine right of genius and monarchy. Baudelaire had undisguised disdain for "the public, to whom," he warned, "one should never offer a delicate perfume. It exasperates them. Give them only carefully selected garbage."[41] In the same vein, he considered aristocracy as the only proper type of social order. The association made aestheticism as corrupt and outdated as the fallen monarchies of the previous centuries in Sartre's strict taxonomy.

Like Sartre, Arab advocates of *al-adab al-multazim* exhorted writers to present clear and accessible texts for the mass public, necessarily avoiding artistic experimentation. Thus, it came as somewhat of a surprise that many of the great realists of the 1940s, renowned for their clean and simple style, became noted for their impressionism in the 1960s, none more so than Mahfouz. In fact, Salama Musa, the early pioneer of 'Literature for the People,' made reference to an established French dictum—"that which is not clear is not French"[42]—in his appeal to Egyptian writers.

So fixed was Sartre on calling writers to action that he refused to stray off on tangents like other forms of artistic expression. He dismissed such questions with "no, we do not want to 'engage' painting, sculpture, and music 'too,' or at least not in the same way."[43] The mission of writing for social change was so pressing that Sartre preferred to let someone else decide in what "way" visual arts could be committed to the struggle. Similarly, like Adorno, Sartre had difficulty reconciling poetry with commitment.[44] The most controversial point in Sartre's formulation of *engagement* no doubt was the initial exclusion of poetry from his definition of committed literature, a point that riled more than a few contemporary poets.[45] In his introduction to an anthology of *négritude* poets, *Black Orpheus*, Sartre reversed his position, applauding the *négritude* poetry as an ideal means for raising the consciousness of the black colonial audience. By appropriating the form and language of French poetry for their own purposes, Sartre noted, the African and Caribbean poets inherently made a significant statement of independence.[46] Thus, questions of genre and style were historically conditioned. While poetry or surrealism might be inappropriate for one social context, they might work well in a different setting.

Finally, Sartre concluded, as did Khuri and the hardliners of *iltizam*, with the proviso that the writer must be free. Sartre found the French Communist Party so tainted by the influence of Stalinism that he advised French writers to avoid the party. In a different country, however, party membership might be a good thing for a writer.[47] Yet coming on the heels of the aforementioned demands, this concession to freedom did not ease the claustrophobia many readers found in Sartre's vision of *engagement*.

Hussein's counterpart in the French equivalent of the debate on *al-adab al-multazim* was none other than Sartre's one-time comrade and long-time rival Albert Camus, who, like Hussein, found the demands of *engagement* at odds with the freedom Sartre supposedly respected. Like his Egyptian counterpart, Camus's standing in French literature gave his dissent undeniable weight. Even after decades of advocating *engagement* over Camus's objections, Sartre found to his chagrin that the works of Camus were much more popular among the student protesters of 1968 in France than those of the ostensible standard bearer of *engagement*. In a particularly biting denunciation, Camus saw 'committed' as the wrong term to describe the literature Sartre demanded:

> Today everything is changed and even silence has dangerous implications. The moment that abstaining from choice is itself looked upon as a choice and punished or praised as such, the artist is willy-nilly impressed into service. 'Impressed' seems to me a more accurate term in this connection than 'committed.' Instead of signing up, indeed, for voluntary service, the artist does his compulsory service. Every artist today is embarked on the contemporary slave galley.[48]

Camus famously objected that the advocates of *engagement* should focus more on commitment in their actions and less on commitment in writing, reminding critics, as did the quote above, that he had seen more action as a civilian in the *résistance* than the former soldier Sartre.[49] To Camus, Sartre was an apologist for Communist Russia, who overlooked its most detestable acts and accepted the dubious 'freedom' of the Soviet writer.

Sartre raised a challenge and a series of questions that Arab writers took up directly in the 1940s. While politically and socially activist writing had been a very strong trend in Arabic literature, particularly since the late nineteenth century, Sartre's call helped solidify committed writing into the movement of *al-adab al-multazim*. Despite his influence, however, Sartre had bequeathed questions rather than answers, and Arab writers would continue to debate the same questions of the writer's role, mission, and relation to the public that Sartre had raised in *What Is Literature?*, as seen in the Hussein–Khuri debate. Sartre had also raised the question of *how* to write for the masses, a question that had confounded Soviet writers as well. Arab writers of *al-adab al-multazim* were profoundly influenced by European styles and genres, and their visions of the most effective approach for reaching the mass public were shaped by European debates on the subject. When Mahfouz cited the influences on his writing style, for example, his preferences and dislikes were almost entirely drawn from European writers of the nineteenth and twentieth centuries (as discussed in chapter 3). In this regard, one of the most important theoretical conversations on the subject of socially engaged literature was the exchange between Eastern European Marxist writers in the mid-twentieth century, under the misleadingly condensed title of the Lukács–Brecht expressionism debates. A brief look at the two competing positions in this debate provides a valuable lens for viewing the evolution of *al-adab al-multazim.*

Brecht and Lukács Debate Literature for Social Change

The evolution and transformation of socially engaged writing between the two Egyptian revolutions was marked by a dramatic change in style and form, from the highpoint of *al-adab al-multazim* in the 1950s to the profound disillusion stretching from the 1960s to the end of the century. Writers renowned for their mastery of classic realism, like Mahfouz and Idris, turned sharply toward impressionist, opaque works in the later period. The continuity in these two periods, however, is best seen when viewed through the lens of the famed 'expressionism debates' between two competing groups of Marxist writers, led informally by Bertolt Brecht and Gyorgy Lukács. As this debate centered on the best literary style for reaching the masses for social change, it directly addressed the same questions and problems that writers like Mahfouz and Idris faced.

The expressionism debates were so named because their catalyst was an exchange of opinions in the Marxist exile publication *Das Wort* on the merits of that style, but the discussion quickly expanded to take on the entire problem of realism in the service of socially engaged writing. While involving a host of the most accomplished Marxist literary minds of the 1930s, the leaders of the competing camps came to stand as the flagbearers for the contending visions. Both were 'committed' writers in the Sartrean sense, as their statements of purpose indicate:

> Lukács: What are the fundamental issues on which the artist must take a stand to be a true artist? The great issues of human progress. No great artist can be indifferent to them. Without passionate commitment he cannot create types or achieve profound realism. Without commitment a writer will never be able to distinguish the essential from the inessential. From the perspective of the totality of social development, a writer who has no enthusiasm for progress and hatred for reaction, who does not love good and repudiate evil, cannot exercise the discrimination essential for great literature.[50]

> Brecht: If we wish to have a living and combative literature, which is fully engaged with reality and fully grasps reality, a truly popular literature, we must keep step with the rapid development of reality. The great working masses are already on the move.[51]

Despite sharing a commitment to social change through literature, they were divided on the thorny concept of realism. For both, social change involved creating an awareness of the true nature of social relations, but how to do this was not immediately obvious. As Marx had described it, an entire substructure of socioeconomic relations kept the masses in their unfavorable position. This substructure was concealed, however, beneath a surface structure that presented the current situation as a natural, unchanging reality. Like Sartre, both Lukács and Brecht saw the need to strip away the illusions, the 'false consciousness' that the upper classes used to numb the proletariat into accepting this unfair system. They parted company, however, on *how* to break that false consciousness. For Lukács, examining and exposing the substructure in clear, systematic detail in a literary work was the answer. Brecht, by contrast, emphasized the need to grab the audience's attention, breaking the illusion of social relations from its familiar context. Their differences came in no small part from the fact that Lukács was a theorist—and one known for his systematic, logical nature of thinking—while Brecht was a practitioner, a dramatist for whom seizing an audience's attention was essential to his success.

Lukács's approach relied upon what he called "critical realism," succinctly defined as "a writer's critical understanding of the world he lives in" and distinct from the "naive," uncritical forms of "modernism" and socialist realism.[52] For Lukács, breaking through the surface level of illusion meant exposing social relations that had become "reified," that is, having taken on the appearance of "things," acquiring a "phantom objectivity" that obscured their true nature. For the unfavorable position of the lower classes to be seen as anything but a deliberate outcome of a socioeconomic system that kept them in their place, those relations had to be attributed to some natural force, like fate, human nature, or divine wisdom. Literature through the ages had done much to entrench this reification. From fairy tales to eighteenth-century novels, stories of social change typically ended by restoring the 'natural' social order. Even when a lowly but virtuous servant triumphed over an evil oppressor, the hero would inevitably be revealed to have been of noble or high birth, somehow mistakenly assumed to be a commoner.[53] True realism could only dispel these misguided reifications by exposing the real, underlying social order in unmistakable detail.

Lukács's realism was much more than just accurate reproduction of surface detail. He recognized that people were surrounded by details all their lives and remained unaware of the social system underlying that detail. In fact, Lukács warned strongly against confusing realism with a fascination for surface detail that lacked attention to the underlying social structure, a fascination that he felt characterized naturalism:

> What is that reality of which literary creation must provide a faithful reflection? The negative response is required first of all: this reality does not consist simply of the immediately perceptible superfice of the external world, nor simply of accidental, ephemeral, contingent phenomena. While Marxist aesthetics makes realism the crux of its theory of art, it also combats vigorously any kind of naturalism and any direction which is satisfied with a photographic reproduction of the immediately perceptible superfice of the external world.[54]

In fact, some of the genres most obsessed with surface detail drew sharp criticism from Lukács. He dismissed the "non-literary literature" of Arthur Conan Doyle as serving merely to prove the "omniscience" of those who guarded the existing social order.[55] Sherlock Holmes may have been adept at noticing surface patterns, but he was blind to the underlying currents of social change. Worse, in Lukács's opinion, was the naturalism practiced by Émile Zola. Despite his exhaustive attention to detail, the naturalist reported as a spectator, not a participant, in the reality around him.[56]

The key to true realism, of "overriding importance," Lukács believed, was its perspective.[57] A proper perspective captures the totality of a given historical situation, while the improper, "modernist" perspective fragments that reality. As he notes, "the question is not: is x present in reality? But rather: does x represent the whole of reality?"[58] In a successful realist narrative, "each section of a portrayed totality is placed in a concrete social context."[59] Lukács was quite exacting in his demands for critical realism, but did he find any actual writers who had achieved these standards? While Lukács was careful not to equate his "critical realism" wholesale with the nineteenth-century European writers most often labeled as 'realist,' the two classifications overlapped significantly. Indeed, Brecht would accuse Lukács of a blanket endorsement of those bourgeois French and German writers:

> [a] small clique, evidently led by Lukács and Hay, is setting up a very specific form ideal implying opposition to everything that doesn't accommodate itself to this form ideal, which is derived from the bourgeois *romanciers* of the past century.[60]

Lukács was well aware of the awkwardness inherent in lauding authors whose backgrounds lay far outside the ranks of the proletariat. Lukács's exemplars of critical realism—Balzac, Tolstoy, and Thomas Mann—achieved true realism without being sent off to labor camps to learn the proletarian way of life. Instead, they offered accurate and thorough depictions of the totality of social and economic relations in their societies as well as the forces of social change. Their personal backgrounds were irrelevant, as long as their social pictures were comprehensive and accurate.

As with Sartre's vision, Lukács's ideal became clearest when he decried what did *not* meet his criteria. Numerous failed literary styles could be grouped under Lukács's umbrella term 'modernism,' which ran the gamut from naturalism to formalism to surrealism. While Lukács's logic for grouping these styles under one banner could be quite flexible—as it would need to be to make bedfellows of Zola and Kafka—at the end of the day, his 'modernism' essentially included any style that was not classic nineteenth-century realism.[61] Modernism failed, in Lukács's opinion, by its surrender to an unchangeable angst. At the depth of this abyss lay writers like James Joyce, who immersed the reader in the jumbled thoughts of a protagonist, detached from the world outside him. Kafka may have shown us victims of an unjust legal system, like the famous Joseph K of *The Trial*, but he chose to focus so completely on the tortured viewpoint of the victim that the structure and inner workings of the nameless authority persecuting him were never explored.[62] Attributing humanity's problems to any kind of unchanging, or natural, force was another sure ticket to the graveyard in Lukács's strict standards of realism. Chief among the wrong turns a writer could take was the catastrophic error that Sartre also derided: focusing on an eternal, ahistorical "human condition."[63]

Brecht, meanwhile, embraced a literary goal much like Lukács's:

> Laying bare society's causal network/showing up the dominant viewpoint as the viewpoint of the dominators/writing from the standpoint of the class which has prepared the broadest solutions for the most pressing problems afflicting human society/emphasizing the dynamics of development/concrete and so as to encourage abstraction.[64]

In fact, Brecht praised Lukács in his text as a source of his definition of effective art. Like Lukács, Brecht insisted on addressing the problems of a particular historical situation, rather than depicting universal conditions. Yet Brecht, as a successful producer of stage plays who understood well the limits of an audience's attention, was much less confident in the audience's willingness or ability to follow a systematic analysis of the social structure. Instead, Brecht's art sought to shatter the illusion of the naturalness of immediate experience that concealed the underlying social structure.

While sharing Lukács's imperative to break the illusion of social relations out of their familiar contexts and expose them for the contrived arrangements they were, Brecht believed defamiliarization rather than analysis was the way to do this. Logically enough, Brecht reasoned that the viewer had seen these unjust relations in their normal context countless times and had not been moved to change them. The audience, he felt, must be made to see social relations in a new light, outside of their normal settings. Breaking with the formal rules of Aristotelean drama, Brecht sought to avoid the cathartic effect that Aristotle had identified in the theater.[65] Catharsis resulted from "identification" with characters, situations, or actions, and played on the emotions rather than the intellect. The resulting effect of catharsis was to reinforce the status quo.[66]

Instead, Brecht's solution to the challenge of bringing everyday relations into the plane of conscious examination was best captured in his most famous artistic innovation, the *Verfremdungeffekt.* The most common English rendering of the term is the "alienation effect," although scholars seem only able to agree that neither it nor any other single English phrase offers a satisfactory translation.[67] Although most often associated with Brecht's distinctly jarring stage techniques, the *Verfremdungeffekt* has a much wider application in its sense of breaking the "illusion" of the naturalness of social relations engendered by the traditional stage presentation or generally raising incidents "above the level of the everyday, the obvious, the expected."[68] The nineteenth-century realism so dear to Lukács was not inherently bad in Brecht's view; rather, it was the familiarity of that style, which could breed complacency, that concerned Brecht. Similarly, Brecht realized that even his own shocking stage techniques worked only because they were new and unfamiliar to the audience. Should his techniques become commonplace, they would lose their effectiveness.

Brecht's point was quite germane to the Arab debates on the nature of effective writing in the mid-twentieth century. During the height of *al-adab al-multazim* in the 1940s and 1950s, the classic nineteenth-century realism that Lukács advocated had not become as commonplace as it was in Europe. The introduction of the novel genre in Egypt is typically dated to 1913,[69] and realist novels on contemporary social issues would gain in popularity only in the 1920s and 1930s. Thus, the advocates of *al-adab al-multazim* need not face immediately the choice that Brecht and Lukács faced; they could, and did, embrace European-style realism for its detailed depiction of social issues, without too much concern about the complacency that style induced in European audiences. By the 1960s, however, Egyptian writers faced the same problem that Brecht had identified—audiences who consumed large quantities of realist literature without being moved to change the social system.

The Lukács–Brecht debates, like the disagreements of Sartre and Camus, or the disputes between Soviet literary organizations, highlighted the predicament of the committed writer at mid-century. *Multazim* Arabic writers picked up an international call to write for social justice, yet they did not receive any clear answers to the numerous problems that vexed that effort. As Khuri and his supporters struggled to walk the same ground that their predecessors had, while trying to avoid falling into any of the same traps, they drew heavily on the lessons from Europe, yet they were left largely to find answers for themselves. The vision of *al-adab al-multazim* that they developed would be uniquely their own.

Chapter 2
Al-Adab al-Multazim: A Distinctive Arabic Model of Committed Literature

When Taha Hussein introduced Sartre's concept of *engagement* into Arabic as *iltizam* in 1947, the term found a receptive audience. Arab authors had been directing their art toward issues of social justice since the late nineteenth century and by the 1920s, many were advocating a consciously targeted 'literature for the people.' Yet answers to the questions of how to achieve this kind of art were no easier to come by in the Arab world than they had been for the Russian or French authors who wrestled with the same issues.

Commitment before *Iltizam*

It's commonplace to trace the emergence of modern Arab nationalism and cultural revival to Napoleon's invasion of 1798, which started the march to the Arab 'renaissance,' or *nahda*, that began in the mid- to late-1800s. Egypt and the Levant were the leading centers of this revival and would remain the focal points of artistic evolution well into the heyday of *al-adab al-multazim*. That socially activist literature developed in tandem with, and often in support of, movements for change in education, gender roles, and, especially, political representation only strengthened the connection of the socially responsible author to the public and political reformers. Writers of activist fiction shared the stage with essayists, translators, and reform-minded educators like Qasim Amin, Muhammad ʻAbduh, Mustafa Lutfi al-Manfaluti, and many, many more. In literature, as in other fields, a central challenge was adopting Western ideas and forms while asserting a distinctive Egyptian, or Arab, identity.

As early as the 1870s, Ya'qub Sannu', an Egyptian educated in Italy, was adapting European drama and short stories to depict the clash of Western and Muslim cultures in contemporary Egypt. In addition to French and Italian, Sannu' wrote in formal and colloquial Arabic, making his work accessible to a wide audience for his day, so much so that he was eventually exiled by the monarchy for the political satires in his popular journal. At the time in which Sannu' worked, Western and Arab literary genres competed for primacy in the Arab world, and there was natural reason to hope that the literature for social change would draw from the distinctive Arabic tradition.

Mahmud Sami al-Barudi, an army officer and very briefly prime minister of Egypt, helped reinvigorate the Arabic poetry genre with his Egyptian and Arab nationalist verse. While al-Barudi's work was written at an elevated level of style, his dual status as a political and literary force for nationalism—enhanced by his exile after the 1882 'Urabi revolution—did much to inspire those who came after him. Muhammad al-Muwaylihi revived the classical *maqamat* genre in 1907 with his *Hadith 'Isa ibn Hisham*, addressing the social problems related to the impact of European culture on traditional Egyptian life. As laudable as al-Muwaylihi's efforts to adapt traditional Arabic genres to the contemporary age may have been, the momentum was definitely swinging toward European forms. The novel genre, a relatively late introduction to Arabic literature, would from its earliest days include a strong trend of social activism. The oft-named 'first Arabic novel,' Muhammad Hussein Haykal's 1913 *Zaynab*, despite the idyllic romanticization of Egyptian peasant life which dominated the majority of its pages, featured a central focus on the structural inequalities in the social and economic system of the day, most notably in the conscription system.

In the 1920s, the Egyptian socialist writer Salama Musa emerged as a leading proponent of an avowed movement of "literature for the people" *(al-adab li-l-sha'b)*. Musa established much of the foundational doctrine that would define committed writing in Egypt through the mid-twentieth century. Editing the journal *al-Hilal* from 1923–29 and producing his own *The New Journal (al-Majalla al-jadida)* over the periods 1929–30 and 1934–42, Musa saw his efforts to reshape attitudes about literature as nothing short of a "revolution" in thought.[1] He advocated a clearly defined style of "modern Egyptian literature," which should stand distinct from classical Arabic writing and which would expose the social problems of the day. In addition to addressing contemporary Egyptian social issues, Musa believed this type of literature could also address "the problems of the world at large." He wanted this new literature to be patterned on European forms—especially the novel and theater.[2] Musa's preference for European styles and forms was unambiguous, yet he advocated not for mere imitation but rather building a distinctly Egyptian literature from European raw material.

A key ingredient of Musa's new literature was the "language of the people." Neither Musa nor his colleagues would ever come to a satisfactory definition of what constituted the "language of the people," yet the concept would become a key mantra of committed writing although it did not necessarily equate to the language *used* by the people. The most obvious language used by the people would have been Egyptian colloquial Arabic, though Musa only allowed for a "flirtation" with colloquial Arabic, to be "conducted chastely."[3] The language of the people, rather, was that which could touch, reach, and move the mass public, and depended far more on an author's shared experience with the public than the dialect in which he or she wrote. However elusive the definition may have been, the change in direction that Musa heralded was unmistakable. Classical Arabic literature, created for the courts of nobles, was intended to serve as a mark of the elite, distinct from the masses, who, after all, could not read. To become an *adib*—that is, a person of letters or a scholar—required specialized training and education to gain the cultural literacy enjoyed by a tiny circle. In his landmark *Literature for the People (al-Adab li-l-sha'b)*, Musa called for a complete reorientation toward the masses; or rather, he codified the change in direction that had been underway since the mid-1800s. The modern *adib* now would be distinguished by his or her ability to write to and for the masses, not the elite.

In fact, this fundamental change in direction shaped Musa's call. Musa sketched the model of his "literature for the people" on a systematic comparison of the classical Arabic literature of the medieval period and the increasingly popular European literary forms. Nonetheless, Musa recognized the need to respect the Arab world's cultural heritage at a time when Arab society was awakening from European rule. Rather than blame classical writers for their failure to write for the masses, Musa excused them on the simple basis that medieval Arab writers had no concept of "the people" *(al-sha'b)* in the twentieth-century sense of the word. The medieval mass public, conversely, was largely illiterate and thus not the intended audience of classical writing. Therefore, the artist focused in both language and subject matter on the elite. "For this reason, we may say that the classic literature was royal," Musa concluded, "guarding the traditions and supporting the orthodoxy of the state."[4] While this type of writing was perhaps suited to the conditions of the medieval period, it was clearly not what Musa considered the appropriate type of literature for an emerging nationalist movement.

Musa further addressed the style of classical literature, attacking its cherished conceptions of proper literary eloquence—its *balagha*. The classical period had produced countless volumes on the art and science of *balagha*, and skilled men of letters had become legendary figures in Arab culture. Rather than condemning the proud heritage of *balagha*, Musa called for a new *balagha*, one suited for the era in which he lived. Invoking the ideas of progress and modernity, he equated the continued use of the classical style to preferring "superstition" *(khurafa)* and "magic" *(sihr)* to modern medicine. His new *balagha* infused the Arabic language with a contemporary social and scientific outlook, unabashedly European in style, and even included some colloquial dialect, European literary forms, and modern scientific terms.[5] Musa even suggested at one point replacing the Arabic script with a Latin alphabet.[6]

Musa also attacked the distinction, which he considered artificial, between "the author" and "the journalist"—for indeed Musa, like most leading Egyptian writers of his time, worked as both. In this artificial dichotomy, the author was supposed to lead "the secluded life of a monk," while the journalist reported on life in the real society in which he or she was deeply immersed.[7] Musa strongly rejected any such separation, and firmly denounced the retreat of authors like Tawfiq al-Hakim and Taha Hussein into what he considered "art for art's sake."[8] Nonetheless, Musa publicly argued for an "open literature" that would be "absolutely free and restrained in no way except by the author's own conscience," although Musa's own comments on the subject reveal that he referred primarily to an author's freedom to violate social and political taboos, rather than being free to write for purely aesthetic purposes.[9] Musa spoke a common warning when he advised that a writer should have a party affiliation but not be subjected to political controls on his or her writing.[10] In practice, Musa's view of responsible literature could be quite narrow, as he frequently took respected figures like Hussein to task for writing about ancient Egypt and medieval Baghdad.[11]

The two leading centers of the Arab *nahda*, Beirut and Cairo, emerged as the dual centers of innovation and development of committed Arabic literature in the early twentieth century. By the 1940s, the overwhelming majority of critical discussion on the subject of committed writing occurred in these two centers, with the proliferation of new paradigms and visions of what writing for the people meant. Writing from Beirut in 1944, 'Umar Fakhuri issued a direct call for committed literature written according to the principles of socialist realism in his book *The Author in the Market (Adib fi-l-suq)*. Also writing from Beirut, Ra'if Khuri, discussed in chapter 1, emerged as one of the most vocal proponents of committed literature, accusing practitioners of 'art for art's sake' of hindering the movement for public awakening and freedom. Khuri, although an avowed socialist, appealed to writers to guide the spirit of the masses without succumbing to the kind of subservience to the state that had marked Soviet writing. Like Musa in Egypt, Khuri recommended writing in simple and clear language to reach the widest audience, eschewing much of the elaborate *balagha* that marked classical Arabic writing.[12] By the time that Sartre's concept of *engagement* found its way into an Arabic journal, Khuri, Musa, Fakhuri, and their colleagues were enjoying a lively debate on socially committed writing, a debate in which assimilating European ideas to fit the Arab movement had become second nature. It was, in short, the perfect time for *engagement* to become *iltizam*.

Iltizam in Arabic Literature

It was Ra'if Khuri's opponent in the famed 1955 UNESCO debate, Taha Hussein, who introduced Sartre's call for *engagement* to the Arab world (as discussed in chapter 1). In 1947, he reviewed Sartre's seminal articles (gathered under the title *What Is Literature?* (*Qu'est-ce que la littérature?*)), coining the term *iltizam al-adib* as the Arabic equivalent of *engagement.* The derivative term for 'committed literature' thus became by extension *al-adab al-multazim*, and the Arabic critical world readily embraced the terms, largely as descriptors for what were already living concepts in Arabic literature. Both *iltizam* and *multazim* were heavily loaded terms with long historical associations in Arab memory, carrying a sharper edge than the corresponding French or English equivalents. *Iltizam*—literally 'duty,' or 'obligation'—had designated a tax collector's commission—a very lucrative yet very dangerously binding commitment a local power holder made to provide revenue to a political sovereign. In choosing that term, Hussein opened the door not only to Sartre's spirit of *engagement* but also to Camus's view of literature being "impressed" as well.[13] Given Hussein's reluctance to conscript himself to the ranks of the 'committed,' as displayed in his debate with Khuri, all the implications of the term seem intended. Activist poet and critic Louis 'Awad was keen to separate *iltizam*, which indicated a voluntarily accepted duty, from the related term *ilzam*, which implied a forced duty.[14] Nonetheless, advocates of literary commitment were not the least bit shy to pronounce their enlistment to the movement. Anwar al-Ma'addawi, a leading advocate of the movement in the 1950s, would not only declare himself "*multazim*" but would also proudly call himself an "extremist" *(mutatarrif)* of *al-adab al-multazim*.[15] For his part, Hussein seemed a bit taken aback that the articles had generated such excitement. Although he would address Sartre's writing three times in a two-year period in his journal *The Egyptian Writer (al-Katib al-Misri)*, each time he expressed surprise that the debate over committed literature had not yet settled.[16] For all Hussein's surprise, Sartre's writings only served to further ignite, rather than settle, the debate on what committed writing meant in the Arab world.

The 1950s would produce the greatest outpouring of Arabic writing on literary commitment, launching new journals, treatises, and schools of writing at a dizzying pace that hardly presaged the rapid decline that was to follow. By 1954, Muhammad Wahbi captured the power of *iltizam* when he stated boldly, "The concept of committed literature dominates the Arab world today."[17] Whether or not his assessment was somewhat hyperbolic, it certainly reflected how *multazim* writers saw things at the time. The "extremism" to which al-Ma'addawi referred, if somewhat tongue-in-cheek, could seem all too real to writers on the receiving end. As noted earlier, despite Hussein producing works like *The Days* and *Tortured of the Earth*, he had been criticized by Musa for writing on historical topics and wound up on the defensive in the Beirut debates of 1955. Al-Hakim, who had written novels about the dysfunctional justice system in the provinces[18] and the struggles of Egyptians for equality among Europeans,[19] also became a target for attack due to his early exhortation for writers to take to the "ivory tower." Fakhuri, the Lebanese creator of *The Author in the Marketplace*, admonished writers not to retreat into that tower,[20] similar to Musa's warning that writers not become like monks. It was a testament to the sway of *iltizam* at the time that al-Hakim felt the need to redefine his conception of the ivory tower in his 1955 rebuttal to Fakhuri. What the elitist-sounding term actually meant, al-Hakim claimed, was only that a writer "not be used as a tool in the hands of politicians, thereby losing his freedom to think independently and without restraints about things." It was an "isolation from politicians and political parties, not from politics or society."[21] Al-Hakim's rhetorical gymnastics spoke volumes for the pressure the movement could assert even on a writer of his stature.

The Beirut journal *al-Adab*, launched by Suhayl Idris in 1953 as an overt platform for *al-adab al-multazim*, became the leading forum for discussion of committed literature in Arabic.[22] Making no bones about the purpose of the journal, Idris's editorial preface "calls for and encourages . . . the literature of *iltizam*."[23] In the second issue of the publication, al-Ma'addawi, the unabashed "extremist" of *iltizam* and leading doctrinal voice of the journal, defined the program of *al-adab al-multazim* in his article of the same name, arguing against both the strict Communist version of controlled literature and the practice of "art for art's sake." Even if his enthusiasm would sometimes get the better of him, al-Ma'addawi nonetheless delineated the two opposite boundary lines that set *al-adab al-multazim* apart from irresponsible writing.[24]

Identifying the antitheses of responsible writing had always been the easier task; describing what constituted engaged writing was the trickier job. Nonetheless, al-Ma'addawi did not shy away from the task, instead seeking to launch *al-Adab*'s mission on as clear a footing as possible. He began, not surprisingly, with a general appeal that echoed Sartre, calling for the writer to raise public consciousness while writing from a personal experience that mirrored that of the people. Meanwhile, he insisted that the writer remain free from political pressures, whether from the state or any political party, or the pressure of strict rules of production. This general appeal was nothing new, of course, but al-Ma'addawi went beyond theory and applied these standards to judge the writing he saw going on around him. He identified six varieties of Arabic writers operating at the time, five of which were acceptable to him. The first type of writer included those who felt that they must always describe current social issues, and made no provisions for wasting one's precious talents on any other subjects. Their duties, however, ended at merely describing the injustices they saw. A second group went even further, not only describing but feeling compelled to find solutions to those social problems. A third group, moreover, agreed with the first two classifications, but did not consider such writing a permanent duty. Al-Ma'addawi then went on to include a fourth set of writers who not only dealt with social concerns but who also expanded their writing to all areas of human life, venturing into those issues of human nature that were not necessarily tied to the current social system. Lastly, there were those who saw no restrictions on literature at all. Al-Ma'addawi saw a place for all these writers in the world of *al-adab al-multazim*, inviting all to apply their talents to the mission of social justice. In the final analysis, he excluded from the movement only the sixth type of writer: he or she who consciously sought to produce socially detached art.[25] Although thorough in his classification of writers, al-Ma'addawi still had not resolved the central dilemma of committed writing. He was left denying only the pure aestheticist, conceding that virtually everybody else in his taxonomy *could* produce committed writing. Coming at a time when even al-Hakim was trying to make "the ivory tower" palatable to the advocates of *al-adab al-multazim*, al-Ma'addawi's classification system offered a place for nearly everybody.

The school of *al-adab al-multazim* centered on Idris, al-Ma'addawi and the board of *al-Adab* faced its stiffest opposition not from advocates of pure aesthetics but from the stricter, Marxist-based school centered around Mahmud Amin al-'Alim and 'Abd al-'Aziz Anis in Cairo, to whom al-Ma'addawi's standards were far too embracing. Al-'Alim would label his school *al-adab al-hadif*, or 'targeted literature,' but it quickly gained the epithet *al-adab al-hatif*—'screaming literature,' a clever change made by substituting one letter, capturing al-'Alim's combative personality well.[26]

Al-'Alim and Anis laid out their literary vision in their 1955 book *On Egyptian Culture (Fi-l-Thaqafa al-misriya)* and launched their own literary journal, *Nationalist Culture (al-Thaqafa al-wataniya)*, as an alternative to the Beirut-based *al-Adab*, distinguishing themselves on principle from Idris's group. Al-Ma'addawi may have called himself an "extremist" of *iltizam*, but that was not enough to satisfy critics like al-'Alim. Unlike Suhayl Idris and his colleagues at *al-Adab*, al-'Alim's school of *al-adab al-hadif* required the author to have a working understanding of socialist principles and to apply those in his or her writing. Far from al-Ma'addawi's embrace of five (extremely broad) categories of acceptable writers, al-'Alim's school required the author to depict social conditions with an eye toward a systemic view of the class struggle that exposed the larger corruption in the social system.[27] Knowing how closely these demands echoed the Soviet writing programs of the 1920s and 1930s, al-'Alim firmly rejected any form of overt control over writers, particularly the kind exercised in the Soviet Union.[28]

Even Sartre was not immune from attack in al-'Alim's theoretical framework. While al-Ma'addawi and Idris at *al-Adab* were willing to accept Sartre's existentialism *(wujudiya)*, for *al-adab al-hadif*, it was the foil with which to compare their committed philosophy.[29] In 1950, another influential Marxist theorist, Shihada Khuri, in his *Literature in the Field (al-Adab fi-l-Maydan)*, had identified Sartre and Kafka as well as "existentialist" views in a long list of misguided paradigms that could distract or misguide the reading public from the social liberation they needed.[30]

Yet for all their disputes on where to draw the final boundaries of committed literature, the competing schools of thought shared some general principles of what constituted writing for the people. It is these shared principles which have left the most lasting impression of *al-adab al-multazim*, and to which we now turn.

An Arabic Model of Committed Literature

Any working model of *al-adab al-multazim* is as sure to spark disagreement today as it would have in the 1950s. Al-Ma'addawi only slightly bent the truth when he declared in 1955, "As for committed literature I do not think there is any longer a need to define it now."[31] Al-Ma'addawi's wise recusal from defining the movement carried a dual-edged message. On the one hand, he knew that no one could precisely define *al-adab al-multazim* without incurring opposition, yet on the other, he knew that committed literature marked a definite movement toward certain shared, general principles. However contentious, a working model provides a necessary framework with which to view the sharp changes in direction of activist writers from the heyday of *iltizam* to the decades of disillusion that followed. In the pages that follow, the aim is not to summarize the theories of al-'Alim, Khuri, or al-Ma'addawi into a single model; rather, the focus is on the key axes upon which the vision of activist writers changed over those decades. As the preceding review of the development of committed writing shows, Arab theorists were keen to position the role of the author carefully in relation to both the reading public and the political authority. The emphasis, therefore, will be on *al-adab al-multazim*'s envisioning of this key, tripartite relationship.[32]

Why were these three parties so essential to the vision of *al-adab al-multazim*? First, all advocates of committed writing saw the essential role of the responsible author as defined by his or her relationship to the mass public. It was on this axis that Musa separated the old "royal" literature from the modern Egyptian literature. It was on this axis also that Khuri and Idris tried to force Hussein to define himself, however adept the latter proved at dodging their imposed dichotomy. In as effective a definition of this relationship as any given before or since, 'Abd al-'Azim Anis stated: "unless a writer accepts his responsibility toward himself, his community, his country, and nationality, his freedom may turn into anarchy and become a means of bringing about the destruction of our social life."[33] Advocates of committed writing intensely debated how the author should write for the mass public, but that he or she should, and could, serve that mass public was never questioned.

Second, all the schools of committed writing that we have discussed buttressed their call for commitment with an insistence that the writer remain free from political control. The shadow of the Soviet experience loomed large over every discussion of commitment as an example of what could happen if this principle was not followed. Musa and al-'Alim, like Sartre and Camus, disagreed on where to draw the line of authorial freedom, with issues like party membership being hot topics, but the importance of the relationship between the writer and political power was unquestioned.

With these key assumptions in mind, we can see that *al-adab al-multazim* was ideally intended to function as a mutual relationship—with constant interaction—between the three parties, without any party usurping the integrity of another. In our current age of global electronic communications, in which writers generally enjoy a direct line to the public, it is easy to overlook the interdependence that once linked these three partners in the mission of socially engaged writing. With government-controlled printing presses, newspapers, and radio a given in the 1950s, the political authority played a key role in establishing and maintaining communication links between the writer and public, and also possessed the power to censor or cut off these links. This power was not absolute, of course; witness the influence of Sonallah Ibrahim's banned novel (discussed in chapter 5), but the era of President Hosni Mubarak's disastrously unsuccessful attempt to shut off the Internet for one day during the 2011 protests was a long way from the days when Mahfouz and Idris published their works in government-supervised newspapers.

In the writer's other key relationship, his or her bond with the mass public brought with it an accompanying set of expectations for style and genre. The genius of the *multazim* writer came from a common union with the public, not from the distance of an impenetrable mind. The *multazim* writer must write in the 'language of the people,' that magic key described by Musa. For most, the language of the people did *not* mean colloquial Arabic, but rather it denoted a manner that captured the experience of the people with absolute fidelity. Although Mahfouz did not use colloquial Arabic, al-Ma'addawi would commend his novels of Cairo life for communicating directly to the heart, rather than the intellect of his readers, a realism that not only seemed true, but "must be true."[34] This type of realism was a stark contrast to the propagandistic idealism that Soviet writers' organizations had instilled through mandatory indoctrination in labor camps and factories. Here again, it was easier to define the 'language of the people' by what it was not. The *multazim* writer would not be commended for stilted, ornamental writing, with obscure references to elite cultural icons or ambiguous, opaque writing. Indeed, while writers like Idris and Mahfouz were exceptionally well versed in classical mythology, European history, and Western philosophy, their realist works produced during the days of *al-adab al-multazim* avoided obvious reference to this knowledge, unlike their later, impressionist texts. To borrow Roland Barthes's distinction of "writerly" and "readerly" texts, *multazim* authors were exhorted to produce the type of clear and unambiguous writing that Barthes classified as "readerly." The "writerly" type of texts Barthes preferred—that is, texts which required the reader to create the meaning[35]—would not serve to enlighten and liberate the mass public.

Putting the relationships of *al-adab al-multazim* into graphic form is particularly useful in comparing the literature of the 1940s and 1950s with that of the 1960s and beyond. The model of *al-adab al-multazim* below is an extension of the Activist-Author Model presented in the introduction.

The spatial positioning of the key components in this model reflects the underlying demands of *al-adab al-multazim*. Three distinct, separate actors are all actively engaged in the mission of social transformation, but without intruding on each other's freedom. The box in the center, though, represents the position of the text in this relationship, a position as important as that between the three actors. Most notably, the model separates the world 'in the text' (represented by the box) from that outside. The only thing an observer would notice in the text was a narrative about 'the people'—that is, the working class—told in the language of the people. One would not be struck by the personal angst of the writer,

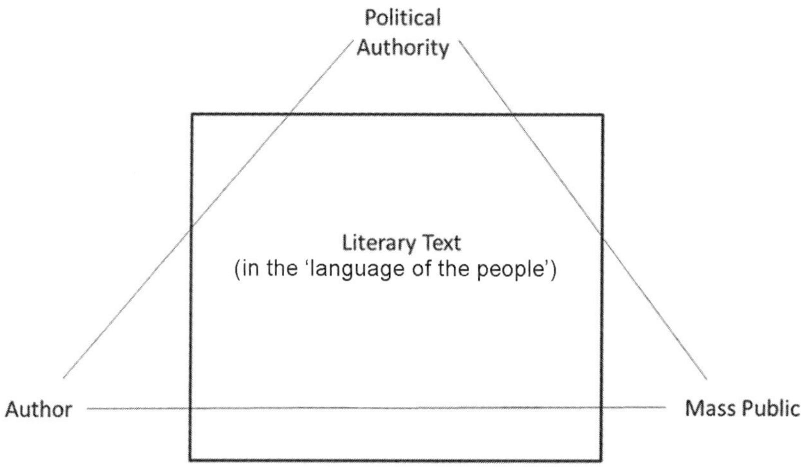

Figure 3: Model of *al-adab al-multazim*

nor his or her stylistic innovations or esoteric knowledge. Nor would one find the active hand of the political power demonstrably intruding on the text. This positioning captures graphically why surrealism or socialist realism failed in the eyes of *multazim* critics: the former for highlighting the internal world of the author, the latter for its obvious state-sponsored propagandizing. Outside their literary texts, *multazim* writers could, and did, discuss the roles of the author, the state, the critic, and the process of producing their art. The world inside their texts, however, was that of the working class, rather than the elite, the political powers, the artists, or the writer him or herself. Outside the text, writers could debate literary criticism or political and artistic theories in a language few in the mass public might understand, but within the text, the 'language of the people' dominated.

Here again, this model is not intended to depict a single theory of *al-adab al-multazim* nor to parse the fine distinctions between acceptable genres and styles on which its advocates dwelled. Rather, its intent is to capture graphically the assumptions that *multazim* theorists held so universally in the early 1950s. That these very foundational assumptions would become the targets of derision and mockery by the 1960s speaks to the drastic change in direction that occurred over the space of the first decade of the Nasser regime.

Al-adab al-multazim was largely an aspiration during the 1940s and early 1950s, as the political power remained in the hands of a foreign-backed monarchy. The 1952 revolution, however, changed the playing field, with an ostensibly socialist, populist leadership in place, openly committed to enlightening and guiding the public. Yet as often happens when a dream comes true, adjusting to the new reality could be disappointing, and the paradigm of *al-adab al-multazim* would not stand long unchallenged in the time of the Nasser regime.

Iltizam in the Nasser Era

No figure in Egyptian history has meant as many different things to as many different people as Gamal Abdel Nasser, a man whose impact is well captured in a scene from Mahfouz's later novel *Before the Throne (Amam al-'arsh)*. In this fantasy tale, Egypt's deceased political leaders, from the first pharaoh to the recently passed president, are brought before the gods for their final judgment, as dictated by the ancient Egyptian *Book of the Dead*. Some find paradise, others damnation, but surely the most anticipated trial is that of Gamal Abdel Nasser, leader of the 1952 revolution and Egypt's first truly independent president. After a heated debate on Nasser's triumphs and sins, the assembled gods split on the legacy of Nasser and find a clear verdict hard to achieve. It's hardly a wonder that ordinary Egyptians have come to no clearer consensus than the gods.

Prominent among the sins identified by the eternals in Mahfouz's book was Nasser's brutal suppression of intellectuals,[36] yet even the committed writers who suffered under Nasser, such as Sonallah Ibrahim, lauded him as "great" decades after his death. For all his oppression of individual freedom, Nasser's funeral still drew a spontaneous outpouring of five million Egyptian mourners, estimated as the largest in history. For *multazim* writers, if the Nasser era was not the proverbial best of times nor the worst, it was certainly the most challenging. While Nasser represented Egyptian independence and national dignity, his regime scarcely fit the role expected of the political power in the model of *al-adab al-multazim*. Mahfouz himself stopped writing for the first seven years of Nasser's rule, no closer to a verdict on the new leader than the fictionalized gods in his novel.

The challenge for *multazim* theorists in the Nasser era was that the regime openly espoused the very same ideals and goals that *al-adab al-multazim* expected from the political power, yet more often than not, it suppressed freedom and expression in the name of those goals. A monarchy with foreign roots and backed by foreign powers was much easier to criticize than a socialist state that threw writers in jail in order to guard the revolution.

From the beginning, the signals from the revolutionary regime on press freedom were mixed. Shortly after taking power, in promising fashion, the new president abolished the old political institutions, including the tainted political parties, and attempted to create a broad national front organization that would mobilize and organize all sectors of the mass public toward the eventual goal of creating a classless society. This broad front organization went through several incarnations, including the 1953 Liberation Rally, 1957 National Union, and 1962 Arab Socialist Union. If this effort recalls the memory of the Soviet evolution of rising and falling cultural organizations, the cautionary tone must be balanced against policy changes that seemed to promise genuine social justice. During that first decade, the regime passed wide-ranging land reform measures, reorganized the political assemblies to include greater working class representation, and began a reorganization of the press to serve the cause of national mobilization. Yet the writers of *al-adab al-multazim* were not naive, knowing well what similar efforts had produced in the Soviet Union. Nasser's consolidation created a powerful, intrusive state apparatus based in the military and security forces and a bloated, inefficient bureaucracy, which absorbed the graduates of the nation's expanded university system.

Writers sat in a precarious position in this evolving regime. Sonia Dabbous's excellent study of Nasser's relationship with the press charts four major stages of press freedom during his rule.[37] From 1952–54, the regime had no clear idea of how to handle the press and consequently imposed and relaxed censorship several times.[38] In the second phase, from 1954–60, the press came under direct censorship from the military leadership of the Ministry of National Guidance. Nasser's stated aims meshed well with the goals of committed writing in the service of the masses, as he claimed, "The social interest of the press did not reflect our new reality. The new reality in our society is that of the village, the peasant, and the workers, and not the Hilton Hotel."[39] In reality, this noble pronouncement served as a blanket justification for locking up troublesome writers.

Beginning in 1960, the government nationalized the press and publishing houses outright. Although both the constitution and Nasser's speeches guaranteed the freedom of all Egyptians to express their opinions without restriction, the president imposed tight controls on publishing and transferred the mission of educating the public on "socialist thought" to a new government department.[40] Given the close ties to and dependency of most authors on the government press, this marked nothing less than the nationalization of *al-adab al-multazim*. Following the 1967 military debacle, Nasser encouraged a popular scourging of Egyptian institutions, allowing increased freedom to criticize the security apparatus. Nasser's sudden death in 1970 left a question as to whether this last phase marked a genuine liberalization or merely a period of scapegoating, perpetuating the mystery and division surrounding the leader's legacy.

Beyond the threat of prison, Egyptian writers were at the mercy of the state for jobs. Since even the top novelists could not earn a living writing fiction, most relied on employment in the government bureaucracy or the state-run press. Thus, the writer in the 1960s walked a tightrope, as Anthony McDermott captured well in his description of Yusuf Idris: "this kind of atmosphere meant that Idris had to be simultaneously a sycophant (he wrote some extravagant articles in praise of Nasser), a hack journalist, and also the dedicated artist."[41] Beirut provided something of a safe haven for writers and critics, but what one said in Lebanon could bear consequences in Egypt. Idris broke his delicate balancing act by criticizing the Egyptian government at a conference in Beirut and was arrested upon his return to Egypt.

It was not only the writer's position toward the political authority that had changed but also his or her relationship with the mass public. As much as the behavior of the revolutionary regime could confound progressive writers, the actions of the public now freed from foreign domination were no less puzzling. Military officers from the lower classes once marginalized in the monarchy and now elevated to positions of power proved as exploitative and opportunistic as their predecessors. And as the 1970s dawned, the public seemed more interested in Western consumer goods than social justice.

For all these reasons, as well as their own fatigue with the realism they had practiced for decades, *multazim* exemplars like Mahfouz and Idris turned to impressionist and surrealist tales of individual alienation in the 1960s, which once again forced critics to redefine the proper boundaries of *multazim* literature. Author and critic Louis 'Awad, who had been exiled under the monarchy, returned as literary editor for the revolution's newspaper *al-Jumhuriya*, where he expounded his vision of a "literature for life's sake" *(al-adab fi sabil al-hayat)*.[42] 'Awad had been an opponent of Hussein and ally of al-'Alim in the 1950s, but by the 1960s, 'Awad and al-'Alim engaged in bitter debate about the proper boundaries of literary commitment. In 'Awad's 1963 *Socialism and Literature (al-Ishtirakiya wa-l-adab)*, the critic surveyed eight "idealistic" and four "materialist" schools of criticism, which constituted two extremes opposed to sound socialist thinking. The idealists sought art for its own sake, while the materialists subordinated art to materialistic purposes. 'Awad, rejecting both extremes, sought a balance. Among the schools which he considered under these extremes, he listed socialist realism, neo-humanism, impressionism, surrealism, and al-'Alim's 'targeted literature' *(al-adab al-hadif)*, all of which were contrary to the socialist literature he advocated. 'Awad's conception of true socialist literature was particularly embracing, though, respecting classical as well as colloquial Arabic, works about the elite as well as the masses, and writers of the distant past as well as the present. Ultimately, he called for the acceptance of every "great" philosophy.[43]

Al-'Alim, by contrast, fought something of a rearguard action for *al-adab al-hadif* in the 1960s, accusing 'Awad of practicing purely aesthetic criticism, a damning indictment under any version of literary commitment. Al-'Alim believed social criticism remained active and healthy in Egyptian literature, even if 'Awad couldn't see it. While this vehemence for social criticism was nothing new for al-'Alim, the places in which he managed to find it were vastly different than those that qualified as committed in the 1950s. In a bitter debate in the pages of the Egyptian journal *al-Musawwar* in 1966, for example, 'Awad and al-'Alim clashed over the general state of the theater in the mid-1960s. 'Awad's readings of contemporary plays, al-'Alim claimed, were superficial, pessimistic, and, worst of all, "existentialist." 'Awad, supposedly, was committing an unpardonable sin in committed literature, that is, seeing individual struggles with personal demons rather than the all-important, class-based social struggles. In the play *The Road to Salvation (Sikkat al-salama)*, 'Awad saw only the story of a lone egotist, whereas al-'Alim found the critique of an entire social class. Indeed, al-'Alim managed to take every play reviewed by 'Awad, as well as other critics whom 'Awad cited (or non-critics that 'Awad "insists on calling" critics), and showed that behind their gloomy interpretations of individual misery, lay general, broad-based calls for freedom and humanity.[44]

'Awad and al-'Alim's debate was not really a contest as to who could better uncover the hidden meaning of plays. Rather, it was an admission that the 1960s works of formerly *multazim* writers no longer presented clear, realist pictures of Egyptian social life. Even the great realists like Mahfouz and Idris were now presenting highly abstract, symbolic visions, such as a bird on a telephone wire,[45] or deluded criminals committing murders in a haze of insanity.[46] In al-'Alim's eyes, 'Awad had shirked his duty by failing to extract the political and social messages from these works. Yet texts that needed a critic to explain them were not what *al-adab al-multazim* had envisioned. If the two critics could divide on what Idris's bird on a telephone wire meant, therefore, so could average readers, assuming in the first place that the mass public would even bother to try to analyze something so symbolic. From the idealistic viewpoint of early 1950s *iltizam*, if the political messages had to come out in the esoteric realm of critical discussion, 'Awad might as well read any message he chose into the texts. The true significance of the 'Awad–al-'Alim debate, then, was not who was correct in their interpretation of the literary works around them but rather as evidence that the nature of writing had changed drastically in a decade. One could not imagine a similar debate surrounding Idris's *The Cheapest Nights* or Mahfouz's *Cairo Trilogy* a decade earlier.

Committed Literature in the Sadat Era

Anwar Sadat's rise to power after the death of Nasser in 1970 brought another promise of free speech, particularly in the new leader's May 1971 Corrective Movement. Political prisoners, including lawyers, journalists, and student activists from both the extreme left and the Islamist right, were released and promised greater freedom, while Sadat put a public spotlight on his curbing of the worst abuses of the security forces. Criticism of the old Nasser regime was quite welcome, but as the years wore on, many writers found Sadat as oppressive as his predecessor, particularly as Sadat considered himself an intellectual and took great interest in what they wrote. The later years of his rule saw escalating crackdowns on dissent. In fact, when Sadat was killed, a large number of Egypt's leading writers were in jail.

Sadat himself proved something of a disappointment with two of his most controversial moves. Bowing to pressure from the International Monetary Fund to relieve Egypt's financial crisis, Sadat lifted basic food subsidies, causing prices to skyrocket and provoking the 1977 Bread Riots. This was shocking enough for writers dedicated to the welfare of the lower classes, but in the same year, Sadat began his famous reconciliation with Israel. On this issue, liberal writers like Mahfouz who supported the peace found themselves at odds with an angry public. During the public protests, Mahfouz and 'Awad published in the Lebanese press their expressions of support for Egyptian student demonstrators that would not have passed the Egyptian censors, and at Sadat's insistence, they were called in for questioning by the minister of information. Going further, Idris was barred from journalism for supporting student protests.[47] Yet Sadat later reached out to Mahfouz, reconciling him to work with the government, to drum up support for the peace initiative with Israel. These conflicting forces made for a difficult time for a writer like Mahfouz—torn by his empathy for the suffering people, stung by the leadership, yet hopeful for a peace that his public seemed to reject.

The writer's relations with the mass public underwent an even greater change during the Sadat period than those with the state. Sadat's *infitah*, his opening to the West, brought a surge of consumerism, as members of the middle class readily joined the ranks of the elite. While the disappointment of seeing the political leadership corrupted by power shook the assumptions of *al-adab al-multazim*, watching the public turn its back on the dream of a classless, just society was also traumatic.

At the same time, the foundations of *al-adab al-multazim* were taking a beating outside Egypt. Arab nationalism and socialism were discredited by the 1967 war, which did much to fuel the rise of Islamism. Beirut, previously the free press center of the Arab world, and not coincidentally the home of *al-Adab*, had been devastated by civil war by the mid-1970s. Outside the Arab world, the pioneers of socially engaged writing had fallen in Arab eyes—Sartre due to his perceived support of Israel and Camus because of his stance on Algeria, both issues that seemed to Arab critics to be clear instances of colonialism on Arab soil. Elsewhere, European and American literary theorists from new critics to deconstructionists had turned sharply against a faith in a discernable authorial intent, a key foundational element of *al-adab al-multazim*. A belief that texts could be endlessly polysemous, always open to reinterpretation and misinterpretation, did not square well with *al-adab al-multazim*'s confidence in a writer's ability to deliver a clear message.

The doctrine of *al-adab al-multazim* had drifted far from certainty and consensus by the early 1970s, even in the pages of the journal *al-Adab*. Critic Suhayr al-Qalamawi, in an article entitled "The Writer and the Problems of *Iltizam*," called for new approaches to art, admitting that critics in the Arab world and outside it had still not settled on a practical conception of *iltizam* after all these years, a far cry from the assertions of al-Ma'addawi in the 1950s.[48] In 1972, a conference of prominent writers and theorists in Damascus considered the age-old problem of *iltizam*: the balance of freedom and commitment of the writer. The opposing views offered no greater consensus than when Hussein raised the issue two decades earlier. Indeed, the opinions of 'Abdallah 'Abd al-Da'im, al-Qalamawi, Khalil Hindawi, and others show a definite broadening of the definition of *iltizam* from the strict categorizations of al-'Alim and Khuri decades earlier. In fact, it is clear that securing freedom for the writer from outside pressure—that is, state pressure—had become a far greater concern than restrictive definitions of *iltizam*. 'Abd al-Da'im's summation of the situation reflected how clearly *al-adab al-multazim* had fallen from the position of power and promise it had enjoyed on the cusp of the revolutions of the 1950s. 'Abd al-Da'im renewed the call for commitment while brushing aside the need to further define *iltizam*. Asserting that a free writer was always *multazim*, he claimed that the true problem was how to provide the writer with that freedom.[49]

Halim Barakat, a respected writer and critic of politically engaged fiction, in 1974 lamented the condition of Arab writing in the face of the myriad crises that gripped the Arab world. Bringing out yet another classification system, Barakat identified five types of novels, four of which focused on the individual while only the last, "revolutionary" writing, targeted systemic social change. Barakat found the majority of Arab writers, including those noted for social commitment, like Mahfouz, writing about individual alienation, instead of societal change. Only Barakat himself and Palestinian author Ghassan Kanafani showed signs of the much-needed revolutionary writing, he believed.[50] Barakat's indictment was even more damning than it appeared on the surface, however, since the works that earned both Kanafani and Barakat their reputations for political commitment dealt with the Palestinian struggle, one of the few 'safe' topics for criticism in the Arab world. If the standard of *multazim* writing was to take on the social injustices within Arab states, Barakat's assessment, then, left no one writing *multazim* literature.

Throughout his writings during the 1970s, Barakat reviewed all components in the model of committed writing. He focused on the relationship between the political leadership and the artist, and identified the ideal state and writer for engaged literature: the "revolutionary" writer and the "cooperative" state, which corresponded largely to the expectations of classic *al-adab al-multazim* mentioned above. In this relationship, the writer was guided and bound by his or her own personal convictions. Unfortunately, Barakat found these to be nonexistent in the Arab world.[51] Instead, the existing relationships between the state and the writer fell into the categories of "indifferent," "persecuting," or "custodial," with only Lebanon in the first category, and the majority of "progressive" Arab states, Egypt among them, in the last.[52] In another blow to the declining fortunes of *al-adab al-multazim*, Barakat differentiated his desired "revolutionary" writer from the *multazim* writer, whom he now saw as limited in scope.

The revolutionary writer looked to the future, beyond political causes to deeper social, religious, and educational change. Barakat's vision reflected how profoundly the doctrinal concept of *iltizam* had become outdated by the changes of the previous decades. While offering hope for the future, Barakat saw that future as guided by a literature wider in scope than classic *al-adab al-multazim*.[53] Barakat was not alone. The clearest indication of the decline of *al-adab al-multazim* lay in its flagship journal, *al-Adab*. Once dedicated to the sole purpose of *al-adab al-multazim*, with its pages full of references to that movement, by the 1980s, the journal had discarded the loaded terminology of *iltizam*. From 1980 to 1989, for example, the term *multazim* appeared only once in the title of an article in that journal, that being a reprint of a 1953 piece in the Sartre tribute issue.[54]

The 1980s, then, saw the demise of *iltizam* as a rallying call. Based on this measure alone, one might be tempted to declare *al-adab al-multazim* a failure in Egypt and the wider Arab world. Yet the 2011 revolution, guided by the power of the written word and influenced by novelists like Alaa Al Aswany, Ibrahim Abdel Meguid, and Mansoura Ez Eldin, surely challenged this gloomy verdict. From the 1960s to the 1980s, *multazim* writers turned away from the style of literature that had "dominated" the Arab world in the 1950s, no doubt. What they wrote, however, kept the questions of *al-adab al-multazim* alive in spirit, if not in form, during those critical years. It is on that treatment of *al-adab al-multazim* which preserved the spirit of literary commitment during those critical years that the remainder of this book will focus.

Chapter 3
Naguib Mahfouz:
The Exemplar of *Multazim* Writing in a Period of Disillusion

Setting the outer boundaries of *al-adab al-multazim* may have divided critics, but identifying the exemplars of socially engaged writing at its core was a simpler matter. Among these, few could outshine Naguib Mahfouz, no matter from which particular school's perspective his work was viewed. This is not to say that Mahfouz sought their endorsement. Over his prolific career, the author transcended genres, styles, and models, and his renowned humility and personal privacy gave him a definite aversion to being pigeonholed into any premade category, whether in his private, political, or literary life. Nonetheless, the critics and theorists of *multazim* literature, among them *al-Adab*'s Anwar al-Ma'adawi, *al-adab al-hadif*'s Mahmud Amin al-'Alim and Ahmad Muhammad 'Atiya, to name but a few, saw in Mahfouz the role model of the committed writer. Mahfouz's pursuit of realism, in the manner of his inspirations—such as Dostoevsky, Tolstoy, and Dickens—suited *al-adab al-multazim* perfectly. In fact, his dedication to writing fiction, rather than engaging in debates about the theories of *al-adab al-multazim*, only strengthened his appeal throughout the 1930s, 1940s, and 1950s. When the author changed direction in the early 1960s, however, it posed something of a puzzle for *multazim* critics. Had he abandoned *al-adab al-multazim* after decades of being a guiding light? Critics were divided on how to read Mahfouz's later works of disillusion, but as this chapter will demonstrate, these works continued to show the influence of *al-adab al-multazim* long after the movement had lost its prominence. Despite dramatic shifts in style, the underlying importance of socially conscious writing remained a constant.

Early Influences

Naguib Mahfouz saw his own career as a combination of unchanging principles and evolving stylistic ideas. Underlying the stable principles was a constant conviction that "there is no contradiction between beautiful art and noble purposes," such that aesthetically pleasing literature could serve useful social goals.[1] Throughout the early years of that career, however, he saw his art directed at a number of different subjects. That career began with his contributions to a magazine headed by the pioneer of Egyptian committed literature, Salama Musa's *The New Journal (al-Majalla al-jadida)*. Mahfouz first directed his literary work to the cause of Egyptian nationalism, which he felt was a primary concern of the public in the early decades of the century. Pharaonic history in particular, he felt, was at the heart of the national identity, and thus his first book was a translation of a work on ancient Egyptian history.[2] He followed with three novels set in ancient Egypt, but with clearly contemporary overtones.

The next, and best-known, phase of Mahfouz's career focused on "the social issues arising from political and economic oppression."[3] 'Atiya, an avowed and outspoken advocate of *al-adab al-multazim*, applauded the engagement in Mahfouz's early works: "In his first collection of short stories, *Whisper of Madness (Hams al-junun)*, published in the year 1938, we find this [style of] art that is sincerely aware of the issues of the people."[4] In the pages of Musa's journal, as early as the 1930s, Mahfouz predicted the rise of socialism as Egypt's leading ideology, followed by the inevitable social transformation of the country, although he warned against violent revolution. Envisioning his role in this social transformation, Mahfouz concluded early on that literature would be his means of effecting change.[5]

Stylistically, Mahfouz embraced the kind of clear, accessible realism that *multazim* critics preferred. His extensive readings of European realists of the nineteenth and early twentieth centuries left him with clear preferences and distastes in approach. While applauding the European realists, he dismissed modernists fairly quickly—Faulkner merited the simple verdict of "he is too confusing," while James Joyce held a particularly low standing. Mahfouz would say bluntly, "In reality, *Ulysses* was not a novel meant for reading. . . . It was an atrocious novel."[6] When his own work later took a noticeable bend toward Joyce, particularly in his use of the interior monologue, Mahfouz quickly downplayed the similarity.

Realism was only one part of Mahfouz's success, however. Mahfouz himself was quick to distinguish "realism" from "reality," noting that "realism equals reality plus art." Thus, Mahfouz justified having his working-class characters speak in formal Arabic *(fusha)*, rather than the colloquial Arabic that their real-life counterparts would have used, noting that "*fusha* enables the author to probe the psychological and material realities to their depths."[7] Reaching the depths was more important than replicating the surface impression. Beyond the surface realism of his stories lay an extensive, systematic view of the totality of the social order, such as Lukács had earlier emphasized. Accordingly, the great Russian realists Dostoevsky and Tolstoy stood above Mahfouz's other models, not only for their realism but for the broad social portraits they offered. Among the works of the latter, Mahfouz particularly admired *War and Peace*, openly confessing, "I shall not rest until I write a novel like it." Mahfouz's massive *Cairo Trilogy*, published in the early 1950s, came as his fulfillment of this dream. Among English works, he admired Galsworthy's similarly ambitious *Forsyte Saga*.[8] Yet even in shorter texts, Mahfouz praised wide-ranging views onto human social conditions, acknowledging that "the comprehensive view in Joseph Conrad's novel *Heart of Darkness* pleased me greatly." Indeed, Mahfouz based his appreciation of the latter work on its totalizing form of realism, noting "the novel tells a very realistic story but at the same times offers an inclusive, comprehensive view. This is what I attempted to do in my latest series of novels."[9]

During the 1940s and 1950s, Mahfouz's literary works, both individually and as a body, painted a remarkably comprehensive picture of Cairo society, one that rivaled what his role models had done in Europe. Even today, one looking for a description of Egyptian society in the early twentieth century would be more likely to quote Mahfouz than a history book. Beginning with *Khan al-Khalili* in 1945, Mahfouz produced a series of novels depicting social life in the old quarters of Cairo, mostly centered on family units. His characters' struggles for survival and dignity were, by necessity, tied to the social and economic structures that governed their environments. As the narratives followed the characters in their battles for survival, the myriad contradictions and injustices in those social structures were exposed. This was the effect that socialist realism had aimed for, but usually failed to achieve. Unlike the stock heroes of Soviet factory novels, Mahfouz's characters were eminently human, often flawed and always unique. Poor workers were as likely to be lazy, greedy, and deceitful as to be honest and compassionate, while the same could also be said for the sons of pashas and beys. In each class, some would end up happy, while others suffered tragedy, even within the same family. Yet the limits and opportunities that all faced were always circumscribed by rigid social laws. That no two among Mahfouz's scores of characters were alike, yet at the same time were all limited by similar factors, was the mark of his genius.

In *Khan al-Khalili*, for example, a middle-class family headed by a low-ranking government clerk—bureaucratic Egypt's equivalent of the Soviet factory worker—struggled to make ends meet in the eponymous neighborhood, famed as Cairo's main public market. The following year saw *New Cairo (al-Qahira al-jadida)* portray another lower-middle-class family, stricken by the retirement of the father for ill health. The novel's protagonist, Mahjub, took a very different route to survival than his predecessors in Mahfouz's earlier novels, in this case submitting to the degrading arrangement of serving as a sham husband for a rich man's mistress. Mahjub's decisions were his own—and distinctly different from those of characters in Mahfouz's other novels—yet one could not ignore the corrupt social system that set the conditions for Mahjub, his patron, and the mistress to make their choices.

Midaq Alley (Zuqaq al-midaqq) from 1947, one of the author's most beloved works, quickly earned a place as a masterpiece of *multazim* literature. In a relatively brief story, the novel offered a sweeping and incisive examination of life in a Cairo alley,[10] painting with exceptional detail the unwritten rules of the various economic systems at work there—prostitution, baking, theft, retail trade, politics, and even the marriage market. Mahfouz's *Midaq Alley* was not a particularly sad place—the author had great affection for such old neighborhoods. Some of its residents managed to carve out happy lives in the novel, while others ended up miserable, largely due to their own choices. The novel's two central characters, in fact, while radically different in temperament, share similar fates when they dare to challenge the social order. 'Abbas, a kind and humble barber, dreams of a better life outside the alley, and sees the employment opportunities brought by the extensive British commercial and military presence as a chance to improve his station through honest, hard work. Hamida, the alley's great beauty, on the other hand, is a thoroughly vain and selfish schemer looking to cash in on her physical attributes without scruple. Polar opposites in nature, both share the goal of breaking out of the social milieu assigned to them—the one impermissible aim in this rigid social structure—and thus, ultimately, both must fail, whether they seek escape through honest work or illicit trade. Leading *multazim* critic Anwar al-Ma'addawi was so impressed with the novel's realism that he thought Mahfouz could not surpass it. Two years later, his mind was changed with the publication of *A Beginning and an End (Bidaya wa nihaya)*, which is discussed in detail in the next section of this chapter.[11]

Speaking in 1946, Mahfouz expressed his still-unfulfilled quest to produce a comprehensive literary picture of his society, noting that "the idea of a long epic novel keeps tempting me. . . . I will devote ten years to this work."[12] The result was his *Cairo Trilogy*, a 1,500-page work that, like the others before it, detailed the experiences of a middle-class Cairene family. The texts span the first half of the twentieth century—focusing in large measure upon the social contradictions during the period of the monarchy, particularly regarding gender relations. In the words of that leading critical voice of *al-adab al-multazim*, al-Ma'addawi: "This family serves as a genuine human symbol of Egyptian society during an extended historical period in terms of social, political, and intellectual development."[13]

While Gladkov's power plants struck knowledgeable Russian readers as patently false, Cairenes knew Mahfouz's neighborhoods reflected the genuine article. In painting his images of Old Cairo, Mahfouz drew from his own experience, the neighborhoods depicted in the novels most often being Mahfouz's beloved Jamaliya or 'Abbasiya. For years, it was possible to visit the neighborhoods described in *Khan al-Khalili*, *Midaq Alley*, and the *Cairo Trilogy* and identify specific buildings in the stories. Mahfouz also spent countless hours in the cafés of Khan al-Khalili (Fishawi's being his favorite), talking to Egyptians of all classes. Not only his chosen form of relaxation, it served as a major source for his research. Mahfouz, therefore, could describe the procedures required to get a bureaucratic job through the back door, or the bribes a drug dealer paid to stay in business, with a fidelity readers accepted without question.

Al-Adab al-Multazim in Practice: Mahfouz's *A Beginning and an End*

While any of Mahfouz's novels of the 1940s could serve as fitting subjects for an examination of *al-adab al-multazim* in practice—*Midaq Alley* and the *Cairo Trilogy* being two of the most frequently identified by critics for that purpose— another of his beloved 1940s works exemplifies the totalizing, realist view of Cairo society that marked his *multazim* output: *A Beginning and an End*, from 1949. Both the Beirut school of *al-Adab* and the Cairo-based *al-adab al-hadif* found the novel to be a landmark work of committed literature. Al-Ma'addawi proclaimed that *A Beginning and an End* reached new heights of realism in its depictions of Cairo life, no small praise coming at the end of the decade that had seen a succession of the author's greatest realist novels.[14] From the other major school of committed literature, the founding critic of targeted literature *(al-adab al-hadif)*, Mahmud Amin al-'Alim, praised this "most mature" of Mahfouz's novels up to the 1950s for its achievements in synchronizing the particular with the general, and the individual with the social dimension. While the principal characters all fit distinct yet identifiable types, al-'Alim noted that their fates were inevitably sealed by social and economic factors.[15] This, of course, was the effect for which committed literature aimed, but rarely achieved.

A Beginning and an End has been, and remains, for millions of Egyptians the powerful story of a family struggling to survive, of greed and sacrifice, of devotion and selfishness, rather than a social commentary. Its characters are well remembered by Egyptians in decades since, not least due to Omar Sharif's portrayal of the novel's central character in the film version of the story. Yet the story also offers one of the most comprehensive and systematic explorations of the lower end of the middle-class social system. More importantly, that social system forms an instrumental part of the story. The general public need not—in fact should not—recognize that they're reading a social analysis and commentary; rather, they can merely notice that they're enjoying a poignant story that resonates with their experiences.

A Beginning and an End charts the paths of the members of the Kamil 'Ali family after the loss of the father, the family's sole breadwinner. A low-ranking government clerk who had shown no signs of being ill, he leaves his family completely unprepared for life on their own. With that single, unexpected event, the children are launched into the world, with little preparation, to seek a livelihood in a variety of professions open to lower-class Cairenes. Mahfouz is too adept at weaving a diverse cast of characters into a realistic social milieu for his novel to bear the overt stamp of the type of social experimentation Émile Zola had used to catalog French society in the late-nineteenth century, but the novel can be considered a social experiment nonetheless. The four children of the Kamil 'Ali family will discover, through hard knocks, what it takes to survive and succeed in the range of professions open to lower-middle-class youth.

Mahfouz sketches in systematic detail each socioeconomic microcosm that the children attempt to enter: from military service, to education, government bureaucracy, prostitution, the drug trade, and the marriage market. The reader sees each social system through the eyes of the characters—hopeful, curious, and easily shocked entrants into a world (or worlds) whose inner workings they do not understand but must grasp to survive. As in *Midaq Alley*, Mahfouz shows no partiality to any social system. The illegal drug trade appears just as rigidly structured as the government bureaucracy, but in the end, no more perilous or harsh to its members. While the characters' aims in the two novels are somewhat different—survival versus enrichment—the final verdict on Cairo society in *A Beginning and an End* is the same as in *Midaq Alley*: those who try to break out of their social milieu will fail, while only those who stay where they are put will survive.

A Beginning and an End offers none of the sentimentality of *Midaq Alley*, spending no time sketching the happier days of the children's youth before their abrupt forced entry into the job market. Instead, that entire period is summed up by level-headed middle son Husayn when he declares, "If only we'd never known comfort, then we could easily handle this new life that's forced upon us."[16] While offering a more detailed and systematic examination of the economic order, the novel's weakness may be its preoccupation with socioeconomic survival. The children's lives seem to have room for nothing but economic concerns.

Without missing a beat, the first scene of this novel announces the unexpected death of the family patriarch, as the two middle children, promising students Husayn and Hasanayn, are pulled from school to confront the shock. Only a few moments are allowed for mourning before their mother, hard-nosed realist Samira, sits the grieving family down to face the stark reality of their financial situation. Without the meager salary of a government clerk, they have nothing. The boys' insular lives as successful high school students are now over. Worse, they learn through a realistically detailed encounter with the government bureaucracy that the administrative procedures necessary to start the father's pension will take months, leaving them penniless. It is to be their first taste of the rigidity of socioeconomic law in Egypt—whether manifest by government bureaucracy, criminal codes of honor, or laws of the marketplace. As one nameless clerk tells them: "there's nothing we can do about the procedures of the Ministry of Finance."[17] Indeed, they will find that there is little that can be done about the procedures of any economic microsystem in Egypt, as the rest of the story turns into a quest for survival: one mother and four children looking for any opening into the myriad trades of Old Cairo.

Hopes initially rest on eldest son Hassan to provide for the family, the logical choice as he is no longer in school. "I beg you to start seriously and sincerely looking for a job," his mother implores, only to hear an assuring "I promise you that. I swear on our father's tomb!"[18] Hassan, however, shows little inclination toward honest living, heading out to gamble rather than find a job. Yet as much as he disappoints his mother to the point of despair, his roustabout lifestyle suits him well. Hassan joins a rough crowd, becomes a hired thug and later a drug dealer. As objectionable as

Hassan's choices may be, Mahfouz is not out to make a moral judgment. Drug dealing provides the family with money for its first months without a father, allowing them to eat—a simple, if inconvenient, necessity. Moreover, Hassan, while ill-suited to honest pursuits, has some skills that make him a valuable asset in this business, not least among them his willingness to beat up rivals. Pairing up with an equally successful prostitute, Hassan becomes a minor power figure in a filthy alleyway populated by criminals. Shedding light on the bureaucratic details of all Egyptian government professions, Mahfouz points out that entry into any legitimate field requires cash, and the only source of cash for this family is Hassan's illegal activity. As Hassan will remind his more noble-minded younger brother, while displaying his ill-gotten cash, "Your life is as dishonorable as mine. It comes from this, I made you an officer with my illegal money from the narcotics trade and from the work of this woman!"[19]

Unfortunately, Hassan's sense of obligation to his family is fickle at best. His rise though the ranks of minor criminals serves mostly his own interests and does not alleviate the pressure on his two younger brothers to enter the job market as soon as possible. Yet Hassan can be counted on in moments of great need, just reliable enough to force his higher-minded brothers to swallow their pride and come begging for his help. Crime initially allows for more rapid upward progression than licit employment, but it also brings the danger of a more rapid fall. "Either I'll be imprisoned or killed. If I'm fated to be killed, then that's a natural way to avoid being imprisoned!" he laughs, knowing well the laws of his profession.[20] Lasting much longer at the top than some of his rivals, Hassan will inevitably be brought down by the violence inherent in his profession, to end up as the first casualty in the Kamil 'Ali family's sad demise. This is no moral tale of the dangers of crime, however, as Hassan's fall is no less arbitrary or cruel than that of his siblings, and for a time, his life seems a lot more interesting.

The second son Husayn, a high school student who once had great ambitions for higher education, realizes he now has few options open to him. With Hassan largely out of the picture, Husayn must secure an immediate salary, and he need not be told where to go for that. The son of a civil servant, his prescribed destiny is that of a civil servant. Alone among his siblings, Husayn is not inclined to challenge his destiny. He dutifully sacrifices his dreams of academic achievement in order to provide for his family in the only legitimate field open to him, the dead-end path that sent his father to an early grave and left the family penniless. Husayn, eminently the most sympathetic character in the novel, is both a tragic figure and the only triumphant one in the story. He had aspired to, and deserved, much more than to repeat the sad cycle of his father's life, but compared to the violent, early ends that every other member of his family will meet, he finishes the novel as the closest thing to happy that the text will allow.

As adept as Mahfouz proves at detailing the inner workings of each social microcosm, he achieves true totalization by showing the interaction of these myriad subsystems in the overall social order. This totalization is most apparent when two or more systems intersect, placing the demanding internal rules of one system in opposition to, or occasionally in harmony with, the demands of another social microcosm. In one cutting plot parallelism, Mahfouz sends honest Husayn on a journey for assistance to two ostensibly contrasting worlds: the home of a wealthy bey and the alley apartment of his elder brother, the openly criminal Hassan. The sole wealthy character in the novel, the distant family friend and well-placed official in the Ministry of Interior, Ahmad Bey Yusri is the family's (and the novel's) only window into the world of the privileged. On the surface, the bey's world seems one of dazzling riches and power to the Kamil 'Ali children, who accordingly assume he has unlimited power to help them. The reader, however, sees a harried civil servant crushed by the backstabbing politics of his occupation and swamped by financial debt from his need to maintain the façade of luxury demanded by his position. Only from the comprehensive panorama of Mahfouz's narrative do we realize that Ahmad Bey has no more sense of personal agency or economic security than a minor government clerk or seamstress.

Having given up all hope of higher education and self-improvement, Husayn seeks only a government job to feed the family, and mother Samira assures him that Ahmad Bey, a dear friend, "can get you a job in the blink of an eye."[21] Ahmad Bey, however, has used up most of his own influence for survival, and his initial reaction to Husayn's request—"a job?!"—is hardly encouraging.[22] Ahmad Bey must strain to get Husayn the lowest-possible position—a clerk in the Delta town of Tanta, a town often the butt of jokes in Egypt, which will take Husayn away from the family and, even worse, require separate lodging, meals, and other expenses. Forever the novel's resident accountant, mother Samira does the calculations and immediately realizes that Husayn's meager salary in this new position will not even cover his living expenses. Thus, the job will worsen the family's economic situation. The scene teems with cruel ironies that all recognize yet none dare express. Both the bey and the Kamil 'Ali family understand that the rich man has exhausted his backdoor capital to get Husayn a job that is worse than nothing at all. It would be humiliating, however, for a man of the rich, ostensibly influential class to admit defeat to a group of lower-class people and return with no response to their entreaties, while equally impossible for them to refuse his offer, however much they may now regret having asked for it.

From the world of wealth and influence, Husayn then travels to the criminal depths occupied by his drug-dealing brother to borrow enough money to afford the move his new job now requires. Visiting a trashy alley apartment that Hassan shares with his prostitute girlfriend, Husayn must listen to his brother disparage his efforts to seek honest employment: "What benefit is this to your mother?" Hassan asks, to which Husayn can only respond: "little benefit, but what can I do?" Hassan, the self-supporting criminal, dismisses Husayn's years of hard work with the remark: "that's the end result of your schooling." Husayn, who has come begging to the unreliable and immoral Hassan, can only smile at what is essentially an accurate summation of his situation.[23] Worse, Hassan will repeat essentially the same speech Husayn heard from Ahmad Bey. As much as Hassan and Ahmad Bey differ in surface appearance, their expositions of the demands and constraints of their respective positions are virtually interchangeable. Times are tough for gangsters as well as elites and both have to maintain an expected standard of living, lest they lose the respect of aggressive competitors. In the end, at least this time, the criminal delivers better than the bey and Husayn gets a pair of the prostitute's bracelets, allowing him to afford the disastrous 'help' he received from the rich bey.

For the daughter Nafisa, school is never an option. As a woman, she has little agency of her own, and coming from a poor, fatherless family, has no one to shepherd her. Her meager earnings in the pariah job of a seamstress help the family to stave off immediate starvation, but the girl has virtually no value in a woman's primary calling—the marriage market. Being poor and ugly, she turns instead to cheap prostitution, recognizing that "ugliness itself is a useful commodity in the market of licentiousness."[24] Nafisa's prospects for survival in this treacherous environment are not promising, but it is her association with her youngest brother, the most ostensibly respectable of the group, rather than her criminal older brother, that will be her undoing.

With his three oldest siblings occupied in ignoble employment for subsistence-level wages, only the youngest son, Hasanayn, has a shot to break free of poverty and deliver the family to a higher standard of living. "The world must change," he asserts. "It is our right, without a doubt, to enjoy a clean place to live, healthy food, and a position of respect. But when I think about our life so far, I don't find anything good in it!"[25] In contrast to the degenerate Hassan and the humble Husayn, birth order gives Hasanayn the luxury of both arrogance and high-mindedness in his plan to make himself the family savior. Seeking admission to the Military Academy, he consumes the earnings—both legal and illicit—of the entire family in a gamble that he can enter the world of the privileged elite without being tarred by his origins in an alley. While Husayn can be humble enough to accept the embarrassing aid of a criminal, haughty Hasanayn has a harder time taking his brother's illegal charity to gain entrance to the Military Academy. Yet Hassan will not let him put up a false front of propriety, reminding him of what everyone else knows: "Thanks to my dishonorable lifestyle, I was able to keep our family from starvation, to provide your brother Husayn everything he needed to work for the government, and to pay the fees that enabled you to become an officer."[26]

For a few years, his dream seems to be materializing. Hasanayn graduates, becomes an officer, and moves the family to a more fashionable apartment. Nafisa can't help but announce, "Now we've really become part of the upper class."[27] Yet arriving at a higher status is not the same as maintaining it. Hasanayn struggles to maintain the illusion of belonging in a class dominated by the elite, even cutting his ties to his beloved fiancé, lest she bring down his status. Yet even drug-using Hassan appreciates how out of place his brother is, calling him "you deluded officer."[28] Hasanayn soon recognizes how correct that assessment is, when he learns that his new comrades in the army disparage him and his family behind his back, and must humbly swallow the support of one of his friends defending him with the assertion that "being poor isn't a crime!"[29] A crime, no—but certainly a curse Hasanayn had thought he had discarded.

Things quickly get much worse as Hasanayn cannot escape the criminal brother and prostitute sister who expose his true origins. The arrival of brother Hassan on the doorstep, dumped bleeding and near death in the respectable new neighborhood, brings the past back to haunt him, as does a call from the police revealing that his sister has been arrested for prostitution. The unwritten laws of the social system seem to provide some mercy for sister Nafisa, as the police recognize her family name from the intricate network that connects military and law enforcement officers. In a gesture no doubt meant as kindness, they contact Hasanayn to claim her and spare her from prison. Yet larger unwritten laws turn this favor into a death sentence for the two siblings. Hasanayn realizes the news will spread to all quarters of his new profession, ruining him forever. His career as an officer is finished, leaving him only the choice between death and dishonor. The rigid laws of the social system have forced this simple choice—the personalities of the individual characters prompt their very different decisions. Hasanayn chooses the former for both himself and his sister; as a woman, Nafisa is not allowed her own choice. When Hasanayn baldly informs her that he intends to kill her to defend his honor, she offers to make things easier by killing herself. Hasanayn chooses the Zamalek bridge as the place and escorts her to it, ensuring she follows through. In the last moments with the sister with whom he has shared his whole life, Hasanayn is concerned only about whether the client caught with her would expose him. Yet even with his sister gone, Hasanayn knows his ambitions are foiled. In the novel's most poignant scene, both the disgraced prostitute and the young officer in his white uniform throw themselves off the same city bridge. Humble Husayn, just as thoroughly shamed by the exposure of the prostitute and drug dealer as his haughty brother, however, takes the latter choice, deciding instead to live out his life as a minor clerk from a tainted family, married to the girl from the tenement upstairs and accepting the limits imposed on him. For all the tragedy that punctuates the novel, Mahfouz never lets it degenerate into melodrama. The outcome of the story is not predetermined. The final combination of one living government clerk and three dead siblings is the result of four individual choices. The options in front of them, however, are solidly fixed by their class.

As discussed in chapter 1, advocates of socially engaged literature could differ fundamentally on how to inspire an audience toward change. Bertolt Brecht had warned that identification with characters could distract audiences from underlying problems in the social system that a work sought to expose. Gyorgy Lukács, by contrast, argued for realistic characters in credible social environments as a way to expose social contradictions. The *al-adab al-multazim* movement in the 1940s and 1950s placed great faith in the power of stories about the working class to draw attention to the larger social and political systems, in a more Lukácsian fashion. Thus *al-adab al-multazim* sought to keep direct reference to the political leadership, writer, and public out of the text and focus instead on realistic characters. In this novel, Mahfouz has opted for the Lukácsian way favored by *al-adab al-multazim*. The sympathetic portrayals of Husayn Kamil 'Ali and his siblings—and even the rich bey, for that matter—are intimately tied to the cruelty of the social system. Husayn's very logical nature draws the reader deeper into the morass of social contradictions, in an attempt to understand the forces that affect him. Al-'Alim bluntly demonstrated the effectiveness of this approach in his review of the novel by pointing out that the story screams the question (about the injustices faced by the Kamil 'Ali family)—"Why, people?"— but without ever posing it outright.[30] Why would anyone take a job, for instance, that would cost them more than they would earn? Why is crime the only way this family can afford to survive? The outrage prompted by the fictional scenario inspires a deeper examination of the social system, in true Lukácsian form.

Throughout the novel, Mahfouz indicts the political powers of the day, without ever bringing them directly into the text. Were there any doubt, Mahfouz himself declared the villain of this novel to be Prime Minister Isma'il Sidqi, a name that never appears in the text.[31] While this sort of direct criticism was quite acceptable, even expected, for a writer speaking outside the novel, within the text, the lives of his characters must carry that message. The blame only lands with Isma'il Sidqi by implication, as the novel systematically pursues the threads that link the classes of Cairo society, leading us to seek the ultimate culpability for their social misery. In fact, the only wealthy figure to appear in the novel, Ahmad Bey Yusri, gets a fairly positive treatment, unlike the stock villains in a Soviet novel. It is rather the unseen pressures that limit the bey's ability to help the family that point us to ultimate guilt in the story.

Reviewing for the flagship journal of *iltizam*, *al-Adab*, Mahmud 'Abd al-Zahir applauded Mahfouz's manner of addressing real political issues through the limited perspectives of individual characters. In his review of the novel, 'Abd al-Zahir devoted considerable attention to the historic events that were unfolding in Egypt at the time of the story. Yet Mahfouz's novel offers only rare mention of historical political events, the chief of these being passing references to the wide-scale demonstrations of 1935. The masses of demonstrators came from the same class as the Kamil 'Alis, agitating for the rights of their class, and indeed, Hasanayn's entrance into the Military Academy would have been due to the increase in native Egyptians commissioned as a concession to nationalist protests. While the young brothers do not go into such detailed discussion of news events and their consequences, they certainly express the spirit of those protests in language suited to their age and perspective. Hasanayn notes at one point that either "all of us should be rich" or "all of us should be poor," and that if such equality is not possible, then "we will revolt, we will kill, and we will steal."[32] The critic 'Abd al-Zahir found Hasanayn's limited—and naive—perspective on his family's position in the social order to be a strength rather than a weakness in the novel. Through this view, Mahfouz brings large-scale political issues down to the very human level of individuals and families. While Husayn and Hasanayn do not debate the merits of socialism, 'Abd al-Zahir found in their divergent life paths a clear call for a comprehensive socialist solution to Egypt's problems. This analysis was fit material for a critical article like that which 'Abd al-Zahir has written, or in an interview with the author, but the novel is more powerful when such direct explication is kept outside the text.[33]

A Beginning and an End keeps the intratextual realm quite free from obvious surrogates for the author or the state. Social analysis, in such limited form as appears in the novel, comes from the mouths of the characters, in language suited to people of their age and position. Mahfouz was not wholly averse, however, to putting some more obvious spokespeople for political views in his novels. Never descending to one-dimensional caricatures like the heroic party representatives of Soviet novels, some of Mahfouz's own novels included a more subtle version, such as the café ideologue or student activist. The *Cairo Trilogy* featured debates between the communist, Islamist, and skeptic members of the al-Jawwad family's last generation, while *New Cairo* saw Ma'mun the Islamist, 'Ali the atheist, and Ahmad the Wafdist argue about the best ideology for the future of their nation.

A Beginning and an End, however, has few such theoretical discussions, as direct contact with the social system takes priority over opinions and feelings. Only rarely does Mahfouz fall back upon the technique that would become a staple of his later work—the interior monologue. While his works of the 1960s involve continuous, ambiguous, and often conflicting interior monologues, the technique appears in this novel only to clarify a point of social law. Why does the romantic Hasanayn, for example, abandon the fiancé that he has spent years courting in order to make an overly ambitious proposal to the daughter of a noble? As the newly minted officer finds himself in the precarious position of being between social classes—above the rest of the family members who could never understand the demands of his position, but unable to discuss his humble origins with the elite members of his new class—he quite logically carries out his deliberations with the only person he feels could understand him: himself.

The credibility of Mahfouz's created world is most noticeable in the few instances where it breaks down. After the disappointing results of Samira's attempt to get help from the family friend Ahmad Bey Yusri, for example, the narrative is interrupted with the assertion that their deceased father "was only a friend of the third degree" to the bey—doubtlessly an accurate statement, but one that bears the obvious stamp of a social analyst.[34] Certainly there would be other terminology available in the 'language of the people' to relate this general law more subtly to the predicament of a starving family. Yet these lapses only call attention to the difficulty of balancing aesthetically pleasing, realistic individual stories with larger social commentary, and remind us how successful Mahfouz has been throughout the novel at keeping this deliberate balancing effort concealed.

Realism, however, need not be reality. As the author was quite willing to discuss outside the novel, *A Beginning and an End* was based on an actual family from Mahfouz's own neighborhood, but the author changed the course of events to make the Kamil 'Ali family story end in tragedy, unlike that of his real neighbors. Mahfouz felt the tragic ending better served to awaken public consciousness to the severity of the social problems depicted.[35] The critics understood and supported Mahfouz's choices, as 'Abd al-Zahir conceded that many Egyptians do escape poverty, yet applauded Mahfouz for not focusing on individual stories of success but rather choosing to capture the general misery of an entire class. Acknowledging the distinctiveness of the Kamil 'Ali family, 'Abd al-Zahir felt the novel represented the reality of life for a majority of lower-class Cairo.[36] 'Abd al-Zahir concluded that the work was "one of the greatest examples of the novel in Arabic literature . . . aware and authentic," calling it a "targeted *(hadif)* novel"—using the term al-'Alim had coined for his version of committed literature.[37] Al-'Alim himself classed this novel, along with the later *Cairo Trilogy*, in a separate category apart from the author's other work, for having reached an unprecedented level of maturity. In addition to its painstaking depiction of social details, such as the seating positions based on class at the father's funeral, the novel went further than any previous work in its comprehensive social portrayals, he believed.[38] Meanwhile, al-Ma'addawi, the prolific theorist of *al-Adab*, cited the novel for reaching unprecedented heights of emotional coloring and reflecting such a realistic "taste" for life as to go beyond the mind and connect to the very heart of the reader. The critic felt that Mahfouz's narrative surpassed a "second order realism" that reflects what could be real, to reach a very rare "first order realism" that indeed resonates as what actually must be real. Invoking the highest term of praise, he noted that Mahfouz had been faithful to his *iltizam*.[39]

A Dramatic Change in Style

In the turbulent years after the Nasser revolution, Mahfouz's realist works provided the new regime with a welcome body of social criticism of the old order. Although written about the monarchial period that ended in 1952, some of Mahfouz's greatest novels, like the *Cairo Trilogy*, were published after the revolution, a time when the new president was still living off the political capital he gained by punishing the exploiters of the past. Mahfouz accordingly won the State Prize for Literature in 1957 and the accompanying acclaim of the government.

The honeymoon, however, wouldn't last long. Deeply disappointed with the course of the revolution, Mahfouz entered a seven-year 'period of silence,' in which he did not write any new novels. As long as Nasser still lived, Mahfouz justified his silence as being due to the exhaustion of writing the *Cairo Trilogy* or the lack of serious social problems to address, but once Nasser was gone, the author left no doubt as to the real cause of his silence:

> I used to say to those who asked me about that period [of silence] that the revolution had achieved the [desired] goals and there were no [social] problems to provoke me [into writing]. This was an explanation intended to clear me of any suspicion, especially since the question as to my silence had political implications.[40]

Lest there be any misunderstanding, Mahfouz expressed his disappointment with the course of the revolution after Nasser's death:

> The revolution brought into our lives a whole new set of ideas. The one thing about which there was no doubt was that the declared goals of the July Revolution, for me and my entire generation, were very pleasing; if only they had been implemented in the manner promised . . . socialism . . . and democracy were something new entirely, and I wanted nothing other than this, but real socialism and real democracy have yet to be achieved.[41]

After he emerged from that silence in 1959, Mahfouz would never return to the old style of *al-adab al-multazim*. Indeed, the output of the latter half of his career bears little in common with that which preceded it. While his first new novel would be banned for religious reasons, the rest of his post-1960 output had a decidedly political bent. Even the president could not convince the author to embrace the old style again. Nasser once dropped the none-too-subtle suggestion to Mahfouz and his publisher to return to his beloved characters from "the old quarters of Cairo," essentially, a return to *al-adab al-multazim*, adding that the author's recent output could land both Mahfouz and publisher Muhammad Hasanayn Haykal in jail.[42] Mahfouz avoided jail, but many of his contemporaries, Yusuf Idris and Sonallah Ibrahim among them, did not.

Meanwhile, *iltizam* was in retreat everywhere during the 1960s and even die-hard advocates like al-'Alim had to strain to find evidence of *engagement* in surrealist works of that era. The turn from realism to impressionism and surrealism in the 1960s was partially due to the fear of the intrusive political leadership. Not only did the political authority not match the expectations crafted in the pre-revolutionary days, expression was actually *less* free than under the foreign-backed monarchy—certainly a tough blow to the dreams *multazim* writers had nurtured. The political authority was not the only player in the *iltizam* relationship to disappoint, however. Disillusion with a public intent on creating a new elite also drove authors from the naive belief that they could inspire social justice through writing. A style designed to reach the masses gave way to one which better suited the author's own anguish.

Mahfouz exemplified this change more than any other author of the period. Indeed, critic Stefan G. Meyer, after citing Mahfouz's mid-career work as the "apogee of the realist novel in the Arab world," notes a change in narrative technique as pronounced "as in that of no other Arab novelist."[43] In the early works, Mahfouz kept his artistic dexterity out of the textual realm, letting the focus fall entirely on his characters' lives. Outside the text, Mahfouz made frequent reference to influences as diverse as Shakespeare, the ancient Greeks, the Bible, and Thomas Mann, while being interviewed about works that eschewed direct reference to any of those sources. By the 1960s, such esoteric references shared the pages with interior monologues by psychotic killers, drug-induced hallucinations, fragmentary notebooks, multiple conflicting narrators or unidentified voices, ambiguous time sequences, and drifts into flashback.

A comparison of styles in *A Beginning and an End* and the 1961 *The Thief and the Dogs (al-Liss wa-l-kilab)*, two of the author's most popular and critically acclaimed works of the 1940s and 1960s, respectively, bears out the dramatic change. *A Beginning and an End* follows a purely chronological sequence that begins with the catalytic event marking its "beginning." From their opening moments, a very different set of narrative assumptions signals our entrance into the textual world of each novel. *A Beginning and an End* opens with a solid rooting in a geographic and temporal context:

> The proctor gave a troubled glance down the long hallway that led to the third and fourth year classes. Pervading the school—the Tawfiqiya School—was a deep quiet. Then, he went to one of the third year classes and knocked politely on the door. He entered, heading directly for the teacher and whispered some words in his ear. The teacher focused his gaze on a student in the second row and called him, saying:
>
> "Hasanayn Kamil 'Ali."
>
> The student stood up, his gaze, full of anticipation and nervousness, alternating between the proctor and the teacher. He mumbled:
>
> "Sir?"
>
> The teacher said: "Go with the proctor."[44]

From the start, the monologic narration offers a concretely defined setting for the fictional story—even the name of the school and the level of classes taught there appear in the first paragraph of the novel. One of the principal characters of the story is identified by name, grade, and position in class. On the next page, the other leading character, Hasanayn's brother Husayn, is likewise called out from his class in the same manner. The scene's minor supporting characters, the school proctor and teacher, while lacking names, are unambiguously identified. Although identifying details greatly outnumber descriptive adjectives and adverbs, even the descriptives present little ambiguity—the proctor knocks politely; Hasanayn feels anticipation and nervousness. Upon arrival at the principal's office on the next page, Hasanayn and Husayn will be presented with the news of the event that will set in motion the rest of the story: the death of their father.[45] The narrator, an omniscient, third-person voice, employs generally simple sentence structure and vocabulary, and while capable of penetrating characters' internal thoughts when needed, avoids direct commentary. This narrator presents descriptive details, events, and character motivations as objective fact. At one point, as Husayn lies on his bed considering the precarious position of his family, the narrative tells us "in truth, his mother was to other women like Germany was to the other nations,"[46] a statement of fact describing his mother's social isolation and economic desperation that is offered without room for dissent. In *A Beginning and an End*, there can be 'truth,' offered without irony or apology that equates the economic struggles of a family to those of European nations. By the 1960s, no such truth exists.

Our entry into the *The Thief and the Dogs*, by contrast, begins:

> Again, he inhales the breeze of freedom, yet the air is choking dust and the heat too much to bear. He finds waiting for him only his blue suit and rubber-soled shoes—these and nothing else. No one is waiting for him. The world returns as the massive prison gate becomes distant, taking its terrible secrets with it. These sun-drenched streets, this chaotic traffic, the passersby, those sitting, the houses, the stores, no lip allowed a smile . . . but he alone had lost so much, had lost four precious years from treachery. He would soon stand before his antagonists. Anger would burst forth and singe, then the traitors will despair until death, and treachery repent on its ugly face. Nabawiya 'Illish. How have your two names become one? You two have reckoned on this day a thousand times. You thought the prison gate would never open. Perhaps you lie in wait, but I will not step in your snare. Instead, I will destroy you at the appropriate time, like fate.[47]

The reader begins The Thief and the Dogs not from the viewpoint of a detached observer but within the internal world of the novel's protagonist—only identified two pages later as Sa'id Mahran.[48] The narration concentrates not on the type of factual details that helped situate Husayn and Hasanayn in their social context but rather on Sa'id's impressions. "No lip allowed a smile," Sa'id noticed, yet what these people actually felt remains unstated, unlike the factually reported "nervousness" in the previous example. We know there was a prison full of "terrible" secrets, but which prison, and what the secrets were, will remain forever "secret." The narrative teems with unanchored references: "the snare," "the appropriate time," or "treachery would repent." Indeed, why Sa'id was in prison will only be gradually revealed, largely by implication. The names Nabawiya and 'Illish seem linked to a betrayal for which Sa'id seeks revenge, but they are only later revealed to be Sa'id's ex-wife and a former underling in a burglary racket. Whether Nabawiya maliciously sold out her husband, as Sa'id believes, or was driven to desperation by fear of his violence remains one of the story's many mysteries.

The narration in this text moves inward, isolating the protagonist from those around him and fragmenting his own world into a series of clashing impressions, unlike the outward, totalizing movement that situated the characters of *A Beginning and an End* in a clearly defined environment. While the Kamil 'Ali family wrestled with clearly defined social rules and constraints, Sa'id's understanding of his place in society stands at odds with what those around him believe. He considers himself another Robin Hood, stealing to help the poor, while the newspapers label him a deranged menace to society. Mahfouz, however, does not provide enough detail to confirm either side of the dispute. Sa'id's principal antagonist throughout the novel, 'Illish Sidra, makes only a brief appearance in the text and offers an ambiguous take on the enmity between him and Sa'id: "It was destiny and chance, duty also, a sense of honor pushed me to what I did."[49] Exactly what 'Illish did will remain a matter for speculation. Instead of an objective, systematic view of society, Mahfouz offers a polyphony of worldviews in conflict, paradigms for understanding society that inherently disagree, and which the narration does not attempt to reconcile.

Al-adab al-multazim had assumed that society had a clear set of rules and structures that could be exposed. Indeed, exposing those structures was the first step toward moving society to change them. The protagonists of Mahfouz's 1940s novels labored toward definite and reasonable goals within a well-defined social system. When they failed, the inequitable rules of that system were to blame. By the 1960s, however, confused loners like Sa'id Mahran breathed hate and anger at a society which repaid their bitterness in kind. Mutual misunderstandings and confusion, which the texts make no attempt to clarify, lead to conflict and despair. This dramatic shift shows clearly in a comparison of two of the key moments in *A Beginning and an End* and *The Thief and the Dogs*. In the former, a long-anticipated school examination for the Kamil 'Ali children—one that will determine their future opportunities—receives a rather sterile, analytical rendering:

> In the following weeks, the two brothers took the test to advance at the end of the school year. Their efforts were crowned with success as Husayn advanced to the fifth year and Hasanayn to the fourth. They both knew that they must succeed; the situation of their family did not allow the possibility of mistakes. They persisted in their efforts with true determination, and the results came as they had hoped. As the summer vacation began—which lasted nearly five months—the mother encountered a new difficulty, this related to the meals for the two young men. The mother and her daughter had usually been satisfied with the most simple food. They usually depended on prepared food from the market, to spare the expense of meat, fat, and fuel. The mother now found herself obliged to modify this spartan practice, despite what she had done to economize. Therefore, they had little happiness from the success, while the harshness and gloom of life seemed to increase in that time.[50]

Mahfouz offers a rather monological and objective reporting of the boys' advancement and its economic impact, as well as the emotional states and calculations of the family before and after the event. "The situation of their family did not allow the possibility of mistakes" neatly summarizes what must have been a nervous period of discussions and preparations. By implication, they had considered the consequences of failure and the costs involved in ensuring success, then made resolutions to succeed and likely feared for the worst when their preparation seemed difficult. Yet all these thoughts are condensed into a sentence that presents the arrived-upon conclusion as factually as one of Newton's laws.

Likewise, the emotional response to achieving success after months of arduous study is a rather sterile net effect of "little happiness," after which life becomes even more oppressive. For two bookish young men who have worked for years for this climatic moment to transition from a state of celebration to resignation must certainly be a bitter, frustrating process. The author can condense it so briefly here partly because his working class readers will immediately understand all that is implied behind the words, and partly because the strict demands upon the Kamil 'Ali children do not allow for long periods of personal contemplation. Mahfouz then builds on the irony in the immediately subsequent scene, in which criminal son Hassan arrives to bestow the fruits of his shady work on his ostensibly successful, but cash-strapped, siblings.[51]

The world of Sa'id Mahran, however, is a far cry from the monologic certainty of that of the Kamil 'Ali family. Sa'id also pursues a long-awaited goal with as much anticipation as the young schoolboys. With single-minded determination, he seeks to kill his two demons Nabawiya and 'Illish, an act that (he believes) will somehow restore his honor and clear his path for the future. "The pinnacle of success is to kill them both," he tells himself.[52] Exactly how any of this will follow is unclear and, given Sa'id's mental state, probably irrelevant. His big 'test' comes on the night he sneaks into the apartment building of his two enemies:

> He took out his pistol and struck a blow at the glass of the peep-window through the grate, shattering it, scattering glass with a sound like a hoarse scream in the silence of the night. He got close to the door, until he was nearly clinging to it, aimed his pistol at the interior of the apartment; he waited with his heart pounding and his eyes immersed in the darkness of the hallway. There came a voice asking, "Who is it?" The voice of a man, the voice of 'Illish Sidra, clear to him despite the throbbing in his temples. A door opened on the left side, a dim light coming from it. Then he perceived the shadow of a man approaching warily. Sa'id squeezed the trigger

> and the bullet flew, with a wail like a spirit in the night. The man in turn screamed and fell, but another struck him before he settled on the ground. Another scream of alarm rang out desperately for help, the voice of Nabawiya. He called back to her: "Your turn will come! There is no escape from me! I am the devil himself!" Then he turned to flee.[53]

Unlike the absolute facts presented in the previous excerpt, this narrative overflows with subjective sensory and emotional impressions. Yet even the scarce information that is presented objectively here will later prove inaccurate. The dead man in the narrative is plainly identified as 'Illish and the woman left in terror as Nabawiya. Indeed, these facts remain undisputed for the next six pages, until Sa'id learns through the newspapers that he has in fact killed a complete stranger. As it turns out, 'Illish and Nabawiya had long since moved out of the apartment and were, in fact, nowhere near the scene of the murder.[54] Hardly deterred by one failure, Sa'id sets out to right the record by killing another enemy, the former revolutionary journalist Ra'uf 'Ilwan, whom Sa'id believes guilty of selling out his principles. Again, the murder of Ra'uf is presented as absolute fact, so certain that Sa'id prepares to write a letter to the newspaper claiming responsibility and—he expects—winning public acclaim. Only in a subsequent chapter will Sa'id discover that he has in fact killed another innocent bystander, while Ra'uf 'Ilwan lives on. Eventually, Sa'id's increasingly paranoid delusions will establish him as a dangerous, irrational killer, even if he imagines himself a hero all the while.

For all his ravings, Sa'id Mahran has much in common with Mahfouz's latter-day protagonists. Isolated and misunderstood, his encounters with society prove disastrous. Even the criminal world in *A Beginning and an End* had clear rules and well-defined paths to success, but by the 1960s, the community has become hostile and unpredictable. The most deluded and dangerous characters are those who seek that vaunted goal of *al-adab al-multazim*—social justice. The crusading Sa'id Mahran, like the rest of the Quixotic figures in Mahfouz's post-1960 novels, brings more harm than those who resign themselves to isolation.

Inverting the Paradigm of *Iltizam*

For all their pained expressions of disillusion, Mahfouz's works of the 1960s have not abandoned *al-adab al-multazim*. Certainly, they reject all of *iltizam*'s assumptions: a caring public, an honest political authority, writers who can inspire social justice, for starters. Yet the model of *al-adab al-multazim* remains central to this disappointment, a painful reminder of what should have occurred after the revolution. Ahmad Muhammad 'Atiya, a strident defender of *iltizam* in the latter part of the twentieth century, still asserted in 1970 that "Naguib Mahfouz is a contemporary, authentic, and *multazim* writer."[55] Few critics, however, would make such a definitive assertion after the 1960s. To be purely *multazim* or not by 1970 was not as clear cut a choice as it had been two decades earlier. *Iltizam* was no longer the guiding method in the creation of these later novels but rather the subject of discussion, usually portrayed in a negative light. The key elements of *al-adab al-multazim*, that earlier doctrine required to be kept outside of the text—such as the hand of the author, the political power, and the writing process—now feature prominently within the text, but in a negatively caricaturized fashion. *Multazim* writers play leading roles in the novels of the 1960s, yet are universally failed, misguided, or defeated artists. *Multazim* stories, plays, and poems feature in many of the novels of the 1960s, but these works, produced by the failed *multazim* writer-protagonists, remain offstage, as important and yet unseen as Hitchcock's ubiquitous "MacGuffin." Rather than the abandonment of *al-adab al-multazim*'s separation of the intra and extratextual realms, these works offer their inversion.

Mahfouz does not attempt to oversimplify the numerous and varied problems that undermined *iltizam*, nor does he lay blame on any single source. Culpability lies among the political power, writer, and public. The wide corpus of disillusioned fiction that Mahfouz produced from the 1960s to the 1980s includes scathing indictments of each of these key players. In each case, Mahfouz shows how *multazim* writers struggle with, and usually surrender to, the corrupt conditions that prevent them from bringing *multazim* works to the public, rather than the written works on which they labor. In this way, the spotlight of blame falls alternatingly on the public, the writer, and the state, rather than on the *multazim* texts themselves. In all cases, *iltizam* waits patiently for a chance to return, but will need a genuinely revolutionary change to bring about suitable conditions.

In the four novels to be examined below, Mahfouz highlights the effect of a disinterested public in *The Beggar* (*al-Shahhadh*, 1965); the disillusionment of the intellectual class in *Gossip on the Nile* (*Tharthara fawq al-Nil*, 1966); and the heavy hand of the state in *Karnak Café* (*al-Karnak*, 1974). Finally, *Wedding in the Dome* (*Afrah al-qubba*, 1981) offers a comprehensive portrait of *iltizam* gone wrong, presenting a domineering authority and a self-serving public deluding a committed but naive writer.

The Beggar

In *The Beggar*, Mahfouz brings about a direct confrontation between the beaten-down intellectuals of the 1960s and the former, revolutionary selves they once inhabited. Rather than employing the magic of time travel, the author secludes one member of a revolutionary cell in prison, while his former comrades remain on the outside to experience the changes in society firsthand. By the time the fiery cell leader 'Uthman emerges from his Egyptian version of a desert island quarantine, the two politically committed writers he left on the outside to continue the battle have long since given up trying to move a public that doesn't care to be moved. 'Umar al-Hamzawi, the poet, and Mustafa al-Minyawi, the playwright, greet their old friend with more dread than joy as they try to explain why their kind of writing no longer has an audience. 'Uthman, they know, could no better understand the demise of the revolutionary spirit than they could have back when they were still young fighters. The novel quickly becomes an extended debate between the revolutionary 1940s and the worn-out 1960s. Mahfouz, as a prolific writer who thrived in both eras, might well have been debating himself.

For unabashedly *multazim* critic 'Atiya, 'Uthman exemplifies the "sincere revolutionary" *(al-thawri al-mukhlis)* in the tradition of the great *multazim* works of the 1940s.[56] Within the text as well, this anachronistic firebrand finds an ally in 'Umar's young daughter Buthayna, a girl who has been shielded by her father from the harsh realities of Egyptian life almost as completely as ‘Uthman has been isolated in prison. Both generations of idealists—the old and the new—struggle to exhort the battered, disillusioned former artists to return to the revolutionary crusade. Buthayna and ‘Uthman, however, are in the minority in 1965 Egypt, as is the critic ‘Atiya who applauds them. ‘Umar and Mustafa bear the unenviable task of explaining that there is no audience for revolutionary messages in contemporary Egypt, a fact they have learned from bitter disappointment. Although the state and the writers receive their share of blame for this unfortunate reality, the novel focuses on a public that has little in common with the yearning masses upon whom *multazim* theorists of the 1940s and 1950s placed their hopes.

Once charged to write about the struggles of the working class, ‘Umar has become a very sad protagonist in a novel centering on his inability to write. From the outset, the novel has turned the paradigm of *iltizam* inside out—the writer is now the subject of analysis rather than the one who analyzes. ‘Umar, moreover, has become the walking antithesis of the *multazim* writer he once was. Previously known as “the radical socialist *(al-ishtiraki al-mutatarrif)*, the important lawyer, . . . the poet,”[57] this man of action who once produced stirring revolutionary poems has turned into a decadent, obese glutton whose misery is hardly assuaged by booze and whores. ‘Umar’s doctor does not hesitate to label him a former *mutatarrif*, a term implying extremism and radicalism, but not unfashionable in the days of the revolution—in the 1950s, al-Ma‘addawi referred to himself as a *mutatarrif* of *al-adab al-multazim*, for instance.[58] ‘Umar has gotten wealthy playing the legal field for the rich and powerful of Cairo, freely admitting that Nasser’s socialist revolution didn’t hurt “capitalists” like him.[59] He specializes, in fact, in helping the rich dodge the revolution’s redistribution policies. ‘Umar may be corrupt, greedy, and decidedly “bourgeois,”[60] but he achieved his dirty success by riding the wave of corruption that his fellow revolutionaries brought with them as they replaced the old elite with a new one.

Not proud of what he has become, ‘Umar nonetheless insists that material gain was not the primary cause for his fall from grace. Only after the public had rejected his revolutionary messages did ‘Umar decide to join them in the pursuit of ill-gotten wealth. In their early days, ‘Uthman had advised him: "Dedicate your poetry to the struggle and you will attract thousands of listeners." 'Umar followed this advice, but the public response was far from encouraging: "No one heard my songs. . . . What meaning is there in calling forth the secret of life from silence, back into silence?"[61] Failing as a revolutionary artist, 'Umar turned on his own values: "When failure tormented me, I turned toward power, the very thing that we had once believed to be an evil and wanted to vanquish."[62] 'Umar insists he would not have sold his soul had the public responded to his poetry, an outcome that he and his comrades had taken for granted.

Lest his old boss conclude that 'Umar is merely a lone malcontent, the third member of the revolutionary trio—the playwright Mustafa, yet another *multazim* writer who gave up his craft—echoes his story. Recounting the lost years to 'Uthman, both note that Mustafa retained his commitment to activism longer than 'Umar, which offers little consolation to the shocked revolutionary. In any case, Mustafa shelved his literary commitment just like 'Umar, becoming an entertainment writer for profit. "I absolutely decided to renounce art and here I am selling seeds and popcorn through the newspapers and television."[63] Like 'Umar, Mustafa advises his old friend to abandon all noble principles: "Let us finally discard any illusions of greatness and the throne of the learned, and satisfy ourselves with famous names and abundant wealth."[64] The holdout *multazim* critic 'Atiya, in his review of the novel, offers heavy praise for the revolutionary 'Uthman, yet finds little to sympathize with in the decline of his two former comrades.[65] Is it any wonder they fail to convince 'Uthman or Buthayna?

At this point, after both sides have argued their positions, the story seems to demand a glimpse at their revolutionary literature, enabling the reader to determine whether their efforts deserved public response or not. Yet the novel does not offer the essential examination of 'Umar's revolutionary poems—the central object of discussion in the novel—nor Mustafa's committed plays. Indeed, only one of 'Umar's poems makes an appearance in the text—not a *multazim* revolutionary work, but rather one of the man's last artistic gasps explaining his renunciation of writing altogether. 'Umar, in fact, disowns the poem as a mere "hallucination" from his "pathological condition," while his former leader 'Uthman, who had once applauded 'Umar's revolutionary poetry, is barely able to control his anger at the pathetic work. 'Uthman dismisses the poem out of hand by saying, "I did not understand anything."[66]

The inclusion of this strange poem—universally acknowledged to be unlike the revolutionary work that established 'Umar as a committed artist—as the only literary selection in the novel hardly seems like an accident. In a story centering on the literary careers of two *multazim* artists, why has Mahfouz elected to exclude all of the works in question? For that matter, why have none of the characters dragged out one of 'Umar's classic poems to revisit it, or why has their discussion not touched on the relative strengths and weaknesses of 'Umar's writing? Their discussions, and by extension the novel itself, focus on the apathy of the public as the cause of the writer's demise. The unpalatably modernist poem that does make an appearance serves to represent what the public will accept—vague, polysemic works of little political import. 'Uthman dismisses the poem, and with it the tastes of a new generation, as "the whine of an age on the verge of passing."[67] Mustafa offers a more sweeping conclusion: "The age of art has passed, expired. The art of our time is amusement and entertainment. This is the only art possible in a time of science."[68]

'Umar retains a corpus of engaged poetry, but it remains deferred outside of the text. Neither his fictional audience, nor, we must assume, the audience of Mahfouz's novel, is ready to receive it. Yet the novel offers constant reminders that this body of work exists, ready to be invoked when an Egyptian public can be made receptive. 'Uthman exhorts 'Umar with his spirit of revolutionary zeal, while the pull of a future generation to action comes in the form of 'Umar's idealistic daughter Buthayna. Neither the exhortations of the past nor the new generation can induce 'Umar to bring his old poems out of storage, but the intergenerational tension speaks to a writer caught between two revolutions.

Giving up on this broken exemplar of the 1960s, Buthayna instead forms a strong bond with the ancient revolutionary leader, which will turn, however improbably, into a runaway romance. Buthayna, full of the burgeoning idealism of a new generation, looks to the glories of the past to bring about change. She conceives a child with old 'Uthman, runs off to start the next revolution, and eventually meets a violent end at the hands of the police state. The 1960s in Egypt were not ready for a new generation of revolutionaries, nor did they offer much respect for the old, but Buthayna's natural idealism speaks to a yearning that future generations will continue to feel for change. Mahfouz, writing in 1965, could not envision that 2011 would be the year to finally bring about the conditions in which someone like Buthayna could succeed and someone like 'Umar could redistribute his poems, but the nascent idealism her youth carries offers the hope of change with each new generation. Providing some sense of optimism, Mahfouz chooses not to end this novel with a clear resolution but rather in an ambiguous fog. The previously clear-thinking, if jaded, 'Umar falls into a fit of hallucination after the police attack on 'Uthman and Buthayna, while their fates are left somewhat vague by his deluded state. The implications of 'Umar's final haunting thought to close the novel—a remembered verse, "Why did you forsake me?"[69]—swims in ambiguity. Does 'Umar feel guilt at having forsaken his political, social, and artistic commitment? Or has the public abandoned him? Or does he hear the voices of two generations of revolutionaries—past and future—calling out to him? *The Beggar* concludes with a once-committed artist drowning in the miasma of the 1960s in Egypt, yet beckoned by revolutions past and future, while his committed works remain in reserve awaiting their place in a transformed future.

Gossip on the Nile

Published only a year after *The Beggar*, *Gossip on the Nile*, one of Mahfouz's most controversial novels, was nearly banned by Nasser. Like the previous novel, it centers on another group of intellectuals who have surrendered their beliefs. While the apathetic public received much of the blame for the demise of *iltizam* in *The Beggar*, the intellectuals themselves get their turn in the spotlight in *Gossip on the Nile*. Here again, an aspiring committed writer of the new generation, much like young Buthayna of *The Beggar*, tries to understand and revive a deadened group of once-progressive thinkers. Samara Bahjat, however, faces a much more daunting task. Rather than two broken revolutionary writers, she confronts a houseboat full of intellectuals who have given up their former dreams to retreat into drug-induced stupor. They include writers, critics, artists, government functionaries, and teachers, all of whom have left their useful years behind them. Like the rest of the group, Samara will eventually sell out her moral and artistic principles and join in, rather than overcome, their disillusion.

Why a rising, avowedly committed journalist like Samara Bahjat decides to join a group of worn-out intellectuals in the refuge of their nightly drug sessions aboard an anchored Nile boat is at first a mystery. Samara comes to them as a friend, not a reporter, but naturally raises the suspicion of the more cautious members of this illegal gathering. Eventually, the group's most pathetic and defeated member, Anis Zaki, finds a notebook that reveals her true purpose: writing a play based on the characters of the boat, though he lacks the energy to be offended enough to do anything about it. Samara's play is to be a postmortem on this dead generation, explaining how they have abandoned their principles, but disillusion proves as powerful a drug as hashish and eventually claims Samara as its victim.

Unlike Buthayna of *The Beggar*, Samara has spent time in the real world and loosened up her moral code considerably. Realizing that a group of drug addicts would be quite reluctant to talk with a journalist—for good reason—she concentrates on winning over the most domineering member of the group, the womanizing film actor, Rajab al-Qadi. Rajab has already gone through a string of mistresses; his older, discarded ones are now placid members of the houseboat group, who also lack the energy to do much more than watch passively as he uses and casts off newer catches. Samara quickly recognizes her avenue to secure Rajab as her key to access the group's secrets. Predictably, Rajab demotes his most recent catch, a girl named Sanaa', to show off the more attractive Samara Bahjat. With the confidence of a committed writer among failures, Samara heedlessly plays with fire, never suspecting that her compromises could leave her like the others. From the beginning, her dual role as Rajab's lover and a writer profiling the group reeks of inherent compromise and contradiction, making her fidelity to either role suspect. She has clearly seduced Rajab to get a story, while at the same time must sell out her journalistic integrity to keep the mediocre actor happy with inflated reviews in the press. The others laugh, for example, at the obvious conflict of interest in her articles praising Rajab's questionable acting. Somehow, though, Samara believes her commitment as a writer is powerful enough to withstand all her numerous compromises.

Although nowhere near the moral idealist, Samara, like Buthayna, still believes fundamentally in the power of political engagement and is willing to argue with these battered survivors of the revolution for commitment. While they were the very people to embrace these ideas a decade earlier, by the mid-1960s, they recoil at the very idea of engagement. One member dismisses Samara outright because her work seems like *al-adab al-hadif*.[70] Yet Samara continues to probe, looking for signs of some residual concern for society behind their apathetic exteriors. She will, however, find none. In one attempt to stir the group's interest in social justice, Samara asks pointedly, "Do you really not care what happens around you?" only to be told by the lawyer in the group, "We sometimes use it as material for our humor."[71] Even moving from the abstract to the concrete produces no greater response, as Samara tries to jump-start the group by telling them that a woman has just thrown herself to her death, only to be told "it's our good fortune to be far from the outside, so we don't hear a thing."[72] Lest she harbor any doubts, they add, "We are neither Egyptians, nor Arabs, nor people. We are not affiliated with anything but this houseboat."[73] She asks of their narcotic waterpipe, "Is it an escape from life?" only to be told that for them, "truly, it is life itself."[74]

In light of this total rejection of any kind of social responsibility, Samara feels well justified in pronouncing judgment on the fallen generation. The play on which she works would no doubt qualify as a piece of *multazim* literature were it ever to be completed. When the notebook falls into the hands of the houseboat residents, the play becomes the center of discussion in the novel. Yet like the revolutionary writings of 'Umar and Mustafa in *The Beggar*, the actual *multazim* work is deferred outside the text. Instead, the notes Samara scratches down serve as our only indicator of why this *multazim* work was doomed to fail.

Samara's play, in her own words, will address a central theme: "seriousness against absurdity."[75] Her term for 'absurdity' is *al-'abath* (and can connote 'frivolity,' 'joking,' or 'nonsense'). She uses it in her characterization of the meaningless banter of the group, in opposition to a seriousness *(al-jiddiya)* she finds lacking, and indicates the negative implication she intends. It is a simplistic dichotomy, one befitting an idealistic writer, and Samara's eventual decision to abandon the project by the novel's end speaks to her inability to complete it. Samara, in her arrogance, and Buthayna, in her innocence, both failed to understand the reasons for the collapse of the previous generation. 'Atiya, however, sees beyond Samara's black-and-white categorization, describing the group's frivolity as a "serious absurdness" *(abath jad)*—combining the two roots she had placed in opposition. He even notes a "committed absurdness" *(abath hadif)*—using the term, from al-'Alim's school, that has been used to represent commitment in the novel.[76] 'Atiya's view offers a good deal more empathy for the position of these battered activists than Samara's, as he sees some commitment and sincerity deep below the calloused surface of this group. While this proposition seems reasonable enough, it is very clear that these tired men and women have no inclination to let the young reporter draw any of that commitment out of them. As with old 'Umar al-Hamzawi, that commitment lies deferred.

Like *The Beggar*, *Gossip on the Nile* features a battle of wills between the resigned generation and the new activists, and in both cases, that battle will end with the defeat of the idealists. Samara's fall, much like her rise, is neither as noble nor as pure as Buthayna's, but it is a failure nonetheless. Samara's moment of testing comes when her lover Rajab kills an innocent person while recklessly joyriding. As Rajab swears all the others to silence, he dismisses Samara's talk of social responsibility in a sentence: "We're here in the real world . . . not on a stage."[77] Buthayna went down fighting for her ideals, but Samara's pretenses of commitment don't survive even the pressure of the egotistic actor she has seduced for her own purposes. Samara abandons her play and acknowledges that her toleration of Rajab's crime means she "won't be useful for anything after this."[78] In a stroke, the new generation has joined the old in its abandonment of commitment. As a final slap to Samara's pride, only the hitherto dazed Anis Zaki—the character for whom she has shown the most contempt—shows a spark of conscience as he declares he will report Rajab to the police.

Samara's literary aspirations have been snuffed out in the harsh cynicism of 1960s Egypt, ensuring that her envisioned dramatic work will never be completed. But what if she had persisted to completion? What would the output of an overtly *multazim* artist in that era look like? The brief hints offered in Samara's stolen notebook give little cause for optimism. In a twist of irony that presages the value of her work, the page of her notebook entitled "Significant Observations" turns out to be blank.[79] The comments she actually has recorded validate this coincidental verdict on her work. Samara sees only the surface of her characters, swayed by the outward charisma and bravado she mistakes for virtue. Rajab, for example, is "like a god" of old and "the hope of the play."[80] While she acknowledges his rough edges, she naively believes he can reach his true potential through "love," with little doubt as to who will provide him with that. Rajab, in the end, reveals himself as the most cowardly and unprincipled of the group, a heel who destroys her to protect himself from justice. Even as she was writing of him in glowingly heroic terms, he bragged of his romantic conquest over her in his egotistic rhetoric: "The greatness of the conquest is measured by the impregnability of the fortification taken."[81] Samara's readings of these characters, like her understanding of social commitment, is painfully superficial. Yet Samara is an acknowledged standard bearer of what is left of *al-adab al-hadif* in 1960s Egypt, and by extension, the negative verdict falls on the entire movement.

Although the group members have produced numerous stories, films, and articles, Samara dismisses their turn from the movement of literary commitment with little interest in its causes. All have since become open advocates of "art for art's sake" *(al-fann li-l-fann)*, in the words of 'Ali the art critic.[82] 'Ali himself is easily dismissed by his friends, his output summarized as "empty words . . . as for criticism, he only criticizes as a courtesy to his friends or attack against his enemies or to fleece a little money."[83] To Samara, he is "a pig" and "a wretch" whose "aesthetic base rests on material enrichment" and who is "not moved to tell the truth."[84] The noted story writer Khalid, in her opinion, merely "takes from society without giving anything" but "the jelly-like art" that betrays his lack of values or convictions.[85] Had Samara any of the respect due those veterans who once championed the principles she holds dear, she might look upon their cynicism with empathy and concern, and at least learn how to avoid the same fate.

More revealing is Samara's interaction with the man who has found her secret and who finally upstages her with his inclination to turn Rajab in to the police, the seemingly pathetic Anis Zaki. Samara dismisses him out of hand with a staccato summary of his failings: "Unsuccessful employee. Former husband. Former father," "half dead" and likened to "a vacant seat." Zaki, to be sure, does not cut a dashing figure in the novel. He is the most apathetic and deluded of the group, as well as the most dependent on drugs. Unlike the others, he appears to live on the boat full time. As the novel opens, the failed government clerk has just written a report with no ink in his pen, not aware as he hands his boss three blank pages. Samara can sum up his value by mere observation of his sorry exterior: "suitable to be exploited in comedy, but there is no positive role for him in the play."[86] Samara cannot anticipate the spark of positive energy within Zaki's rotten shell. She has heard the sad story of Zaki's decline, yet did not consider it worth recording in her notes. Like the reader, she learned that Anis Zaki was once a poor medical student from the countryside who struggled to become a doctor. She likewise knows that economic pressures forced him to abandon medical school and take a dead-end bureaucratic job, while the poverty of their conditions killed his wife and young daughter. She also knows that as a young activist, Zaki was nearly killed in demonstrations during the revolution. To Samara, however, he is but "a vacant seat."

Samara does not lack for opportunities to probe Zaki's soul. During their long, private conversation after Zaki discovers her secret notebook, Samara asks Zaki only about the most banal facts—such as her missing fifty piasters—while Zaki drops hints that should have raised the ears of a *multazim* writer. "Your ideas are empty, trust me,"[87] he warns, yet she doesn't think to ask why. He mocks her simplistic character sketches with "you imagine that you are able to comprehend in a few days what I have been unable to understand after many years,"[88] yet Samara does not ask for further explanation. Ostensibly, she seeks to understand the fall of a generation, yet when presented with continuous provocations from a perfect exemplar of that fall which call for further discussion, she remains deaf. Samara will never know what Mahfouz has revealed to the reader, that in his hallucinations Zaki often rails at the old pharaohs and Egypt's recent leaders for the injustices and failings of the ages. Like 'Umar and Mustafa, Zaki knows that something has gone horribly wrong with the revolutionary movement he once served. For him, the old ways of commitment are no longer sufficient. In the words of 'Atiya, Zaki's reading of Samara only reinforces his opinion that "committed literature rings out insufferable slogans, but even the committed will end as ashes."[89]

Gossip on the Nile ends with a spark of life from within the shell of the most defeated relic of the old revolution. It is little more than a spark, as even Zaki wavers on going to the police or not. Yet *Gossip on the Nile*, for all its heavy atmosphere of gloom, confirms that a spark still exists. 'Umar al-Hamzawi's poems rest on a shelf, ready to be dusted off when conditions are right. Similarly, Samara's disastrous play project could become a real work of activist drama if the battered souls of Zaki's generation were ready to join forces with a new revolutionary spirit. In these 1960s works, their spirit is dormant, awaiting a true revolution to revive it.

Karnak Café

Conspicuously absent from the scathing portrayals of *The Beggar* and *Gossip on the Nile* is an indictment of the role of the state in wrecking the ship of *al-adab al-multazim*. True, government corruption provided the money to fund 'Umar's slide into decadence, and government indifference to the drug abuse on the houseboat on the Nile contributed to the demise of the former activists in those novels, yet the heavy hand of Nasser's police state operated mostly in the background. The injurious role of the third partner in the *iltizam* relationship—the same political power that threatened to lock Mahfouz up—finally takes center stage in his 1974 novel *Karnak Café*.

Mahfouz's reasons for delaying this scalding review of state oppression were quite practical. Nasser had personally threatened Mahfouz and *Gossip on the Nile* was delayed and nearly banned until it received Nasser's direct approval. While the reserved Mahfouz avoided provoking Nasser too much, plenty of his contemporaries did end up in prison.

By 1974, however, Nasser was dead, and the new president Anwar Sadat opened the door for criticism of the old regime, ostensibly in the name of press freedom, but also with an eye toward deflating Nasser's personality cult. The belated indictment of the old regime in Mahfouz's *Karnak Café* suited the needs of Sadat's campaign so well that it was soon turned into a "highly opportunistic and propagandistic film," in the words of Roger Allen, who nonetheless notes that the novel resonated with a public that had lived under such oppression.[90]

Like *Gossip on the Nile*, *Karnak Café* centers on a group of once-committed intellectuals who have lost their zeal, resigning themselves to waste away their time in virtual exile. The eponymous *Karnak* café serves the broken men and women of that novel as the same type of refuge as the houseboat provided for the drug-addled refugees of *Gossip on the Nile*. In *Karnak Café*, however, the characters have been drained of their spirit by a single, unmistakable force—the arbitrary brutality of Nasser's security apparatus rather than the general malaise that crushed their counterparts in *Gossip on the Nile*. Mahfouz's characterizations in the two novels clearly distinguish the groups. *Karnak Café*'s characters make no jokes about the pain of their lost idealism, nor do they have the drug-induced escape of the houseboat group. The patrons of *Karnak Café* are described as "phantoms" or "ghosts," suggesting a condition brought about by murder, or the theft of their souls, rather than a self-imposed intoxication.

Our entry into the world of *Karnak Café* comes through a first-person narrator-protagonist, an unnamed author surrogate trying to understand what has happened to this lost generation. While his mission parallels that of Samara Bahjat, unlike her, we learn little about him and he will never become more than a lens in the story. In the previous novel, which depicted the decline and corruption of the intellectual class, Samara Bahjat, as a writer, was as much a part of the story as those she profiled. Here, Mahfouz's take is far more sympathetic to his subjects. They are merely victims—quite innocent ones, in fact—and Mahfouz does not wish to take the spotlight off the sins of the state in order to focus on the fallibility of the chronicler-observer. The narrator, as an author surrogate as well, offers some justification for Mahfouz's belated criticism of the Nasser regime. After a long, introspective paragraph in which he compares the brutality of the secret police to the Inquisition and insane Roman emperors, the narrator attempts to justify his previous inattention to the role of the state and, by extension, explain why Mahfouz is now supplementing his previous indictments of the corrupted intellectuals and the apathetic public by finally giving the state its due. This narrator claims, however improbably, "My information had long come solely from my imagination, until it was granted me after many years to have these closed hearts opened in very different circumstances. This presented me with the frightening truths and explained to me the events that had been beyond my understanding at the time they occurred."[91] Yusuf Idris and Sonallah Ibrahim from their prison cells might have decried such belated engagement with the old regime, but however unconvincing the narrator's justification, it does serve to illustrate that the critical role of the state must be added to that of the public and the intellectual in the story of the fall of *iltizam*.

In sharp contrast to the shells they now inhabit, the young men and women of *Karnak Café* were once full of zest for life and the revolution. "To the majority of them, history starts with the revolution, which left behind it a despicable and incomprehensible period of ignorance. They are [the revolution's] true children,"[92] the narrator-protagonist explains. True to this description, these characters, led by the young activist Isma'il al Shaykh, fill the first section of the novel with idealistic, socialist platitudes. They grant the state a great deal of latitude, willing to forgive the excesses of the government in its pursuit of social transformation—"You say bribery, embezzlement, corruption, oppression, and terrorism? So? It has to be. It is a necessary injustice."[93] Even after three incarcerations, Isma'il's faith in socialism remains strong, although the state no longer embodies true socialism for him. "There was no true socialism in our life. Therefore, I did not forsake socialism, although I would like to cut off the hands that applied it,"[94] he laments.

Whereas *al-adab al-multazim* had envisioned a world in which rules and powers were out in the open and clearly understood, the revolutionary regime has imposed an atmosphere of darkness and phantoms. Isma'il, the first to tell the tale of his imprisonment, describes his captivity as an immersion in a world of shadows. Confined in an empty, dark cell, where he can navigate only by feel, he perceives the guards who intrude upon him like ghosts. When he is let out of the cell, his eyes are blinded by the light, only dimly able to perceive the shape of the vicious interrogator Khalid Safwan before him. Yet despite the dismal, threatening surroundings, Isma'il recalls feeling a sense of optimism when finally brought before Safwan, recognizing him as an official of the state, and harboring a hope that somehow this representative of the government would give him a chance to set the record straight. That hope is quickly dashed, as Safwan comes to represent for Isma'il and the others only abuse and injustice. While the interrogator wears a mask of friendship, he commands unseen torturers to deliver blows from behind the victim. This is certainly not the political power that *iltizam* called for.

The most perverse trick of the state, however, may be its appropriation of 'the language of the people' that *al-adab al-multazim* held so dear. Safwan taunts the young socialists by describing his actions in terms of friendship, protection of the revolution, and the good of the people. The discourse of revolution has now become a coded language of threat and menace. Scenes of torture and abuse are punctuated by ironic statements about "friendship" and a shared brotherhood in the revolution.[95] The police also redesignate signifiers of benevolence as marks of guilt. Isma'il's crime, for instance, is donating a piaster *(qirsh)*—the smallest unit of currency—to a religious charity that Safwan suspects of being linked to the Muslim Brotherhood. Likewise, the other evidence of Isma'il's guilt is the telltale sign of an Islamist—a beard. With wasted breath Isma'il points out that the beard has grown during the time he has been locked in a dark cell with no hygiene facilities. By condemning this socialist as an Islamist, Safwan thus ensures that Isma'il will suffer not for the values he actually holds but for those which are anathema to his own. Upon releasing Isma'il, Safwan recodes his entire stay in the prison, ordering Isma'il to remember the time as "days of . . . hospitality," repeating twice to never forget he received "pleasant treatment," a scarcely veiled threat as to what will happen if he does not so describe his stay.[96]

Safwan likewise corrupts Isma'il's girlfriend, Zaynab. Prior to her arrest, Zaynab treasured her virtue as well as her political ideals. Rejecting rich suitors, she kept herself pure for Isma'il; the pair was, in fact, about to be married when Zaynab was imprisoned and subjected to brutal interrogation from Khalid Safwan. Similarly plunged into a world of shadows and phantoms, she is first humiliated by confinement for days in a cell with no toilet, forced to live among her own waste, certain that guards are watching the spectacle for their amusement. After being brutally raped by Safwan's ghostly thugs during her interrogation, she assumes the role forced upon her, now willing to have sex with the men she rejected before, even for money. Zaynab, once virtuous, openly labels herself a prostitute and considers herself unworthy of a decent man like Isma'il. Menahem Milson's study of character names in Mahfouz's novels points out that Zaynab is the instantly recognizable eponymous heroine of the often-cited 'first Arabic novel,' a beautiful peasant virgin who represents the Egyptian nation.[97] What the state has done to Zaynab, it has done to the nation.

The transformation imposed by the state is both perverse and pervasive. Safwan not only tramples the ideals of the young people and steals their language but also appropriates the relationships that bind these people together. He forces Isma'il and Zaynab to become informants and spy on each other, and sets traps to ensure they actually follow through with the task. Isma'il attempts only once to shirk his duty as an informer against his friends, merely succeeding in getting them all in trouble. Having been turned into instruments of mutual destruction, the former lovers realize that the only way to protect each other is to keep their distance and say nothing. The resulting picture of the former revolutionary idealists sitting together in the café, carefully restricting their conversation to idle, emotionless chatter, offers testimony to the state's power to stifle communication. *Al-adab al-multazim* had looked to the political power to preserve the conditions for enlightening communication; instead the government has done just the opposite.

Like *Gossip on the Nile*, *Karnak Café* involves a literary project that never comes to fruition. Hilmi Hamada plans to write a text based on the café owner and renowned dancer Qurunfula, detailing the rise of the woman from her humble beginnings to her embrace of the revolution and her transformation of belly dancing into a respectable, national art form. But "its aim is more serious" than dancing, he warns. As Qurunfula enthusiastically boasts, his text will detail "the men of Egypt and their women in their hidden lives" and "people of the past era," but also those of "the present!"[98] Both Hilmi and Qurunfula realize the danger of this undertaking, acknowledging that "it will cause an uproar when it is published." Qurunfula's term to describe the seriousness of the project—*akhtar*—implies not only 'more significant' and 'weightier' but also 'more dangerous.' The narrator-protagonist adds the warning of "if it is destined for publication,"[99] which turns out to be prophetic. When repeated incarcerations and torture cannot completely break Hilmi's resistance, Safwan has little reserve about not only killing Hilmi but forcing all the others to watch his dead body dangle from a rope.

Once again, as in *The Beggar* and *Gossip on the Nile*, a work of *multazim* literature is prevented from coming to the public. Whereas 'Umar had withdrawn his poems because of public apathy, and Samara aborted her play because of her own moral failings, Hilmi's book project is terminated by the heavy hand of the state. Taken together, these novels show the collective failure of all three partners in the *iltizam* relationship: author, public, and political power. With such a disastrous combination, is it any wonder that *al-adab al-multazim* went into suspension in the Nasser era?

Karnak Café concludes with a controversial anticlimax, which has caused its share of division among critics. Throughout the text, the destructive power of the state has been embodied in the metonym of Khalid Safwan. In less than subtle fashion, the narrator states baldly that Safwan is the very "symbol in our lives" of government control, an effect bolstered by the fact that Safwan is the only government agent they have ever identified. The narrator captures the sense of oppression and paranoia that they all feel in a chilling image—"let's speak as if Mr. Khalid Safwan were here keeping company with us."[100] This absurd image solidifies their fears through its pure improbability. The reader, by this point, can imagine Khalid Safwan in a number of contexts: deep in his prison fortress, or perhaps bursting into the café to round up the suspects again, or even somehow caught out on the street on his own in a vulnerable position. Khalid Safwan sitting in their midst, a casual companion of their social conversation, however, does not fit within the realm of possibilities that Mahfouz has established up to this point.

That is, not until the day Khalid Safwan actually walks in the door of the Karnak café. No longer an interrogator, having been incarcerated for three years in the purges following the 1967 defeat, Safwan seeks a place to rest out his days of social exile. Although the former interrogator and his captives instantly recognize each other, the novel presents neither remorse on Safwan's part nor hostility from the others. Only at one point does Qurunfula—notably not one of Safwan's former prisoners herself, but an outside observer—try to engage the subject of Safwan's past. In a rather circular exchange, she is told repeatedly, "We are all victims and criminals. If you don't understand that, you won't understand anything."[101] Instead, after some vague philosophical discussion on life itself, the narrator notes that "we prepared to accept him if he actually decided to become a part of al-Karnak,"[102] and indeed, by the story's end, Khalid seems to have become rather popular.

Mahfouz biographer and critic Rasheed El-Enany points out that this "bizarre twist" is inherently "unpalatable within the logic of the novel,"[103] and indeed it is this very unpalatability that shocks a reader seeking catharsis and closure. El-Enany notes that Mahfouz's intent in writing *Karnak Café* may well have been to make a political statement, and thus caused him to "abandon every good principle of fiction writing" in the novel. While El-Enany considers *Karnak Café* as a whole to be "artistically negligible," he belives that "posterity, however, will certainly treasure" *Karnak Café*, which despite its turn from traditional literary conventions, offers "a priceless source for the social and political history of the Egypt of their day."[104] No doubt, Mahfouz has rejected all the traditional forms of resolution that the story demands, whether tragic or cathartic. The "unpalatable" ending to the story, in fact, prevents the reader from swallowing exactly what the state has presented: Safwan as an offering to satisfy the public lust for revenge. Certainly, had Mahfouz, his characters, and his audience satisfied themselves with retribution against Safwan, the Sadat-era purges would have accomplished their goals. Instead, this "bizarre twist" leaves outrage intact and directs attention at the larger failings and injustices that have destroyed a generation.

The lack of closure recalls the alienation effect posited by Bertolt Brecht. Brecht understood that the emotional pull of the individual characters could overwhelm and obscure the greater social lessons in the literary work. In other words, Safwan's blood on Isma'il's hands might bring closure—a satisfying catharsis of the reader's anger at the injustices against these young people—but, in the end, would only obscure the recognition that the police state is much bigger than an individual like Khalid Safwan. Whereas his earlier, realist works had been firmly Lukácsian, *Karnak Café*, like Mahfouz's later output, is decidedly Brechtian, provoking thought by alienating its audience. Significantly, the "propagandistic" film that Allen cites replaced this anticlimax with a more traditional condemnation of Safwan and rousing declarations of new freedom in the Sadat era. In the novel, however, Mahfouz's verdict on the contemporary state of Egypt is left ambiguous. Egypt in 1974 was still not ready for a return to *iltizam*. The suspended projects of Hilmi, Samara, and 'Umar remained deferred, despite the public purges, awaiting a genuine revolution that would replace not only Khalid Safwan but the entire security apparatus of which he was a part. Such a revolution lay far in the future.

Wedding in the Dome

Despite Mahfouz's assertion in the previous three novels that Egyptian society of the late twentieth century was not ready for the return of *iltizam*, in the early 1980s, the author offered a vision of what an attempt at *al-adab al-multazim* might look like in that corrupt environment. In 1981's *Wedding in the Dome*, Mahfouz offers such a damning vision of the collision of pure *iltizam* with a corrupt society as to make the reader glad that Samara Bahjat never got to finish her play.

By the late 1970s, the focus of criticism of the state's corruption of society had come to center on the economic corruption of Sadat's *infitah* (opening) policy. Capitalizing on the adoration he had achieved in the West, Sadat had invited a flood of Western commercial investment that permanently altered Egyptian society. Much like the fruits of Nasser's socialist reforms, the profits from the *infitah* went to a new elite. Accordingly, the novel *Wedding in the Dome*, yet another work to take brutal aim at the failures of the partners in *iltizam*—public, author, and political power—focuses its criticism of that power on an agent of economic corruption and consumerism that represents the ill-effects of the *infitah*, in this case, a corrupt and dictatorial theater company. The theater company constitutes an all-encompassing community in which the characters of the story spend their entire lives. The protagonist is born and raised in this tight society, over which the theater manager rules like a despot. Like the state, the theater should facilitate the work of the *multazim* artist. Yet here again, that power does more to prevent effective communication.

Wedding in the Dome, like the other works in this study, involves a *multazim* literary work that is never seen by the reader. Unlike Samara Bahjat's unfinished play or Hilmi Hamada's aborted biography, young 'Abbas Yunis's drama not only comes to publication, but becomes a public hit. While Mahfouz's previous novels explored the reasons why such texts could not be presented to the public, *Wedding in the Dome* imagines what would happen if they were. The novel, then, is the story of public reception, a reception that serves to validate the doubts that 'Umar and Mustafa had earlier expressed about the capability of the public to swallow a revolutionary message. Still, not one word from 'Abbas's play—the object of discussion in every scene of the book—appears in Mahfouz's text. The deferral of the work outside of the novel, then, creates a more glaring absence than in the earlier texts. Indeed, Mahfouz's novel even shares the title of 'Abbas's unseen play, as if to trumpet the missing piece upon which the novel centers. Once again, the quality of the written work will not be allowed to intrude into what is clearly a study of the relationships of an author, public, and authority.

Using a narrative format with which he had achieved success in the 1960s in the novel *Miramar*, Mahfouz presents a quartet of narratives that consider 'Abbas's play and its impact from four different viewpoints. Once again, the novel's structure prevents any conjecture about the 'truth' of 'Abbas's play. The play means four completely different things to four different characters, and Mahfouz is satisfied to leave the ambiguity in place. Such haziness is alien to the realist style of Mahfouz's classic 1940s texts, like *A Beginning and an End*, in which a single, uncontested reality is assumed. To further emphasize the priority of audience reaction over the playwright's intent in this story, Mahfouz offers 'Abbas's narrative as the last of the four. By that point, 'Abbas has been slandered by the others as a criminal, a betrayer, a political opportunist, and an ungrateful child, and his play seems—to these narrators—a brash admission of his sins. The play has wrecked homes, enriched exploiters, and slandered the innocent before 'Abbas ever gets a chance to tell his story. When the novel reveals 'Abbas as a naive idealist who believes his play to be a great *multazim* work that will inspire social justice, his failure has already been firmly established.

The play has put the idea of justice into the mind of the first narrator in the quartet, the outraged actor, Tariq Ramadan, though certainly not in the way 'Abbas intended. Although 'Abbas's play gives the struggling theater troupe its only hit in years and single-handedly revives Tariq's career, the actor is not amused. Tariq has suspected 'Abbas of stealing his lover out of spite, killing her and their infant son, and sending his own parents to prison. The play, in Tariq's mind, is an unabashed confession to all these crimes, so clear in fact that Tariq wishes to use it as evidence to call the prosecutor and have 'Abbas locked up. "Playwright? . . . What is he but a criminal!"[105] Tariq rails. Indeed, the novel opens with a livid Tariq Ramadan combing the alleys in order to drag the playwright to justice, a scene which does not presage the triumphant return of *al-adab al-multazim*.

'Abbas does not fare much better in the subsequent narrative, presented by his own father, Karam. The older man agrees with Tariq's accusations about his son, but does admire the play for setting the record straight about the misfortunes of Karam's own life. The poor father, we learn, has been saddled with an ungrateful child and a wife who makes no secret of prostituting herself with the other members of the theater group. As 'Abbas drags their scandals out into the open, Karam finally feels that justice has been served. "In this moment of shame, I have achieved a victory over both my wife and son!" he declares.[106] Even though there will be no legal retribution against 'Abbas or his immoral mother, at least part of the public feels vindicated by 'Abbas's work.

The next to tell her story, 'Abbas's mother Halima, also recognizes the bald depiction of her character surrogate as a shameless whore and realizes the play is her public scourging. She, however, remembers the events that inspired the story quite differently than her husband. Coming from a rural area to the city seeking honest work, Halima, like many young, attractive women, was lured into the theater company by the aggressive manager, Sirhan. Her interview with Sirhan quickly turned into a rape, ruining the reputation of a girl who had previously guarded her virginity. In a desperate attempt to preserve her honor, she married Karam, as he offered her a place to live and was willing to conceal her disgrace. Yet Karam turned out to be a rather worthless degenerate—a drug addict who insisted on turning their house into an opium den for profit, in the process exposing Halima to advances from other men. Young 'Abbas frequently witnessed Halima being taken behind locked doors by the male customers of their drug house. Lacking any other information, he concluded what the circumstantial evidence seemed to imply—that Halima was prostituting herself—and his play solidly attacks her for it. 'Abbas has no doubts about her guilt: "She is my primary enemy. My father is crazy; he's an addict, but my mother is the orchestrator of all the evil."[107] Yet the glimpse behind closed doors that only Halima's narrative can provide shows that she not only refused to have sex with those men but that she had actually become completely frigid from her earlier trauma.

The character names give the story a larger, allegorical context: Halima ('gentle,' but the etymological root also alluding to dreaming as well as reaching sexual maturity, all involved in her downfall), with a family name "al-Kabsh" ('the ram') is devoured in a passage into the world of theater by Sirhan ('wolf,' but coming from the etymological root for 'play,' 'drama,' and their associated terms), and is then rescued from shame by marriage to Karam ('noble' or 'beneficent'), in his act of mercy rather than attraction. The introduction of such a symbolic level into the story serves to further distance the narrative from objective truth. The characters' accounts of their pasts conflict fundamentally, and while the symbolism in their names would seem to validate Halima's perception, the novel is ultimately unclear. There will be no unambiguous victory for the power of *al-adab al-multazim* here.

'Abbas has taken such a beating in the first three narratives that the picture that emerges in his own account seems to depict another person entirely. Instead of the selfish heel that others see, his values make him a paragon of a *multazim* writer, one who thinks he clearly and unambiguously sees the moral decay in his society. Some of his pronouncements are so naively idealistic that he appears from a world far removed from all others in the story. "For me, art is not merely art, but rather a substitute for the kind of work an impotent idealist dreams of accomplishing. What have I done to oppose the evil surrounding me? What work do I have, if I am impotent on the only battlefield I have been granted, and that is the stage?"[108] he declares, sounding as though he has swallowed a volume of Salama Musa. When asked about his desire to become a playwright, he explains, "I am addicted to a dream, the way my father is addicted to opium—my dream of changing everything and recreating it. . . . I would demolish the old houses and put tall buildings in their place. I would enlighten the police, raise up the level of behavior of students and teachers, produce food out of thin air, and eradicate drugs and alcohol."[109] There is an unmistakable note of awakening and instructing in his vision, as befits one who believes ignorance to be the main cause of social injustice. 'Abbas intends to *ahdhib* the police, a word embracing the idealistic aims of purifying, enlightening, instructing, correcting, and refining. Yet from its direct action of teaching society, 'Abbas's vision jumps immediately to producing material results out of nowhere. The logical gap in 'Abbas's reasoning is the same as in *al-adab al-multazim*, which also assumed ignorance to be the cause of suffering and thus public enlightenment to be its cure. Mahfouz has preceded this idealistic talk with three other narratives that provide clear evidence that the public instead will extract from his work whatever messages it needs to serve its own interests.

The power figure in this little world is the theater manager Sirhan, who exploits his position for profit and the systematic deflowering of women. Like Halima, many other virtuous young women, including 'Abbas's wife Tahiya, have found that sexual favors are the price of admission into the troupe. Sirhan the wolf has his pick of the new actresses as they come in, passing his castoffs down the chain of power, stopping next with the lead actor, Tariq Ramadan. Eventually, most hit bottom with a wreck like Karam. Tahiya, however, seems to have found escape. After being used up by Sirhan, then physically abused by Tariq, she finds the naive and gentle 'Abbas. Together, the two briefly build a happy family. Both Tahiya and their baby die tragic deaths from disease as a result of their poverty and inability to get adequate medical care and 'Abbas turns to writing, pouring his grief into his work. The resulting drama—an exposé of the corrupt theater troupe itself—becomes a major hit for this *multazim* artist. Were we given only 'Abbas's narrative, we might conclude that *iltizam* had finally won the day.

Unfortunately, 'Abbas's play seems to have set the cause of social justice back decades. The exploiters have been uniformly vindicated while the victims Halima and Tahiya are defamed as manipulative tramps. Tariq Ramadan has wrapped himself in a blanket of self-righteousness supported by his egotism. The play proves to him the villainy of both Tahiya and 'Abbas and inspires him to demand justice: "She deserved to be killed anyway," he tells 'Abbas, "but you also deserve to hang!"[110] Halima is crushed and shamed while Karam can celebrate the public flogging. Meanwhile, the corrupt theatrical power takes the profit, as Sirhan makes plain he doesn't care what the play says, as long as he makes money. The absence of any direct excerpting from 'Abbas's play leaves the ultimate culpability unresolved. Is the play merely poorly written, or has the audience just extracted what it needs to reinforce existing injustices?

The recollections in 'Abbas's narrative indicate that he may have been the victim of manipulation by the local power. To his credit, there is some suggestion that 'Abbas tried to stick to reality in his early drafts of the play, although here again, the reader is denied any access to those texts. More important than the actual text of 'Abbas's early play is Sirhan's flat refusal to produce a piece of melodrama. The theater, he explains, is no place for pathos, and if 'Abbas intends to see his play on stage, he had better spice it up. Sirhan makes no secret of his distaste for the commitment 'Abbas holds dear. He rails to the actors: "There is no one more cruel than the idealists. They are responsible for worldwide slaughter!"[111] "Don't talk to me about life . . . don't philosophize. I hear that every night on the stage until I can't stand it."[112] In the play, Halima becomes a saucier character, while the ever-faithful Tahiya becomes an adulteress, who dies with her baby, not from poverty and sickness, but rather at the hand of a raging 'Abbas. "It's an exciting play that promises to succeed and that's the limit of my concerns," Sirhan notes.[113] Somehow, the crusading moralist 'Abbas has been co-opted into Sirhan's Machiavellian system without quite realizing it.

Samara Bahjat surrendered her idealism after her own moral compromises. 'Abbas, however, remains committed to his art. The inflamed public reaction forces him to leave town, and even entertain thoughts of suicide, but his conviction triumphs. Sitting in a Helwan park, the artist reaches an epiphany about his life and his noble mission. Brimming with excitement, he rushes back to Cairo. Meanwhile, the theater manager, the actors, and the critics are eagerly waiting to see 'Abbas's next offering.

Wedding in the Dome validates the messages that have permeated Mahfouz's post-1960 works. All the actors in the *iltizam* relationship have either abandoned their roles or deluded themselves into believing that self-serving distortion serves some noble purpose. In the era of *al-adab al-multazim*, those actors remained outside of the text, responsible only for ensuring a realistic portrayal of the world of the working class. Now, the entire model has been turned inside out. The actors of *iltizam*—deluded artists, corrupt authorities, and an uncaring public—are the center of the story. Meanwhile, the *multazim* works produced or envisioned by those artists must stay outside the text. The plays of Samara, 'Abbas, and Mustafa, the poems of 'Umar, and Hilmi's biography do not belong in the world of late-twentieth-century Egypt. The fate of 'Abbas's drama shows what would happen were such texts introduced to Egyptian society. Even as Mahfouz uses 'Abbas's work as an object lesson, he keeps it deferred outside the novel. Yet *multazim* writing has not been abandoned. Mahfouz keeps *iltizam* very much alive and under discussion, but always deferred, waiting for the moment it can return. That return would require fundamental change: a sweeping away of the political authority, the re-engaging of the public to the power of the written word, and a new generation of activist writers to move the masses. That world looked as far away in the 1960s as it did in 2010, but *al-adab al-multazim* remained in waiting throughout, in the inverted model of committed writing that Mahfouz offered.

Chapter 4
Yusuf Idris:
A Writer of the Revolutionary Era

Despite their common commitment to social justice, *multazim* writers could be a very diverse group. The stylistic differences among great *multazim* writers and the heated debates that animated them exemplified the artistic freedom that *al-adab al-multazim* treasured, in sharp opposition to the forced unanimity of Soviet style writing. No two Egyptian writers better demonstrated this healthy diversity than Naguib Mahfouz and Yusuf Idris. While they were both heavily lauded as exemplars of *multazim* writing, they differed fundamentally in style, genre, and approach as well as in personality. That so many common threads underlie their early *multazim* works, as well as their sharp turns to disillusion in the 1960s, only serves to underscore the parallels in the rise and decline of *al-adab al-multazim* among leading Egyptian writers.

Truly, Idris would be the first to deny that any similarities came from conscious imitation of the writer sixteen years his senior. When virtually all Egyptians celebrated Mahfouz's selection as the first—and still only—Arabic writer to receive the Nobel Prize, Idris marked himself as "The Lone Dissenter" in a scathing letter to *al-Wafd* newspaper, in which he mourned that Mahfouz's selection had set the cause of Arab writers back thirty years. Idris pronounced himself as the intended recipient of the prize, claiming that Mahfouz had been substituted at the "last moment" because of his appeasement and accommodation of the Jews—about as damning an accusation as could be made in the Arab world.[1]

Idris had long tread a different path than Mahfouz. He had little use for the kind of expansive, panoramic views of society that Mahfouz produced in his elaborate novels. Idris felt that novels on the scale of Mahfouz's *Cairo Trilogy*, with their extensive, intricate attention to detail, distracted the reader from the important social messages buried within. Idris, instead, made his name as the master of the Arabic short story, offering in each a brief glimpse of a particular slice of Egyptian life that, in his own words, struck like "the nuclear bomb in its smallness and efficacy."[2] Idris was something of the "nuclear bomb" himself, his political passions leading him on a far more confrontational trajectory than the quiet and humble Mahfouz. Idris came of age in the final throes of a weakened monarchy, being imprisoned for his participation in student demonstrations and for his revolutionary publications. Trained and licensed as a medical doctor, Idris initially pursued his writing career in tandem with his medical practice, his first stories appearing on the eve of the revolution in 1951 and his first collection in 1954.

He eagerly supported the 1952 revolution, although his honeymoon with the Nasser regime would not last long. Critic 'Abd al-Rahman Abu 'Auf notes with some nostalgia, "Truly, Yusuf Idris was the towering literary expression of the dream of national liberation that reached its peak in 'Abd al-Nasser's project of resurgence, emancipation, and justice, and the most impressive of his fictional and dramatic works were born in the bosom of that project."[3] Yet not long after, Idris freely admitted his disillusionment with the revolution. After speaking against Nasser's domineering governing style at a literary conference in Beirut, Idris was arrested upon his return to Egypt and spent a year in prison. While in prison, he joined the Communist Party, only to part ways with the Communists in disappointment shortly thereafter. After emerging from prison, Idris joined the Algerian guerrillas against the French occupation and was wounded in combat.

Despite starting out in the medical field, Idris turned exclusively to writing as his means of bringing about social change. He noted that the true beauty of literature was measured by the impact it had in "changing the mentality of the people," convincing the reader of "opinions which he would otherwise never have embraced."[4] With such a strident expression of *iltizam* as his guide, it is little wonder that Idris tended toward the ambitious *al-adab al-hadif* school of Mahmud Amin al-'Alim at points in his career. Al-'Alim, in return, offered high praise for Idris's work, saying it was guided by a fundamental "principle of uncovering truth"[5] and an ability to capture the spirit of the distinct "historical, social, Egyptian moment" in which he lived, highlighting its "struggles" and "contradictions," while always speaking to a larger, "deep humanism."[6] Al-'Alim saw Idris's work as "that kind of art that lifts people above their sorrows . . . as a power of resistance, a humanitarian power to confront the prevailing poverty; truly, it is a power of social unification."[7] As frequently happened, Idris would become disillusioned with *al-adab al-hadif*, as he had with Communism and Nasserism. Ultimately, he felt his duty to his art and his people went beyond any particular school or doctrine.

Idris's committed writings gained attention outside Egypt as well. The Soviet author Yuri Nagibin, prefacing his Russian translation of Idris's 1957 collection *Isn't That So? (A-laysa ka-dhalik?)*, describes Idris as "a pure, progressive artist who loves the people," one who had "lived in an exploitive, bourgeois society, and as a pure and noble artist, boldly lifted the veil from the evils of that society."[8] Idris even openly identified himself with socialist realism at one point, although by the 1970s he would deny such an association just as vehemently.

Like Mahfouz, Idris drew on his own distinct life experiences to craft his portraits of Egyptian life. Just as Mahfouz had sketched extremely accurate pictures of the quotidian life in the old Cairene neighborhoods in which he grew up, Idris, the medical doctor and one-time health inspector who was posted to many locations throughout Cairo and the rural villages, frequently explored public health issues in his work, profiling both village and city life. While Mahfouz often showed the biases in the social and economic systems that structured neighborhoods, Idris's stories examined issues like the lack of birth control, poor hygiene practices, inadequate rural medical facilities, and failings of the mental health system—issues which could have been greatly improved through public awareness and civic action, he believed. In both cases, the writers drew from their experiences with the people, to address serious social issues in the language of the people. For all the differences between the two writers, though, it is not hard to see why critics like 'Atiya saw both Mahfouz and Idris as standard bearers of *iltizam*. The underlying principles of *al-adab al-multazim*—as described in chapter 2—were visibly manifest in the works that both men produced during the prime of *iltizam*. Their stylistic differences only spoke to the artistic freedom that kept *al-adab al-multazim* free from the shackles of formulaic, Soviet-style writing.

The *Multazim* Writing of Yusuf Idris: "An Errand"

To highlight the underlying spirit of *iltizam* in Idris's work, I turn now to a representative piece of Idris's fiction from the 1950s. Unlike one of Mahfouz's panoramic novels, the 1954 story "An Errand" *(Mishwar)* runs only fifteen pages, describes only two days of narrative time, and centers on two individuals, rather than a family. Yet like Mahfouz's work, the story exposes social injustices and contradictions through its realistic narrative. "An Errand," was furthermore part of a larger body of work, one of many stories that explored particular social welfare problems from the 1954 collection *The Cheapest Nights (Arkhas layali)*. The title story from that collection, for example, dealt with the cycle of poverty and irresponsible childbearing in lower-class communities. Two years later, Idris's first novel, the 1956 *A Love Story (Qissat hubb)*, despite the seemingly romantic title, would become one of the landmarks of realist *multazim* literature, placed by critic Sabry Hafez in a class with Mahfouz's *Cairo Trilogy*.[9]

In "An Errand," Idris crafts his protagonist, al-Shubrawi, as a lower-class everyman with dreams less ambitious than even those of Mahfouz's Husayn Kamil 'Ali. A minor policeman in a rural village in the Delta province of Daqahliya, al-Shubrawi's fortune is a fifty-piaster note hidden under a pillow that cannot even buy him one night in a cheap hotel. His only glimpse of the world outside his hamlet came through that universal Egyptian passage to manhood as a conscript soldier. Now back in his sleepy village, he is haunted by the memories of such mundane pleasures as the grilled meat sold on Cairo streets, the visits to a real movie theater, and rides on a packed streetcar. Idris's attention to sensory detail in depicting these very commonplace trappings of everyday Cairo life give added punch to the humble aspirations expressed in the exclamations of his hero—"I would sell my life for an hour in you, Dear Cairo!"[10] For Mahfouz, whose world was Cairo, such a desire may have sounded awkward, but Idris understood a different set of aspirations belonging to the rural poor and could express those in the language of the villager.

Is al-Shubrawi's dream of an hour in Cairo too much for a poor rural policeman to ask? Certainly, his meager earnings could never allow him to afford a trip to Cairo, but his honest work for the village seems to offer an unexpected chance at his dream when he is assigned to escort a mentally ill woman from Daqahliya to Cairo for admission to a hospital. Public service, just as it did in his years as a conscript soldier, now offers the rewards of Cairo for al-Shubrawi's service.

Al-Shubrawi needs no further encouragement. He immediately grabs the pittance that constitutes his life's savings and fills his head with dreams of riding the streetcar and sitting in a Cairo café again. Meanwhile, a huge procession of concerned family members leads the patient, an older woman named Zubayda, to the train station. Powerless to protect their own relative because of economic constraints that prevent them from traveling, they must rely on the mercy of a government official. Their pleas to the policeman to take good care of the sick woman bring al-Shubrawi's assurance that he will treat her as if he were "her brother, as if from the same mother and father."[11] Fortunately for them, al-Shubrawi is true to his word, endeavoring to protect the sick woman, even when out of sight of the villagers. Between al-Shubrawi and his two goals of helping Zubayda and enjoying his brief trip to the city, however, lie the Egyptian bureaucracy and medical system. He is but one link in that bureaucratic chain and will soon come to understand the impotence of a single link in an overall dysfunctional chain. One low-ranking policeman is hardly a match for the systemic hurdles of the monolith of Egyptian bureaucracy.

Al-Shubrawi's assignment would seem a simple enough task. He has been charged merely to deliver a patient from one point to another. Yet nothing is simple in the Egyptian bureaucracy, as anyone who has stood in the infamously long lines at government offices knows. With an unruly hysteric in tow and only a few piasters to travel through the city, al-Shubrawi bounces back and forth between the governorate building, the hospital, and a police station, repeatedly meeting minor bureaucrats who refuse to accept custody of the woman, echoing the mantra "that's a responsibility I cannot assume." In frustration, al-Shubrawi begins to curse "responsibility," and feels as though he "carries the weight of the entire world on his head."[12] Al-Shubrawi spends a dizzying day going back and forth between hospitals and police stations. Eventually penetrating into the asylum, al-Shubrawi discovers that the doctors will not commit Zubayda without one of her relatives present, an impossibility given the distance to the village and the lack of money for transportation.

With credible and clear detail, "An Errand" exposes contradictions that would resonate with any victim of the Egyptian bureaucracy. Society says a woman like Zubayda belongs out of the public eye, yet no responsible actor is willing to give her a place to stay. The legal system assigns a policeman, not one of her family members to escort her, out of concern for public safety. Yet the same system refuses the policeman the authority to commit her, reserving that right for the family. No individual actor is willing to take "responsibility" for Zubayda because no actor can guarantee the cooperation of the next link in the chain. These contradictions, while not officially enforcing discrimination, overwhelmingly affect the poor. A wealthier family would have been able to afford transportation for the sick woman, a police escort, and several family members, and thus have avoided the whole mess. Moreover, a truly wealthy family would be dealing with a private hospital and not need to deal with the public health bureaucracy at all. Al-Shubrawi is no less the responsible hero than a "hard as a sword" Soviet-style industrial champion, regardless of his confronting a dysfunctional political authority rather than a malfunctioning piece of machinery. Yet it is not herculean efforts from the workers that his example calls for but rather simple changes from the bureaucrats.

With no food and no place to stay, al-Shubrawi wanders the streets, getting near to a breakdown himself from the ranting of the sick woman he refuses to abandon. He finds no sympathy from the city dwellers, and the small pittance of savings earmarked for his big day on the town cannot even rent them shelter for the night. In a cutting insight into the constraints of social laws upon decent people, the protagonist notes that he could not get a room in a hotel, due to the scandal of sharing a room with a woman.[13] Of all the things an exhausted al-Shubrawi might worry about, his concern is particularly revealing of the moral strictures that dominate his thinking. Al-Shubrawi's decency prevents him from taking a room that he would use for the strictly humanitarian purpose of getting a sick woman off the street, but even though he has absolutely no sexual interest in her, sexual mores make this act of kindness impossible. In a few sentences, the author has managed to combine economic constraint, social customs, and an individual's personal kindness and morality into an insoluble contradiction.

The exhausted al-Shubrawi finally finds refuge in a mosque for the night, giving him enough strength to confront the medical bureaucracy the next day. After a standoff with inflexible doctors, Zubayda goes into a hysteric fit in the hospital courtyard that succeeds where all words of reason and persuasion have failed. Finally moved by some combination of compassion and fear, the doctors admit her to the hospital. If the story's conclusion offers hope for social change, it also implies that this monolithic system can only be awoken by a violent outburst.

Yet al-Shubrawi does not emerge unscathed. In her last violent fit of the story, Zubayda clamps a painful bite on the hand of the policeman who has guarded her. The hitherto patient al-Shubrawi finally succumbs to his anger and slaps the woman. While it is unlikely that she will remember the act, al-Shubrawi appears permanently scarred by guilt, feeling a "shame like he had never known in his life."[14] Immediately moved to sympathy by a remarkably lucid appreciation of her situation given that her teeth were clamped on his hand moments earlier, "he realized, after Zubayda was placed in the straightjacket, that she was truly insane; that she did not comprehend a word that she was saying, she was not at fault for all that had happened and that while she was with him, she had not eaten or drank since they left the village. A strange sense of sympathy touched him as he saw her rolling and banging her head on the ground."[15] Although he has finally discharged his official duties, al-Shubrawi no longer has any desire to see Cairo, and his dream dies.

Of course, it's the bureaucracy, rather than Zubayda, that deserves to be slapped, but al-Shubrawi cannot strike it any more than Hasanayn Kamil 'Ali could have taken the contradictory social mores of the officer class and thrown them off a bridge instead of himself. Critic Abu 'Auf praises the sympathetic identification Idris inspires for the victims trapped in this system through his straightforward narration in this story: "We are not able to prevent our indignation, which the book arouses with simplicity."[16] Herein lay the essence of *multazim* writing: arousing the public, but "with simplicity." The diehard *multazim* critic 'Atiya found a parallel in Idris's use of the poor and mentally ill character Zubayda to illustrate social injustice to Mahfouz's unfortunate characters, despite the obvious surface differences in Mahfouz's and Idris's work.[17]

"An Errand" relies heavily on the relationship of the three partners in *iltizam*—author, political power, and public—to convey its message, without the direct intrusion of any of these three actors into the textual realm. Idris, a medical doctor and health inspector, wrote from a position of authority about the national healthcare system, without the direct appearance of authorial commentary or a character surrogate. Indeed, the fleeting glimpses of medical officials in the story are hardly flattering to the author's first profession. Not even a brief statement from a fictional doctor to express the frustrations and constraints of practicing medicine in Egypt graces the text. Idris downplays his own professional experience within the text in order to focus on the experience of the common man, as a *multazim* artist should. Outside of the fictional text, Idris remained an outspoken critic of the system through his nonfictional work, a reputation which doubtlessly bolstered the credibility of the story.

Idris grounds his story in a confidence in the mass public as well, without recourse to direct appeal to that public. Unlike Idris's later works, which usually centered on isolated, alienated heroes, "An Errand" speaks to collective social engagement. Al-Shubrawi is an everyman, an upstanding if humble member of a village society who can be trusted because of his ties to the community. His history, life experiences, aspirations, and frustrations are common to lower-class Egyptians and the problems he faces call for unified social action. He is a victim not because of his alienation or oddity, as Idris's later characters would be, but rather due to a harsh system that could victimize any Egyptian of his class. As Abu 'Auf noted above, the plight of one ordinary Egyptian activates the collective dignity and compassion of the mass public. Idris's later works would question the concern of the public for any individual, but here that concern is assumed.

Similarly, Idris's story deals with the third actor in the *iltizam* relationship, the political power, without direct intrusion of that power into the text. The true villains in this story, those responsible for the failings of the healthcare system, were well known to the author, yet remain outside the text, like Mahfouz's unseen "villain" in *A Beginning and an End*, Prime Minister Sidqi. Instead, the only government officials to appear in the story are low-ranking, impotent links in the chain—marked by their inability to "take responsibility." The protagonist's slap of frustration against a woman he immediately recognizes as an innocent victim stands as testimony to the absence of any truly responsible or guilty party in the text to whom he can address his anger. The author indicts officials responsible for the entire healthcare system by focusing on the fictional everyman. As Abu 'Auf points out, the text causes us to demand answers, to seek those responsible, without ever making direct reference to them.

Idris would find it more difficult to keep the political power out of the text as the revolution gave way to an entrenched police state. Unlike Mahfouz, Idris had no 'period of silence' in the 1950s—indeed, the concept of silence seemed wholly alien to Idris. As his disillusion with the Nasser state grew, Idris began to engage the regime more directly, while upholding the formal tenets of *iltizam* ever more loosely. His 1956 story "Farahat's Republic" *(Jumhuriyat Farahat)* is a case in point of Idris's transitional period, marked by indirect, allegoric criticism of the regime, yet still anchored in realistic detail. In this story, a tired but dedicated policeman—bearing no small resemblance to the protagonist of "An Errand"—shares with a visitor his dream of a just and prosperous nation. The visitor to the police station seems to be a man of importance, inspiring the officer Farahat to describe his vision of an imagined leader who will build a socialist utopia for the people of Egypt from humble beginnings. Starting with a fleet of ships, the imagined leader garners the capital to invest in industry, then in agriculture. Not stopping with economic growth, this model ruler builds huge workers' communes and provides for the needs of his people, never getting sidetracked into pursuit of personal glory.

Farahat's dream strikes an immediate parallel to the socialist vision for 1950s Egypt. Beginning his project with Egypt's maritime commerce, Farahat's leader echoes Egypt's long-standing grievance against the West: European ownership of the Suez Canal. Not coincidentally, Nasser's greatest achievement as a national hero came in his seizure of the canal, part of a multi-step plan to provide the economic stimulus to invigorate the nation. Farahat's ideal leader strengthens the nation's defenses against external threats and increases its self-sufficiency, much as Nasser is credited for doing in Egyptian lore, then goes further, using that power to enact widespread domestic reforms.

Arab critics applauded the clear expression of a common "Egyptian dream" in Idris's story. *Al-Adab*'s Tawfiq Hanna considered Farahat's vision a "charter" for the desired Egyptian state, presented by the author in a pure Egyptian language.[18] Similarly, al-'Alim called the story an expression of "resistance and rebellion," conveying a dream of a world in which "freedom and justice reign."[19] The story, however, ends in disappointment. Rather than the man of influence that Farahat imagined him to be, the visitor to the station turns out to be a prisoner, dispelling Farahat's temporary feeling of euphoria. "Let's forget it, mister. It's just talk. You didn't really believe me, did you?"[20] Farahat never directly equates the visitor with his ideal leader, but the disappointment of someone turning out to be less than what he at first seemed and Farahat's quick rejections of his dream offer a sense of mounting disillusion.

A Turn from Realism

Just as *multazim* critics applauded Mahfouz's realism, they applauded Idris's early writing for its contextual authenticity and "pure Egyptianness." In reviewing Idris's second anthology, *al-Adab* critic Tawfiq Hanna cites more than ten times in one page the distinctly Egyptian picture Idris paints, while also mentioning the particularly "Cairene" view of the city scenes. The physical details of a fictional police station, for example, recall "every police department in the cities and the countryside." Invoking familiar slogans of *iltizam*, Hanna links this authenticity to Idris's "consciousness" of and "zeal" for the Egyptian people.[21] Similarly, after citing the failures of previous artists in depicting the peasant, even categorizing their errors into several mistaken tendencies, *al-Adab* critic Muhammad al-'Antil praised Idris's fidelity in "overturning the heaps of Egyptian society" to expose the contradictions and problems in the environment of the masses. He felt that Idris carefully organized and crafted his picture of the peasant from material of the society around him in such a way as to stir the emotions of the reader and call for a better future.[22]

Like Mahfouz, Idris changed direction stylistically in the 1960s from classic realism to modernist experimentation. While the former emerged from his long 'period of silence' with a radically different style, Idris, who kept writing throughout the 1950s, shifted more gradually. Yet a comparison of representative works from the mid-1950s and mid-1960s reveals a profound change in style. The detailed, empathetic presentation of al-Shubrawi that opened "An Errand," for example, stands in sharp contrast to the protagonist introduced in the opening lines of the typical 1966 story "*al-Shaykh shaykha*":

> God's lands are wide and many, and each village is full of young and old, male and female, individuals and families, Muslims and Copts; a vast world, governed by rules and disturbed by rules. Occasionally, an aberration comes out of this system, as in the case of our village, which stands out from the rest of God's lands because of that creature that lives within it; that creature who cannot be counted among the people of our village, nor among its creatures or beasts. Nor was he the missing link between them. A creature standing on his own, but with no name. Sometimes called Shaykh Muhammad; sometimes Shaykha Fatima. Yet this was only at times, for convenience. In reality, he lived without a name, without a father, without a mother. No one knew from where he had come, nor who gave birth to that solid body. . . . He had human features: two eyes, two ears, and a nose. He walked with his two legs. The problem was, however, that these features took a shape that was in no way human.[23]

From the outset, this story begins in a setting only vaguely connected to contemporary Egypt. Unlike the firm geographic and sensory orientation that opened "An Errand," with its fantasies of going to "the National Cinema," and dining at "Mu'alim Ahmad's" in Cairo,[24] this unidentified village is as unrooted as its strange protagonist, with only the mention of Copts and Muslims suggesting Egypt. The story does not contemplate the bureaucracy of Cairo healthcare, typified by its rules for committing a woman to an asylum, but rather a "vast world governed by rules"—timeless laws of nature, like the required number of limbs to be classed as human. The central figure of the story is not, like the protagonist of a *multazim* work, constrained by the rules that govern his world; he is rather defined by his position outside the laws. While al-Shubrawi's character had been molded by the experience of conscription and four years of service in the rural village of Daqahliya, the nameless protagonist has no lineage, no history, nor even a biological connection to anything outside himself. The Arabic title is deliberately contradictory and ambiguous in its identification, citing both a male and female, definite and indefinite, term of respect *(shaykh)*, when clearly none of those can be applied to this character. Likewise, the pronoun *huwa* used to describe the character would be ambiguous in Arabic, meaning either "he" or "it."

As Idris continued toward the surreal and absurd, *multazim* critics had a difficult time with his 1960s output. 'Atiya, one of the most strident advocates of *al-adab al-multazim*, launched a vehement appeal for a return to *iltizam* in his 1974 book *Commitment and Revolution in Modern Arabic Literature (al-Iltizam wa-l-thawra fi-l-adab al-'arabi al-hadith)*, including a chapter with the stinging title "Yusuf Idris: From Commitment to Neutrality and Pessimism" *(Min al-iltizam ila al-hiyad wa-l-tasha'um)*. While lavishing praise on the committed, optimistic, and realistic works of Idris's early period—works that advanced the ideals of socialism without slavish adherence to socialist realism—the critic lamented Idris's turn toward generalized, "humanistic" subjects rather than specifically Egyptian issues, as well as his embrace of symbolism and his overwhelming sense of pessimism. Cataloging Idris's 1960s works into two broad categories he labeled "committed" and "not committed," he found the author to be vacillating between the two poles and asked him to make a decision between them. 'Atiya's final words—also the title of an article he wrote in *al-Adab*—asked plainly: "Where to, Yusuf Idris?"[25]

Other critics went to greater lengths to accommodate Idris's change in style. Writing in 1966, the novelist Bahaa Taher noted of Idris: "having established his reputation as one of the leaders and staunch advocates of the social realist school, he then proceeded to divest himself of all that and of any other 'school' approach and entered an experimental phase."[26] Taher lamented that many critics couldn't appreciate Idris's new work, noting that "the list of rejectionists now includes the supporters of the realist school, the supporters of art for art's sake, and opponents of the use of the colloquial language and of any kind of experimentation." He added, "Yusuf Idris's most recent works have yet to receive a genuinely perceptive and objective evaluation."[27] Al-'Alim, one of the last persistent defenders of *iltizam* in the 1960s, accused pioneering critic Louis 'Awad of making "existentialist" interpretations of Idris's works of the period, invoking that damnable term that had come to stand for everything that *iltizam* was not. Idris's 1964 play *al-Farafir*, which had deeply divided critics, was a case in point. The absurdist play, which violated conventional rules of drama in presenting a pair of gravediggers over a thousand years' time, marked a definite departure from the realism of Idris's 1950s works. 'Awad's criticism of the play, al-'Alim felt, rested on an inadequate, surface reading of the work. Al-'Alim, instead, urged a deeper view:

> We don't say, therefore, of "*al-Farafir*" only that it embraces an anarchistic, existentialist conception of the movement, as Dr. 'Awad says, and then say that we should stop at this statement. Rather, we do say that much about "*al-Farafir*" but then we add: while "*al-Farafir*" has such a view, it also offers a vision of unrestricted freedom and progress in the society around the *farafir*. . . . The important thing is to be a guardian of progressive values, insisting upon them, directed always at more growth and progress.[28]

Whether al-'Alim was ultimately correct in seeing progressive social criticism under Idris's surrealistic pictures or not, Idris had clearly moved from the unambiguous, realistic portraits that *multazim* critics had so admired in his earlier work. "Al-Shaykh shaykha" and *al-Farafir* definitely did not resemble the author's classic *multazim* works like "An Errand," nor did they present a wide public with easily accessible, realistic stories of the social environments in which typical Egyptians lived. They may well have presented revolutionary social and political commentary, but if two leading critics like 'Awad and al-'Alim could debate their meaning, then the mass public was sure to have a tough time. Yet underneath the alienation and absurdity that marked these works, a continued concern for the artist, the public, and the political power as well as the possibility of communication for social change shaped Idris's later works. As in the case of Mahfouz, the assumptions of *iltizam* had been inverted, but remained essential to Idris's texts. I now turn to five of the author's many stories of the 1960s through the 1980s that capture this inversion of *iltizam* in practice.

"The Alif in al-Ahrar"

Five years before Mahfouz presented Anis Zaki writing blank pages in a mindless government job in *Gossip on the Nile*, Idris's 1961 "The Alif in al-Ahrar" *(Alif al-ahrar)* offered a protagonist similarly relegated to the production of meaningless words as a cog in the massive public sector paperwork machine. The hopeful architects of *al-adab al-multazim* had dreamed of a day when a socialist state would provide a fertile environment for the free expression of intellectual aspirations. The revolution initially expanded education, especially for the lower classes, seized control of publishing houses and newspapers, and officially guaranteed freedom of speech. Yet by the early 1960s, a stifling bureaucracy had absorbed most of the country's college graduates, while others fell under government-run publishing enterprises.

The protagonist of "The Alif in al-Ahrar," Ahmad Rashwan, a graduate of "the Cairo University Business College," has so been absorbed, now serving as one of the countless civil servants and industrial secretaries filling the most menial of writing positions—a member of a typing pool, that pre-computer-age monument to directed, derivative writing.[29] In Ahmad's history alone, Idris aims several barbs at the state's failure in its national economic project. All varieties of writing in Egypt had by this time come under government control or influence, including publishing as well as the massive written output of the bureaucracy and economic corporations, like the one in which Ahmad labors. Most Egyptian writers, including Yusuf Idris, Naguib Mahfouz, and Sonallah Ibrahim, worked during the 1960s in one or more branches of this massive government publishing system, for even the top rank of Egyptian writers could not earn a living on their fiction works alone. President Nasser dogmatically trumpeted that government control of publishing served the best interests of the nation, directing output toward the true social problems of the masses. Plugging thousands of otherwise unemployable university graduates into mind-numbing jobs in a bloated bureaucracy and inefficient public-sector economy to produce untold reams of meaningless paper, therefore, evidenced the collective failure in all these aims.

Ahmad experiences an understandable frustration, having previously been an aspiring writer, who even succeeded in publishing some controversial opinions in his student newspaper at the university. The political power, under the model of *al-adab al-multazim*, was supposed to have empowered writers like Ahmad, giving them the means to reach the public with messages of enlightenment. Yet Ahmad himself is partially to blame for the demise of his writing career. Not exactly fitting the definition of the committed writer, he considers himself "better than" the other members of the typing pool, infamous for his aloof manner and social separation from the other workers. Indeed, Ahmad is a bit of a joke to the colleagues who laugh when the perfectionist gets in trouble with the boss. The narrator warns that "it was inevitable that Ahmad would find himself in an ordeal" at seeing lesser individuals doing the same work as a man of his education.[30]

Ahmad also prides himself on his perfect classical Arabic, not only speaking the language in casual conversation with his counterparts, but conducting his two-hour interview with the student newspaper in that language, audacious enough to correct the editor on grammar before allowing his words to be published. Writing in classical Arabic is one thing, any Egyptian would know, but speaking for two hours in the language, with correct formal grammar, is quite another, as conversation of that style is so uncommon as to appear a pure artifice. This left-handed compliment carries a strong subtext coming from Idris, a writer outspoken in his view that the language of the people required colloquial Egyptian, rather than purely formal Arabic.

Ahmad is detached from the society around him, because of, rather than in spite of, the educational system that produced him. He is frequently referred to not simply as *muta'allim* ('educated' in a general sense, coming from the same root as 'science' and 'the world'), or even *muthaqqaf* ('cultured,' also a common term for an intellectual), but rather the most *mu'addab* worker to be found. This term comes from the same source as *adab* (as in *al-adab al-multazim*), which long before being chosen to represent the imported concept of literature, meant the 'good breading' and 'manners' that set the elite apart from the masses. The detached Ahmad seems to represent the latter implication of *adab*, rather than that which the authors of *al-adab al-multazim* embraced. The indictment worsens, however, with the acknowledgment that Ahmad comes from the business school at the modern Cairo University—one of the few places actually identified by name in this story—founded to be a more progressive institution than the antiquated bastions of classical Islamic education that had dominated Egypt before the twentieth century. Ahmad cannot relate to his colleagues due to "the constant consciousness" that his education makes him better than them. The term *wa'y* (consciousness) invokes the Marxist sense of a 'false consciousness,' and Ahmad is certainly numbed by his false consciousness of superiority.[31]

Indeed, Ahmad appears to be a perfect example of the success of the state in co-opting intellectuals into numbed servitude. This once-aspiring writer, who should have been—according to *al-adab al-multazim*—using his talents for social change, has become "the most refined employee in the entire world," exhibiting a "total regard for rules, whether right or not."[32] No one can recall the boss, a volatile taskmaster named 'Abd al-Latif, ever directing any of his overabundant wrath at the efficient Ahmad. If Anis Zaki reluctantly surrendered his revolutionary impulses and unhappily resigned to a life of office slavery, Ahmad Rashwan bought into his servant role willingly, his only resentment directed at the co-workers whom he considers less efficient than himself. Ahmad's habitual duty, nonetheless, sounds even more meaningless than Zaki's, the mere copying of memoranda "exactly like the original to the letter."[33] In just a few years, Ahmad and the thousands like him would be replaced by copy machines, yet even now he seems like a machine.

At the most immediate level, Anis Zaki and Ahmad Rashwan serve as metonyms for the abdication by both the political power and the writer of their expected roles. The state, rather than using its control over the education and publishing systems for public liberation, as promised, uses it to numb the intellectuals into mindless compliance. Those intellectuals become cogs in a machine designed to enforce the false consciousness of an anaesthetized society that never questions whether regulations truly are right. These once-promising intellectuals, meanwhile, like the casts of characters from Mahfouz's 1960s novels—'Umar, Mustafa, 'Abbas, and the entire houseboat crew—have abandoned their responsibilities and been co-opted.

Yet, like Anis Zaki, Ahmad still contains a spark of energy. His *multazim* spirit has been silenced, but not extinguished. Having typed thousands of words that he didn't author, on subjects he didn't choose, to people he didn't know, Ahmad unexpectedly reaches his breaking point over the single letter *alif* in the word *ahraran* ("free") on a memo. The sentence upon which Ahmad is working at the time reads, "We are free to proceed according to all of our rights granted to us as a corporation."[34] Coming in a piece of departmental correspondence, the sentence certainly must have referred to some type of legal procedure, but taken out of that context as the only sentence we are given, it has an Orwellian ring to it. The implication of authorizing someone a nominal "freedom" to act in synchronization with a group according to a set of rules parodies the tightly controlled and censored expression that was all too common in socialist states. Ostensibly, Ahmad "did not know why he chose that [word—'free']"—to modify, the narrator speculating that it may have been the sound of the typewriter keys rather than its fairly obvious signification that prompted him to refuse to produce that word for the company.[35] Even if he didn't consciously recognize the motivation, something in Ahmad's dormant spirit has reacted to this absurd mockery of his "rights."

The typist defies the system that has educated him, silenced him, and turned him into a piece of a mindless bureaucracy. The ensuing confrontation, which occupies the lion's share of the text, attains ridiculous proportions in both its triviality and its repercussions. Such a minute act of defiance seems virtually pointless, yet it brings the entire office to a standstill as Ahmad is brought to the palatial office of the general manager and summarily dismissed for his refusal to type the single letter.

Ahmad's defiance goes beyond the simple letter, to encompass his very identity within the system. Discussion centers on his persistent declaration "I am a person" prefaced by colloquial Egyptian, rather than the classical *fusha* which characterized his previously arrogant speech. The general manager, after exhausting polite and gentle means of deflecting the objection, must finally tell him the truth: "you are a machine and 'Abd al-Latif, your supervisor is a machine, and I am a machine. We are all machines."[36] Nonetheless, the manager kindly explains, the outburst can be forgiven and the typing error likewise forgotten, as long as Ahmad renounces his claim to individuality. Refusing the offer of clemency on principle, Ahmad instead allows himself to be fired.

"How did the notion come into his mind?" Idris's narrator asks. Flashing back to the psychological turmoil that preceded Ahmad's breakdown, the author shows us that behind the calm façade of a compliant intellectual, Ahmad had long suspected he was really no better than a machine. Yet it was not the type of systematic, Lukácsian social analysis of Idris's early period that enlightened Ahmad to the truth but rather "unbelievable" images that appear to him in a bout of physical and emotional weakness. Imagining himself as a machine—an idea that comes to him from being bitten by a flea, rather than the countless hours he spends typing—Ahmad ponders the absurd inquiry, "What is the difference between him and the typewriter?" Frantically, he searches for differences, eventually forced to conclude that there is "nothing at all" to distinguish him from a machine.[37]

Ahmad's thought process is something of a demonstration of Brechtian logic in action. He follows a fundamentally absurd thought process that nonetheless gives him an enlightenment that breaks his false consciousness. Alternately shouting that his conclusion is "unbelievable," yet undeniably true, Ahmad is able to see past the physical differences between himself and a typewriter—differences that would blind anyone looking only at the surface level—to isolate their essential similarity in terms of their function in society. At one most desperate point, Ahmad falls back on his proudest asset—his intellect—arguing that the typewriter "is never able to act by itself . . . I am a person who can think and act according to my will."[38] Unfortunately, Ahmad realizes that by not exercising his own will, his actual function does not differ from that of his Continental typewriter, however much his potential might. The dehumanizing division of labor has alienated him from his larger self—the diversity of talents and abilities he does not exercise. The conclusion has a decidedly Marxist ring to it, yet it is not a systematic examination of the socioeconomic structure that leads him to it, but rather an absurdity inspired by a flea.

Once awoken to his own exploited and alienated position, Ahmad immediately turns his attention to the false consciousness around him. How can the rest of society fail to recognize its own alienation? Ahmad—in this philosophizing role a scarcely disguised mouthpiece for the author—has no doubt that only the most haphazard experience separates him from the rest of his deluded counterparts:

> Thousands of these thoughts come to thousands of people thousands of times in a single day, but they do not stick in their minds very often. . . .
>
> This might have happened to Ahmad Rashwan, to discard the idea and return to his pursuing thoughts or the attempt to sleep . . . but he tarried over the thought a little. Beware any one of us who tarries over an idea, for that tarrying might change the direction of his life. . . . The famous Newton did nothing more than tarry one day in front of an apple that fell of its own accord from the tree.
>
> Ahmad Rashwan was just the latest to tarry over an idea.[39]

Ahmad's conclusion certainly does not offer an affirmation of the efficacy of a totalizing, systematic examination of the social structure. Rather, it supports a hope for enlightenment through radical defamiliarization, alienating the object of study from its place in a well-ordered structure in order to consider it in a process of deliberate reasoning. True enlightenment, he concludes, comes from comparing things which logically defy comparison: a randomly falling, powerless apple with the most certain, determined force in the natural world, or equating a human with a passive instrument. The key repeated verb in this description of Ahmad's awakening speaks to the attitude necessary for breaking false consciousness. Ahmad and Newton—but not the "thousands" of others—"tarry" *(talakka'a)* long enough to notice their surroundings. The verb does not imply a deliberate contemplation or examination; rather, it often connotes an idle, lazy, or hesitant lack of progress, being the base from which 'loitering' and 'tardiness' are derived. Keeping Ahmad constantly engaged in mindless typing is the state's way of preventing him from tarrying in front of any idea, such as the word "free." Only the disturbance and disruption caused by the insect gives him the chance to pause long enough to recognize his position.

Ahmad, at this point, might have been on his way to becoming an activist for social awakening of the type *al-adab al-multazim* envisioned, even if his method for achieving that awakening had been quite different from that embraced by *iltizam*. Having recognized that his talent has been wasted in a state-run paper mill that absorbs the energies and skills of thousands, he draws the line with his bosses, refusing to comply with their directions any longer. He understands that he will face expulsion from the state's commercial apparatus for this type of thinking and this will leave him penniless; but now enlightened, he willingly accepts the punishment of the state in order to educate the public. To his colleagues, Ahmad is nothing more than a crazy man. His prospects for achievement on the outside seem even bleaker. The boss takes away "everything in his custody,"[40] that is, only his Continental typewriter, stripping Ahmad of the means of producing written words, reflecting in not-too-subtle fashion the state's control of the means of written production.

As he leaves his office, Ahmad's co-workers look on sympathetically, offering appeals to convince him to return to his place in the bureaucracy. Ahmad rejects their concern, instead feeling compassion for the workers remaining behind. "In the depth of his heart, he pitied them. He felt that he alone was the human, and that they, from the office boy to their general manager, were merely machines." Out on the street, Ahmad finds himself truly adrift. "The street swelled with people, cars, and bicycles.

The people were racing the cars, the bicycles were racing people. He walked, not racing the bicycles and the cars did not pass him, without direction and without purpose." For the first time, also, Ahmad truly considers the regulations that guide this massive, purposeless movement. "He could not prevent a childish notion from seizing him and prompting him to read the sign as if he were seeing it and contemplating it for the first time." Suddenly, unable to contain his newfound knowledge, Ahmad rushes into the street, proclaiming the message that has awoken his consciousness, "I am a person!"[41]

How does society react to this enlightened messenger, who has given up everything to bring this essential truth to the masses? One commuter shouts that Ahmad has gone crazy; a second person speculates that he is on hashish, while another merely laughs at him. Far more are upset at the disturbance in their traffic pattern. "A car horn roared to make Ahmad get off the street. All this only took but an instant. The traffic in the street lost no time in returning to its previous state, as though nothing had ever happened."[42] Unfortunately for Ahmad, the story ends on these words. No glimmer of hope slips in to mitigate the absolute pronouncement that Ahmad has failed to register an impact on the society around him. Idris's choice of idiom for the crowd's behavior explains much of the cause of Ahmad's failure. The traffic *"lam talbath 'an"* (meaning "lost no time," but literally "did not hesitate in") returning to normal. The verb negated in this phrase parallels in meaning that used to describe Ahmad and Newton's processes of discovery—to tarry, linger, or pause. The inverse parallelism speaks plainly: the crowd disregards Ahmad, they even go so far as to erase him from memory as if he "never happened," because they, unlike him, do not pause from their demanding routines to contemplate their environment. Keeping society busy, keeping intellectuals typing and readers occupied with state-written news all help discourage this tarrying.

"The Alif in al-Ahrar," in painting the state of a lost intellectual in the 1960s, depicts the *iltizam* partnership gone awry. That partnership envisioned the political power working to facilitate the writer's mission of enlightening the people. The Nasser state, as seen in this vignette, cannot be accused of ignoring that mission. It has pumped millions of pounds into the creation of a public education system and a massive bureaucracy charged with ensuring the welfare of the masses. It has further filled that bureaucracy with the intellectuals who emerged from this education system. On paper, at least, it seems like the fulfillment of the dream of *iltizam*, and even a proud academic like Ahmad feels comfortable in this machine. Ahmad has been co-opted into a false consciousness that concealed his true function as a tool in a bureaucratic corporation, employed largely for the sake of subduing and taming his spirit, while cloaked in a false sense of intellectual superiority. He is, after all, a university graduate from a modern faculty of commerce, a master of the classical Arabic that distinguishes the intellectual elite, and "free" to act in accordance with the rules set for him. "Thousands," he eventually realizes, persist in this state, draped in the trappings of free intellectual will, unable to see that they are, in effect, little better than machines as long as their words remain governed by the state.

Only a burst of enlightenment that comes from stepping outside the system awakens him to its true nature. The bureaucratic–educational complex exists to produce a semblance of meaningful communication—the reams of paper that give the surface appearance of a society in constant dialogue. Yet the final villain in the story is the mass public—a public far removed from that envisioned in *al-adab al-multazim*. They have been so thoroughly numbed by the state-run system that they "don't linger" to consider the world around them, much less listen to the ravings of a mad writer.

In reality, Ahmad was hardly the lone voice that the story makes him out to be. Ahmad's sudden conclusions would have shocked few Egyptian readers of the time. Egypt's bureaucracy, by the 1960s, was the butt of countless jokes. Nor would Egyptian newspaper readers find it much of an exaggeration to claim their daily news was nothing more than a daily glorification of Nasser. Ahmad's frustration lay rather in his complete impotence to act on what he now understood. Having been denied the means of communication—his Continental typewriter—and shut out of the massive government publishing industry, how could a single writer make an impact? It would be decades before Twitter and Facebook would offer a means of circumventing the state's monopoly on mass communication. When that day finally arrived, it was little wonder that the tens of thousands who gathered to protest did so in front of the notorious Mugamma' office building on Tahrir Square, center of the government bureaucracy. For Ahmad, though, and for Yusuf Idris as well, such a day seemed far off.

A later story, written after Nasser's sudden death, offered a more direct indictment of the state's monopoly on communication. Idris's allegorical 1971 piece "The Deception" *(al-Khuda')* used a ubiquitous, intrusive camel's head as a device to represent the regime's harassment of the people. The unmistakable Arabic pun made no attempt at subtlety, with the word *jamal* (camel) bearing obvious resemblance to Nasser's first name, Jamal (pronounced 'Gamal' in Egypt). The camel's head, with its mocking smile, follows the protagonist everywhere—even interrupting his sexual activities. When the protagonist attempts to read a newspaper, the words disappear and the camel's glaring smile replaces the newsprint, appropriate since Egyptian newspapers were, in fact, little more than a smiling face of Nasser. It would hardly be lost on Egyptian readers that Idris had lost his job as editor of Egypt's leading state-run newspaper, *al-Ahram*, after publishing his short story "The Journey" *(al-Rihla)*, a clearly allegorical attack on Nasser which depicted a devoted son who finally realizes his need to abandon the decaying body of his beloved father.[43] Abu 'Auf, having noted Idris's once great support for the revolution, saw his later work as "criticism of the negative aspects of the revolution in the era of 'Abd al-Nasser, totalitarianism, and one-party rule [which] led to a type of oppression and subjugation of the intellectuals, despite their having stood for nationalism and liberation and revolution."[44]

Beyond Idris's indictment of the partners in the *iltizam* relationship, these stories mark another change in approach from the author's earlier works. No longer do the writer and the political power stand outside the narrative, allowing the focus to fall on the working masses. Instead, the writer and the state are the story. The public, as Ahmad learned, is too busy to be involved in the narrative, serving rather as a bustling stream of indifference. As Mahfouz had done, Idris turned *al-adab al-multazim* inside out, now focusing on the external actors who were supposed to be producing stories about the masses.

The Black Policeman

"The Alif in al-Ahrar" depicted one aspect of the state's suppression of meaningful communication: co-optation of intellectuals into a massive bureaucratic system. Idris's 1962 novella *The Black Policeman* (*al-'Askari al-aswad*) focused on a much darker type of governmental suppression of expression. Published a decade before Mahfouz's *Karnak Café*, *The Black Policeman* parallels that Mahfouz novel in its depiction of violent police oppression. As in *Karnak Café*, Idris's story is told by a first-person narrator seeking explanations for the fall of a former revolutionary into passive surrender. Writing during the Nasser era, Idris based the story on the case of a former torturer of the old regime that had been widely publicized in government newspapers after the revolution. Although the Nasser regime had used that case to illustrate the evils of the old monarchy, Idris adhered to Albert Camus's dictum "for the artist, there are no privileged torturers,"[45] as his story depicts torture as a destructive psychological weapon, regardless of context. With the police brutality of the Nasser regime a widely known—if never openly discussed—fact, Idris's wholesale condemnation of state violence certainly leveled indirect criticism at the Nasser government.

The novella's central figure, a Cairene medical doctor named Shawqi, bears more than a passing similarity to the author. As Idris once did, Shawqi works as a government health examiner dealing primarily with poor clients. In medical school, he was a political firebrand who led the student opposition to the monarchy and British occupation, actions which landed him in jail. If Shawqi's history reads almost like a carbon copy of Idris's résumé up to the point that the latter began writing, then recollections of Shawqi's personality likewise invoke comparison with Idris. Shawqi believed he was "commissioned . . . to rescue our country and change the fate of our people in a fundamental way forever"[46]—the Arabic term *mab'uth* (officially dispatched as a deputy or agent) implying a sense of duty, much like the term *iltizam*. Possessing "a terrible power of will"[47] and "clinging to his opinion and viewpoint, occasionally to the point of committing a crime,"[48] Shawqi exhibited boundless energy and optimism, attracting people with his ever-present "confident smile."[49] The target of Shawqi's political crusade was the same against which Idris fought in his student days: the "occupying armies carousing in our land."[50] Neither Shawqi nor Idris was deterred by the prospect of prison for their open rebellion.

After prison, however, Shawqi's life diverged sharply from that of the author. Like the "phantoms" of *Karnak Café*, Shawqi returned to society a haunted and broken creature. His face had become "like a mask," with a "meaningless smile" to "cause your gaze to slide by and not rest upon him—as if it did rest on him, you would recognize his secret and know what was in him."[51] The "attraction belonging to a firm believer in a truth that illuminated his entire being . . . concentrated as a light in his eyes," had "disappeared . . . leaving in his eyes only the trace of life common to any living thing."[52] Shawqi returns to society a bitter creature, his callous treatment of patients shocking a narrator who cannot associate such behavior with the concerned and compassionate activist he once knew. Outside of work, Shawqi, once the life of the campus social scene, isolates himself from family, friends, and, above all, politics. Yet rather than attracting sympathy, the others "despise" him as "a target of repulsion and hate."[53] Indeed, "his misfortune was that he had to continue to live among those who terrified him," the prison experience leaving this one-time champion of the rights of his fellow citizens believing "all people . . . were against him and would not rest until they caught him."[54]

If Shawqi's early life recalled Idris's medical career, then the novel's true protagonist, the first-person narrator who seeks to understand Shawqi, resembles Idris in his later incarnation as a writer. The story centers on the narrator's quest for understanding, even more deeply than it follows the story of Shawqi or the eponymous "Black Policeman." Sharing virtually the same biography as Shawqi—and Idris—minus the prison term, the narrator, a colleague from Shawqi's student days, embarks on a quest to understand his own emotional and psychological separation from his former friend. The confident, omniscient narration of social conditions that marked "An Errand" yields to uncertainty as the author begins with a confession of his own confusion: "I talk about the secret which confused me about Shawqi, and I don't know its cause or its explanation."[55] While *al-adab al-multazim* applauded authors who could write about the experiences of the masses with genuine empathy, Idris's narrator-protagonist begins from a position of alienation from his subject.

Even the aim of his writing project lacks the noble ambitions of *iltizam*: "I confess that in sitting down to write what occurred, *I have no aim* [hadaf] *except a single hope*: to achieve through writing what I have failed to do through imagining . . . who knows? Perhaps if I finish I will explain everything, and arrive at the truth which has left me dizzy for my efforts [until now]."[56] *Hadaf*, the noun for 'target' or 'goal,' is directly related to al-'Alim's 'targeted literature,' the school of writing with which Idris had been most closely associated. Now, a former proponent of 'targeted' literature offers a writer-protagonist who writes not for clear goals with confidence but is rather chasing a dim "hope." The narrator joins the ranks of a character type prevalent in the works of disillusion produced in the 1960s: the committed figure trying to understand a loss of revolutionary spirit, like Mahfouz's characters the young Buthayna Hamzawi and her older lover 'Uthman from *The Beggar*, Samara Bahjat of *Gossip on the Nile*, and the narrator of *Karnak Café*. The narrator goes on to mock the confident assurances of social analysis that had characterized *al-adab al-multazim*: "If only man were like that. If only he were like an accounting case or engineering exercise that followed a single rule or some theories could explain him. If only he were not that being who, the more we know about him, the harder he becomes to understand."[57] Coming from the author who once described the role of the committed writer as no less than that of a "prophet," or "the eye of society,"[58] these admissions by the author's surrogate send a clear signal that we have left the confident world of *al-adab al-multazim*.

In the world envisioned by *al-adab al-multazim*, meaningful communication would be valued, even the bitter, angry communication between political enemies, like Shawqi and the narrator. The narrator notes, as if revisiting a rare phenomenon that once seemed commonplace: "we were friends without any reason for friendship,"[59] having virtually "no connection in our ideas about politics, or people."[60] Politically, their passionate commitment to opposing factions was so strong that the author recalls "our mutual cursing almost led to fighting."[61] From his clashes with Shawqi, the narrator developed a zeal to "celebrate every sincere act, even when coming from one who differed in opinion or was against me in belief."[62] Shawqi's loss of passion thus stuns a narrator who had previously been "certain that Shawqi was not one of the type that a few months in prison would suffice to change him and cause him to give up his beliefs."[63]

Like that of the broken characters of *Karnak Café*, Shawqi's revolutionary fervor has been crushed, despite the strength of personality that once seemed unbreakable. Rather than turning his prison experiences into a narrative to rally his comrades, Shawqi has locked away the memories and shut out his former brethren. Although he suffered at the hands of a regime that has since been overthrown, the coming of the Nasser revolution produced no change in Shawqi's condition, nor did the public condemnation—or offering, rather—of the notorious police interrogator 'Abbas al-Zanfali, "The Black Policeman."

The narrator, who never experienced the horror of the Black Policeman, eagerly devours the news reports that Shawqi refuses to acknowledge. He learns of a villain so feared that prisoners instinctively recoil at the sound of his key in the prison locks, as well as the distinct sound of his footsteps in the hall. Scarcely human, this sadistic giant known for his coal-black complexion earns his terrifying reputation through the reports of the horrible sounds of suffering emanating from the torture chambers of the prison and echoing throughout the building. To spice up the character profile, the newspapers include scandalous reports of his sexual adventures as well. Declining to join in a discussion that should have established him as a heroic survivor, Shawqi, when pressed insistently about the news reports, only reluctantly comments, "The Black Policeman was for us something entirely different."[64] It is only when Shawqi and the narrator are assigned to perform a medical check on the now-decrepit al-Zanfali does Shawqi finally confess, "Do you know who it was that the Black Policeman was beating in the jail morning until sunset? . . . It was me."[65]

The state had transformed Shawqi into a soulless, powerless phantom, but it first had to transform 'Abbas al-Zanfali into "the man degraded among humanity"[66] to carry out its will. Just as the narrator struggles to understand how police pressure can neutralize Shawqi, he has difficulty comprehending how the same police apparatus could turn 'Abbas into a sadistic interrogator. Reading through the man's medical file, the narrator expects to find evidence that 'Abbas belonged to a different generation, or social background, or even species, than Shawqi and himself. The file offers no such comforting excuses for his deviance. The narrator is shocked to learn "to my surprise that he was *from the same confused, miserable generation as us*."[67] Indeed, the narrator discovers that "The Black Policeman" is not "black" in complexion like the newspapers claimed, nor the giant they made him out to be.[68]

In a macabre bit of irony, in fact, when Shawqi and the narrator finally encounter the once-terrifying interrogator, they find a psychotic wreck, a "shell of a man" wracked by depression, drug abuse, and violent fits. The narrator finds his descriptions of the wrecked 'Abbas virtually matching those he gave of Shawqi, down to the lifeless eyes.[69] While the state had drawn Shawqi and al-Zanfali from the same social pool, then transformed them into enemies for its own purposes of political control, it finally cast them both aside into the same pile of broken humanity. Although the state-run newspapers had offered up al-Zanfali—or rather a sensationalized version of him—as an offering to mollify the public, the narrator has a hard time seeing the broken figure as the source of evil the newspapers claim. The party responsible for Shawqi's demise is not the deranged shell of 'Abbas al-Zanfali but rather the faceless police apparatus that continues its work hidden behind prison walls.

Much like *Karnak Café*, *The Black Policeman* leads to an anticipated confrontation between the victim and torturer. Hardly by chance, medical officer Shawqi is assigned to examine 'Abbas al-Zanfali, a purged and discarded police interrogator now consigned to the mercy of his former victim. While Mahfouz's characters refused to take the bait that the government offered, Shawqi is finally stirred from his years of silence by the opportunity to condemn his former persecutor in person. Flying into a rage, Shawqi exposes his horribly scarred back and harangues the catatonic 'Abbas, straining, without effect at first, to provoke a response from his lifeless adversary. The Black Policeman eventually emerges from his dazed state, only to bite savagely into his own arm, providing a haunting image of gouged flesh and streaming blood as the narrator and 'Abbas's wife try to subdue the man from his crazed acts of self-punishment. After this gruesome scene, the narrator hopes that 'Abbas's breakdown will satisfy Shawqi's pent-up anger and allow him to move on with his life. He convinces himself that Shawqi "will discard from himself this terrified, wounded personality. He is certainly on his way back to us . . . without a doubt I wouldn't leave this room without the old Shawqi that all my efforts so far had failed to bring back to life."[70]

Shawqi does, in fact, seem to gain new life from the confrontation. Choosing to pursue the path of socially responsible writing, Shawqi launches into a project he believes can leverage his experience to help heal Egyptian society. He adds scientific research, diving into references like "The Philosophy of Beating" and "Causing Pain is a Weapon with Two Edges." Meanwhile, the previously silent Shawqi now willingly discusses his experiences with objectivity, even extending empathy to his former antagonist: "Did you know that when you injure another person, you injure yourself without recognizing it?" he asks in one typical exchange.[71] Shawqi's revival builds a sense of optimism for the healing of society through writing.

Unfortunately, Shawqi's writing project will go no further than Samara Bahjat's play or Hilmi Hamada's biography. Shawqi's recovery proves short lived, leading the narrator to comment: "I realized that the condition that I saw Shawqi in, and which filled me with hope, was like the awakening before death."[72] Shawqi slips back into his depression and his writing project perishes. Delivering his final verdict on Shawqi, and indeed, the only conclusion that this confused narrator is able to extract from his agonizing search, he notes, "having once lost his human security, he would never return as a human like us again."[73] Al-'Alim had once cited an inherent belief in the power to change as a distinguishing feature of Idris's stories,[74] but *The Black Policeman* offers none.

The narrator's quest to understand the demise of a revolutionary spirit ends with a gloomy proclamation. The heavy hand of the state has silenced revolutionary voices, replaced passionate, open debate with a system of enforced compliance, and left human beings withdrawn into paranoia. Yet what most disturbs him is the inadequacy of the revolutionary spirit the narrator once embraced to withstand such assaults. The stark contrast between the naive optimism that could not understand how a man like Shawqi could abandon his beliefs and the clear evidence of the overwhelming power of the state to silence anyone has left this writer humbled. In such a condition, constructive communication of the type envisioned by *al-adab al-multazim* cannot develop.

"The Aorta"

Shawqi was a casualty of state oppression, but to some extent, his alienation from the public he once loved contributed to his demise. Idris could be as exacting in his criticism of the public—his other partner in *iltizam*—as of the state. In the 1965 story "The Aorta" *(al-Aurta)*, another victim of state oppression finds himself adrift in an unfeeling Cairo street crowd, as Ahmad Rashwan had found himself at the end of "The Alif in al-Ahrar." Told this time from the perspective of the urban mob, the story presents an unsympathetic, greedy public that pounces upon weakness and difference. Beginning its narration from within the teeming mass, this story offers a frightening glimpse of the bustling crowd in its opening lines:

> The important thing was not that there was rushing, the important thing was that it was in more than one direction, it was in nearly every direction, as if it were the great day of rushing. A very strange kind of rushing, for it was not running in fear, nor hurrying, nor running for safety. An errant rushing, as if the people were scrambling to find the start point to begin running, and as such, no one knew the goal of the other person, nor his intent.[75]

The narration lingers over the description of the crowd, establishing through the chaos three underlying features of the mob's behavior. First, the random, individual jostling, when viewed from a sufficient height, presents a picture of overall calm, as if looking at a paved surface. Conversely, a society that appears tamed when viewed from the lofty vantage of the state can conceal much individual conflict and suffering. The unnamed narrator reports being repeatedly struck with "crushing, painful strikes" in the crowd, but must conclude when writing his narrative that when viewed from a macro perspective "no one knew whether there really were any strikes or not."[76] Second, this crowd is aimless, full of unguided individuals motivated only by a paranoid fear that someone else may know what they're supposed to do. "Therefore, you were also seeing the people rushing as if insane, like the madman trying in vain to discern the footsteps of the others and their direction."[77] Like the narrator in *The Black Policeman*, this crowd has no "goal"—yet another allusion to *al-adab al-hadif*. Last, this crowd full of charged particles bouncing randomly off one another can, at times, become galvanized, directing its energy at a single object. The narrator, swimming in a directionless blur, finally detects a subtle current in the crowd and finds that it is slowly and barely perceptibly forming itself around a single entity, in fact, a single human being. This offers the first calming sign in a frightening vision of a dangerous, unguided mass that is certainly not the public that *al-adab al-multazim* assumed to be highly organized and living in accordance with strict social laws. Unfortunately, this galvanized public turns out to be more destructive than in its previously unfocused state.

At the center of the crowd stands a lone man, a quiet and frightened person, whose principal liability is to be noticeably different than the rest of the crowd. 'Abduh appeared "strange, as if he'd never found a home." Yet in this chaotic mass where no one seems to have a resting place, 'Abduh's sin is weakness, as he is "extremely thin, his eyes never once exhibiting an angry look." Nor, the narrator informs us, "did he ever once stand up to another for the purpose of proving his existence or defending himself. He was good, with that pallid, negative sort of goodness." 'Abduh's vulnerability, above all, his detestable "goodness," attracts the crowd like sharks. In fact, the crowd, narrator included, feels an uncontrollable urge to "grind him and chew him up," confessing, "I felt my fangs chew his flesh and limbs, satisfying their yearning." The crowd seethes with rage: "We sons of Adam have a need to bite. We harbor feelings of hatred, but cannot assuage them in a natural way."[78] The mindlessness of the crowd's fury only amplifies the terror and the alienation that its victim, 'Abduh, feels.

His fear notwithstanding, 'Abduh attempts to communicate with the aggressive crowd. To explain his weakness, he tells them that he has been picked up by a government patrol on the streets and taken away for examination. Deeming him a public threat for no apparent reason, the chief government surgeon ordered a patently impossible operation: severing his aorta and removing his heart. Wrapped in bandages and given a cane, the heart-less ʻAbduh was released on the streets of Cairo, where his injury immediately attracted the attention of the angry mob. ʻAbduh, then, is a surreal Shawqi. Take away the scientific absurdities that mark the story and we have here also a man who has been cruelly and arbitrarily victimized by an oppressive state, yet who can find no comfort from society. Instead, both are marked as outcasts, a reaction that only strengthens the power of the government to neutralize its opponents.

Worse, the crowd is moved by a rumor to believe that ʻAbduh is carrying money. Despite ʻAbduh's protests of innocence, unanimity develops that he has the money concealed on him and the crowd will not stop until it gets the cash from him. Shaken down and searched, ʻAbduh's pockets and wallet yield nothing of value, but the crowd persists, believing that his bandages contain the money. Unable to find a sympathetic ear, ʻAbduh's fate in the hands of this mob is sealed. As events turn toward the macabre, the crowd carries him to a butcher shop and hangs him on a meat hook. The narrator notes that ʻAbduh was left with "no power and no strength, like a slaughtered animal or a hanging, skinned sheep."[79] The crowd, laughing and mocking the victim, and driven by lust for the money they expect to find, opens ʻAbduh's chest to reveal an empty cavity with a dangling aorta.

Through the impossibility of ʻAbduh's medical condition, Idris reveals the devastating alienation that police brutality forces upon its victims. A medical doctor like Idris could have chosen any number of frightening but realistic surgical procedures in place of the severed aorta. ʻAbduh's operation, however, contradicts the scientific beliefs held by the mob and, of course, the reader, but not those of the state and its victim. In other words, only one who has been victimized by the state can comprehend the scope of its cruelty and transforming power. To the mass public, "neither a child nor a fool could believe" ʻAbduh's story.[80] Thus, as cruel as the state may be, it finds a willing, if unwitting, partner in the mass public. Idris does not follow the final, gruesome image of a slaughtered ʻAbduh with any indication of hope or expression of remorse from the public. Nor is there any reason to doubt that the seething crowd that tore 'Abduh apart searching for wealth will now direct its energies toward another target.

Rather than the positive cooperation envisioned in *iltizam*, "The Aorta" exposes the complicity of the mass public in silencing voices of reason. Egyptian society in 1965, with its combination of excessive busyness, materialistic greed, and state-induced paranoia, and further lacking any effective means of mass communication, appears as a completely hostile body. When viewed as a collective entity, this community is thoroughly alien to everything assumed by the theorists of *al-adab al-multazim*. Even the nameless narrator offers neither regret nor remorse, much less responsibility, for the destruction of an innocent individual. Yet if Idris has rendered a scathing verdict on Egyptian society as a whole, he is no less harsh when zeroing in on the individuals that make up that whole, as the next story reveals.

"The Sunken Mattress"

In contrast to the macro perspective of "The Aorta," Idris provides a micro view of Egyptian society in the 1969 absurdist tale "The Sunken Mattress" *(al-Martaba al-muq'ara)*. Having given the bureaucracy, the education system, the police, and even the public's herd instincts their shares of the blame for the sad condition of Egyptian society in his previous stories, Idris now considers the role of individual responsibility. The story is starkly pessimistic, with Idris allowing no room for the intrusion of mitigating factors in its indictment of public apathy. If the married couple portrayed in the narrative has some excuse for their complete indifference to the world around them, then Idris is not interested in addressing it in the text.

Rather, the sheer baldness of the narrative serves as one of its defining characteristics. "The Sunken Mattress" suppresses background detail and contextual description to allow nothing to take our focus off the two lazy individuals who occupy the text. Starting on the wedding night of a nameless—and thus generic—Egyptian couple, the narrative traces the entire wedded life of the couple, a simple enough task given that they accomplish absolutely nothing during that time. The man spends his entire married life lying on the eponymous mattress, while his wife, only slightly more active, spends her time looking out the window. His only action is to ask the same question periodically: "Look! . . . Has the world changed?"[81] If he is too lazy to be bothered to even look out the window himself, she is hardly more engaged, choosing to respond in the simple negative each time. Having no desire to seek any clarification, the man goes back to sleep after every "no" answer.

As the story progresses, the man's lethargy increases, while he resolves to remain in bed first "for a day," then "a week," until finally declaring he will stay in bed for an entire year. His declarations mean nothing, however, as in each case he actually stays in bed far longer than he proposes—his "year" in bed, for example, lasting ten years. As fruitless as it seems, this man's dull life actually offers three lessons. First, his disengagement from society grows longer after each disappointment, as he resolves to wait even longer until his next awakening. This progressively worsening sense of detachment speaks to the gradual process of public desensitization. The longer one goes without seeing any change, the less likely one is to look for it. Second, the lazy husband always sleeps far longer than he plans, yet there is no indication he realizes or cares about the actual duration of his slumbers. Apathy turns out to be a much more insidious condition than its victims realize, with one's inaction having a more debilitating effect than recognized. Last, this man, despite doing absolutely nothing, has left a permanent impression on the mattress, ruining it with the deep body print of sixteen years in bed. No matter how useless the man's life has been, he has had an impact, albeit a negative one, on some aspect of the world.

The wife, surprisingly, does not protest or question his behavior, merely content to perform her periodic cursory examination of the world outside. When her husband finally dies, after sixteen years of lying dormant, she spares herself the effort of a burial by having him thrown out the window along with his mattress. Only then does she suddenly exclaim "Dear God! . . . the world really has changed."[82]

Here, neither police brutality nor the demands of busy city life are responsible for the couple's apathy. Instead, the blame for their degraded conditions lies in the personalities their actions reveal: the man expects social change but is unwilling to do anything himself to bring it about; the wife spends her time watching society, but likewise does nothing herself to impact it. Meanwhile, neither person seems to care at all about the other. Idris is careful to begin the story with their wedding night, lest we conclude that this couple somehow got bored with life after years of dull marriage. These two appear, in fact, a perfect match. As if to cast further light on the self-imposed insignificance of this duo, Idris chooses to name the story not after either them or their lifeless marriage but rather the only thing they have affected in sixteen years—a worn-out mattress.

While the story lacks any other characters, the oblique picture of the public outside is hardly encouraging. As the woman watches the mattress land in the street, she notes that it has hit "its last resting place."[83] She has spent enough time looking out her window in the last decade and a half to realize this decaying corpse on its lumpy mattress will stay out in the middle of the street, without anyone bothering to move it.

The woman's cryptic exclamation at the story's end—"the world really has changed"—is hardly encouraging. Having watched the outside world for sixteen years, the only change she has ever seen is the presence of a corpse in the middle of the street. Although no dates are ever mentioned in the story, tracing the timeline of the narrative back from the publication of the story shows the couple's marriage to correspond roughly to the years of the revolution. She has merely watched passively during that time, expecting change, but doing nothing. When change finally does occur—a gruesome and polluting change that she has largely brought about by her own action—she again reacts passively, as if an outside observer in her own story. For a *multazim* writer who once depended on an active, engaged public, Idris paints a very damning picture of the Egyptian public.

Yet in this gloomy ending, there remains a glimmer of hope. The woman *has* reacted to the world around her, albeit with the weakest of reactions. She has recognized for the first time that the world *can* change, and she seems genuinely shocked to learn this. Perhaps the removal of her husband—a veritable vacuum for human energy—has finally given her a chance to live. Possibly she realizes that by throwing him into the street she has finally taken action to cast off a burden that held her down. For the first time, she has even called on the name of God in her contemplation of society, if only in an expression of horror. For whatever slight encouragement these interpretations may provide, the wife is certainly no al-Shubrawi, battling a monolithic bureaucracy for public good. She is not even a Farahat, dreaming of a true socialist state. The glimmer of hope in this dark tale is just that—a faint glimmer that indicates how much Idris's expectations from the public had diminished.

The ambiguous ending of the story likewise represents a change from the style of "An Errand." Although an additional sentence could have clarified the woman's remark, Idris lets the reader's reaction to the story determine what message to take from it. This satiric couple, speaking for passivity and denial of responsibility, now demands the reader's action to make sense of their lives. Applying Roland Barthes's terminology, Idris supplies a decidedly writerly ending, the type that classic *iltizam* eschewed. 'Atiya, long a defender of *al-adab al-multazim* after others had moved on, felt the once rock-solid *multazim* writer Idris had, by the late 1960s, reached a crossroads in which some of his work remained true to *iltizam* while some represented experimentation outside *al-adab al-multazim*. The very compactness and starkness of this story, 'Atiya felt, placed it in the latter category.[84]

'Atiya wanted to see a return to the *iltizam* of bygone days. While that was clearly unrealistic by 1969 in Egypt, it would be equally shortsighted to overlook the strong relationship that an absurdist work like "The Sunken Mattress" bears to *al-adab al-multazim*. The concerned public that served as a foundational assumption of *al-adab al-multazim* is now a question at the center of the text. Social change—a goal once assumed possible—is also under question in the text. While Idris sounds a note of distinct pessimism, his story actively probes issues of great importance to *iltizam*.

"The Piper Dies"

The 1970s did little to assuage Idris's gloom about the direction of the revolution, Egyptian society, and the role of the writer. By the early 1980s, Idris, also suffering from deep depression, had turned to open despair. A 1982 story about an Egyptian so alienated from society as to lose his identity, his face, and his ability to communicate with anyone, bore the heavily loaded title "19502." The digits of the story's title speak for themselves—the year of the Egyptian revolution, but with a void between the date, which is much more visually striking with the Arabic numeral for zero, a small dot. This aims the story clearly at the hollowness of the revolution's promise and the devastating impact that disappointment with the revolution had on the Egyptian psyche. "The Piper Dies" *(Yamut al-zammar)*, another story in the same 1982 collection, however, marked Idris's most pained expression of anguish over his role as a writer in Egyptian society.

From its opening lines, "The Piper Dies" blurs the division between the intra and extratextual realms, placing itself precariously between fiction and autobiography. Beginning with a confession, Idris admits that he attempted yet found it "impossible" to let a fictional character play his protagonist in this "very personal story." The "I" in this case is Idris himself, yet the work is nonetheless a "story."[85] Despite the heavily autobiographical qualities of the story, it flaunts improbabilities and makes Idris something of a satiric figure throughout. Idris's choice to place himself in the center of a story and then blur the distinction between his functions as a character and an author stands far removed from the transparent hand of the ideal *multazim* writer who stood outside the text.

The author-protagonist begins by sharing the early motivations that led him to become a writer on the eve of the revolution:

> My dream of writing was like my dream of the revolution, and like my dream of the miracle capable of curing each and every sickness . . . in my age I would see the disappearance of the barefoot, while all the people would be clothed, the disappearance of need, while those in need are made content. This was the oasis in my time; I took refuge in it whenever the wellspring of my imagination became exhausted.[86]

His vision sounds like the manifesto of the classic *multazim* writer, but his life's experience has shattered that vision. He confesses starkly that all his years have taught him only "the total lack of value of writing. Not only my writing, but all the writing since man learned to write."[87] Writing has not improved humankind one bit, he concludes. Indeed, the human progress of which writing has been a part has produced a society more barbaric and destructive than ever before. A world that can produce conflicts like the Vietnam War or the Lebanese Civil War, he concludes, can only be a world that is getting worse, not better. Revisiting the same conflicts that once engaged Shawqi in *The Black Policeman*, the medical doctor Idris concludes that even scientific writing designed to help humankind ultimately produces "means of torture reaching the very core of the marrow, striking the sensitive nerves."[88]

In light of this wholesale rejection of the very soul of *al-adab al-multazim*, Idris takes the only reasonable action—to "renounce writing altogether."[89] Going further, he decides to renounce reading as well, out of the fear that reading might lead to writing. His colleagues who choose to remain active in the field merit only contempt. He likens them to "Xerox machines" putting out volumes of paper, "every day on each and every subject from politics to fiction to science to memories to love" with so little emotional commitment that their blood pressure stays a level "120 over 80."[90]

Worse than occupying the masses with meaningless words, these writers have inspired a false sense of optimism, creating a public "holding onto the myth of dreams which never come true."[91] Giving the public hope for a better future was once a key duty of the writer, a duty Idris had once embraced. Now, he equates this action to a sin against the public. Moreover, Idris describes the deceptive ideas foisted on the public as *khurafa*, meaning 'fairy tale' or 'myth,' but also the same word Salama Musa had used decades earlier in his landmark treatise on committed writing to describe the attitudes of those who opposed his school of 'literature for the people' (*al-adab li-l-sha'b*). Here, Idris has thrown the ideas that Musa once championed into a pile with those against which he fought. In fact, Idris makes the ultimate resignation as a *multazim* writer, rejecting "the responsibility of changing a world which does not change."[92] These pages offer, in no uncertain terms, a point-by-point condemnation of *al-adab al-multazim*.

Turning contemptuously from writing, Idris decides to pursue a career repairing videocassette recorders, that early 1980s symbol of Western commercialism. The VCR offers derivative, mass-produced entertainment, its end product being inauthentic (and quite often illegal) copies of anything from artistic works to news reports. Having trashed the human "Xerox machines" of the writing business, Idris has no qualms about facilitating the public addiction to American television icons like the *Six Million Dollar Man*, and *Dallas*'s J.R. as a VCR repairman.[93] In his new occupation, there is no pretense of artistic or social commitment and no danger that his labor can lead to actual production of original work of his own. Idris boasts rather proudly of his skill at working with different videotape machine formats, a rather satirical portrait of his brief dalliance in the frivolous world of materialistic Egyptian society.

Eventually unable to satisfy himself in the vapid world of VCRs, Idris instead decides to emulate the contemptible anti-hero of his earlier story "The Sunken Mattress" and take to bed full time. Like that character, he finds his body wasting away, and through the grace of his medical expertise, can recognize that a blood clot is slowly bringing him the death he now desires. Idris is ultimately unwilling to settle in that role, however, and decides on his deathbed to make a fight for life. With knowing references to the inefficiency of the Egyptian medical system, Idris escapes death by making "impossible" phone connections to hospital numbers that are always "busy, busy, busy."[94] Rushed into a hospital, he eventually recovers despite the medical prognosis. The comments about the improbability of his medical experiences serve to distance this story from a pure autobiography, but they also highlight that something in Idris's makeup—beyond that observable to doctors, and perhaps even some hand of destiny—keeps him alive.

That source of life, of course, is writing. As a writer, writing forms an essential part of his atomic structure and he has no choice but to write, whether society responds or not. "The piper" in the title of the story, according to folklore, "dies with his fingers playing the flute."[95] Thus a writer must die at his typewriter. Neither death nor resignation is his due; he returns to the only function allotted him: writing. Yet his will not be the writing of a *multazim* writer. He writes not for the benefit of the people but only for his own self-preservation. He writes not because of a passion to cure social ills but because he has to, because he has been destined—or one could say *condemned*—to do so.

The most interesting question in the story at this point should be *what* the restored writer chooses to write. Having gone through the agonizing exploration of the role of the writer in this new society and concluded he must now write, Idris must have discovered what to write for this new public. Has he returned to classic *iltizam?* Is he producing the kind of "Xeroxed" entertainment that his co-opted colleagues churned out so reliably? Or has he discovered a new style? As is so consistently the case in the works we have examined so far, his text is deferred. He writes, but what he writes either does not matter or cannot be explained. Idris's death shortly thereafter left this question permanently unresolved.

Earlier in his career, Idris had confessed, "renewal of writing is a natural, spontaneous and ingrained process which the author pursues unconsciously . . . development in writing will only occur as the consequence of this struggle with oneself."[96] True to this creed, Idris never ceased this internal struggle, constantly challenging the beliefs about writing that shaped his career. From the 1960s on, this author, once passionately committed to *iltizam*, conducted an unflinching inquiry into all the elements of *al-adab al-multazim*, inverting that model of writing and examining all its components. Having thoroughly condemned the political power in his earlier works, as well as indicting the uncaring public, Idris turned to the final actor in the *iltizam* relationship—the writer. Despite having the best of motives, writers turn out to be wholly inadequate for the mission *al-adab al-multazim* assigned to them. Writers have instead done harm, he finds, deluding the public in their attempts to help. Given Idris's rather magnified opinion of himself as a writer, and his disdain for even his most talented peers, Mahfouz chief among them, this negative verdict must be taken as a wholesale condemnation of all writers, their good intentions aside.

Had Idris lived to see the renewed spirit of revolution that swept Egypt in 2011, he would certainly have been heartened. The active role of writers in shaping public opinion during the revolution, as well, would no doubt have pleased him greatly. Yet for all his bitterness, Idris's shocking and somewhat satirical portraits of Egyptian society challenged the public to throw off the apathy of "The Sunken Mattress" and rediscover that revolutionary spirit. However dormant the spirit of revolution may have seemed between 1952 and 2011, it continued to motivate and inform the works Idris produced, works that will continue to remind the audience of the difficult challenges that follow revolution.

Chapter 5
Sonallah Ibrahim,
Son of the Revolution

Amid his own struggles as a committed writer in the disappointing atmosphere of post-revolution Egypt, Yusuf Idris announced the arrival of a literary talent who had given voice to the indescribable malaise of a generation. The "great pride" and "true joy" Idris felt in introducing the first novel of Sonallah Ibrahim owed much to his common experience with the new writer, a friend of "over ten years."[1] Like Idris, Ibrahim had gone to prison for his opposition to the Nasser regime and emerged to find a society quite different than that for which he had sacrificed his liberty. Ibrahim's 1966 first novel *That Smell (Tilka al-ra'iha)* expressed an emotion so overwhelming as to leave the renowned writer Idris at a loss for an appropriate term to describe it, finding the capacity of the words "disgust" *(al-ishmi'zaz)* and "alienation" *(al-ghurba)* quite insufficient.[2] The Egyptian government banned the powerful novel, while critics and readers puzzled over it. Yet some, like Idris, would applaud its bold new approach to political and social criticism, and Ibrahim would eventually receive the Arab world's highest award for novelists.

Naguib Mahfouz had established himself as a master of *multazim* fiction in the period before the overthrow of the monarchial regime, and Idris launched his career as a committed writer along with the promising revolution, but Ibrahim was a child of the revolution, taking up fiction writing well into the period of disillusion that the other two experienced during the 1960s. Born in 1937, Ibrahim became an active socialist and Egyptian nationalist early in his life. By age twenty-one, already in the seventh year of Egypt's revolutionary regime, he went to prison for five years for his involvement in the outlawed Communist Party.[3] With his characteristic frankness, Ibrahim expressed the profound disillusion he experienced after he emerged from confinement to find Egyptian socialism to be far removed from that for which he went to jail. Its society transformed by the "social revolution Gamal 'Abd al-Nasser put in place at the beginning of the 1960s," as well as by the spread of materialist culture and television, Ibrahim described 1964 Egypt as "a different world, therefore, than that of which I had dreamed." "Classes had fallen and other classes had risen," he acknowledged, but ultimately, he believed, a petite bourgeoisie had adapted socialism to benefit itself, meanwhile seizing control of the media to ensure that art, publishing, and public dialogue adhered to its own beliefs.[4]

Ibrahim decided to become a writer while in prison, finding that writing gave him a sense of freedom that defied the confinement of prison bars. Nonetheless, he struggled with a fundamental issue—the role of the writer in a transformed society. Reviewing the sweeping changes in Egypt, he asked, "What about the novelist? What does he do?"[5] Beginning his career in the turbulence of the mid-1960s, when established writers of *al-adab al-multazim* were also questioning their roles, Ibrahim spent many years deliberating on the proper style and direction to pursue, pondering over literary approaches from Chekhov to Gorky to Joyce, but finding no adequate style to meet the challenges of his time among the countless literary approaches of the past. In listing the possible models that he considered in his lengthy research into literary styles, Ibrahim named one modern Egyptian—Mahfouz. Placing him together with Balzac and Zola, Ibrahim acknowledged the realist style of *multazim* writing championed in the previous two decades. Ibrahim gave that style due consideration, but ultimately rejected it, feeling, like Brecht, that classic realism's intense focus on details and histories could obscure the larger, hidden social reality. Eventually, he decided to avoid all imitation and tradition, particularly eschewing the style of socialist realism that he felt "embellished and counterfeited" the truth. Rather, he drew upon Marx and Freud in crafting a style that would show the way to open the reader's consciousness to social truths that would otherwise be missed.[6] This intensely personal search for the place of the concerned writer in a new Egyptian society would become the focus of Ibrahim's early novels, a search conducted by his semi-autobiographical protagonists and mirroring his own self-questioning.

In his early efforts at writing after prison, Ibrahim worked as a journalist in the state-run wire service and later spent three months studying the conditions of workers on Egypt's massive development project, the Aswan High Dam. In 1968, he went to East Berlin as an Arabic-language editor for the East German press and eventually landed in Moscow, returning to Egypt in 1974. In the meantime, he began work on his first novel, but like nearly all Egyptian novelists, needed to maintain employment in the public sector to survive economically.[7] Even out of prison, Ibrahim's relationship with the state remained turbulent. The government confiscated his first book after printing, while illegal copies circulated for years. His most celebrated confrontation with the state, however, came in 2003, when he publicly rejected Egypt's highest literary award with the explanation, "it comes from a government that oppresses our people and protects corruption."[8]

Long after Nasser's death, Ibrahim continued to enjoy something of a love–hate relationship with the regime that imprisoned him. Even in prison, Ibrahim reportedly wrote letters of support to Nasser and decades later fondly displayed a picture of the leader in his apartment. While his stark depiction of the dehumanizing conditions in Nasser's prisons got his work censored, he still looks back on his jail term as a useful learning experience, bringing him into contact with suffering people from different walks of life. For all Nasser's failures as a leader, his image remains nonetheless associated with a revolutionary spirit that Ibrahim, like many Egyptians, prefers to the bland subservience to the West of the Sadat and Mubarak regimes. Ibrahim once asserted, "Despite my long detainment under Nasser's regime, I was never against his policies. . . . What I was opposed to was his police system and his refusal to share power with anyone. Nasser's accomplishments cannot be denied. He protected the dignity of Arabs and we are all proud of him."[9] Charles Freund described this not-uncommon sentiment as a yearning for "Nasserism without Nasser."[10]

Ibrahim's first three novels, written over the space of a decade and a half—*That Smell* (1966), *August Star* (*Najmat Aghustus*, 1974), and *The Committee* (*al-Lajna*, 1981)—share a common, largely autobiographical focus on a writer in search of his proper role in a changed Egyptian society, a search paralleling Ibrahim's own. The prolific critic of *al-adab al-hadif*, Mahmud Amin al-'Alim, considers the three works to form a "trilogy of rejection and defeat," with the unnamed protagonist in each being the same character at least in spirit if not in body.[11] Al-'Alim's classification provides a useful conceptual device to link the themes that run through each of the novels, as all three detail the tribulations of a writer-protagonist adapting to his new life out of prison. In each novel, Ibrahim explores the relationship of writer, state, and public that Mahfouz and Idris had also questioned. Here again, this quest presents *al-adab al-multazim* turned inside out—an examination of the conditions necessary for committed writing, while that writing remains deferred.

That Smell

Ibrahim's first novel, *That Smell*, had a long and difficult path to public dissemination. Although censorship had officially been lifted in 1964, the secret police took interest in this 1966 novel after its publication and confiscated the existing copies. In her detailed study of the novel's publication history, Marina Stagh notes that censors had a difficult time with the seemingly banal novel and initially missed much of the content that prompted its belated banning. A censored version appeared in Lebanon in 1968 and another in Egypt in 1969, but the first uncut edition of the novel was its English translation in 1971. Ibrahim faced opposition not only from the political authority, however. He received chastisement rather than support from fellow Arab authors, including the eminent Yahya Hakki, for the provocative content of his work. While *That Smell* was still under censorship, even the editor in chief of *al-Adab*, Suhayl Idris, refused to publish Ibrahim's next novel.[12]

In the opening lines of the novel, the unnamed protagonist, like his authorial creator, emerges from a prison term for a political offense only to face the practical questions of his destination and purpose in the world outside prison. Throughout the novel, he will agonize over where he belongs in his transformed society and how or, indeed, *if* he can write in his new environment. Rather than disavow the parallel to his own experience, Ibrahim confessed that his personal style of writing always "stands on the edge of autobiography," building a "unity" of reality, author, and storytelling that blurs the line between fiction and reality.[13] Idris confessed the need for a similarly autobiographical presence in his story "The Piper Dies," but for Idris, this resignation to the necessity of blurring of intra and extratextual worlds marked a failure, after repeated effort, to keep himself out of the text, as he had done for so long. Having never written during the peak of *iltizam*, with its emphasis on the transparent hand of the author, Ibrahim felt no such need for an apology. He, instead, began his career in a period in which *al-adab al-multazim*'s dictates were no longer sacred.

The style of *That Smell* initially disappointed and confused some critics and readers; Ibrahim was, after all, a virtual unknown at the time and his works were not given the latitude of a Mahfouz or Idris text. The novel seems at first to say almost nothing and contains virtually no traditional plot action, but beyond the surface banality, it fulfilled Ibrahim's goal of bringing out the larger reality hidden behind the minute details of life.[14] Detailing the apparently pointless wanderings of its protagonist around Cairo, the novel hardly seems to rise above the dullness of its endless enumerations of mundane tasks like taking the train or eating. The story's deadpan narration of some of the seamier aspects of life in the city—two allusions to masturbation, a brief, flatly narrated paragraph of prison sex, and the narrator's admission of his inability to perform with a prostitute among them—shocked both censors and critics alike and ostensibly served to justify the confiscation of the work. No doubt these brief glimpses aimed sharp barbs at the false propriety of Egyptian society, but they remained secondary to the major thrust of the work. The protagonist's numbed, emotionless depiction of these short narrative moments, undistinguished from his narration of riding the metro or staring out his window, fits seamlessly into a tight narrative that paints the droning monotony of life for a man who feels no connection to the world around him. Although the narrator tries to pursue a writing career, he is a far cry from Mahfouz, who spent his days in a street café communing with everyday people and turning their experiences into novels. This protagonist understands neither the jargon nor the concerns of those he meets, and consequently, cannot put a word on paper. The novel's central question, then, jumps out from the minutiae of daily life, asking how this one-time activist lost his passion and became so alienated from the public. Although he does not consciously look for answers in the model of *al-adab al-multazim*, the protagonist nonetheless must examine his position in relation to the key partners in *iltizam*—the political power and the public—to determine where he fits.

His complete unrootedeness begins in the opening moment of the text, depicting his release from prison in a scene that hardly speaks of the joy of freedom:

> The policeman said: "What is your address?" I said: "I don't have an address." He looked me over in surprise: "Where, then, will you go? Or where will you stay?" I said: "I don't know. I don't have anyone."[15]

Although he has no connection to the public, he learns immediately that he has a permanent relationship with the state. As various friends and relatives refuse to take him in, the police put him in a brutal local jail as a vagrant and keep him there until a sister agrees to claim him. The state, while intrusive and confining, nonetheless provides a structure to his daily life throughout the novel. Once freed, the police inform him: "It is necessary for us to know where you are located, in order to come to see you at night."[16] This daily ritual comes to dominate the protagonist's life of supposed freedom—a policeman signing his confinement log every evening to enforce his limited house arrest. The curfew effectively restricts his integration back into society, causing him to miss important events and terminate social engagements to rush back for his daily police check.

The protagonist's relationship to the state also hinders his attempts to pursue his chosen art. The protagonist finds himself constantly incapable of the task of writing, leaving the policeman to do the only writing in the novel. Yet far from being a mere annoyance, the officer's writing ritual captures the protagonist's attention and fills much of his narrative. Every day, at exactly the same time, the agent of the state produces the exact same words according to his government-directed formula. The reliability of this government agent matches the regularity of the state-run media, which produces equally predictable, tightly controlled words in newspapers, radio, and television every day. The object of the government-controlled writing remains the same in both cases—communicating its position of control rather than providing any new information to the recipient.

Roman Jakobson's typology of communication describes well the true utility of this state writing system. Jakobson identified six different functions that can apply to a communicative act. All of these could be operative in state-run communication, although the referential function, in which information is provided about something, is the primary expected function of state media, particularly the media of the kind of responsible state that *al-adab al-multazim* envisioned. The emotive function—expressing a speaker's attitude—and the directive function are also often necessary tasks in state-run communication. The policeman's daily writing, however, falls squarely into the phatic function, that is, a communicative act designed solely to ensure the other party's presence on a channel of communication. The familiar example of phatic communication is asking "are you still there?" over the telephone, a function that seems pointless unless tied to one of the other, higher functions. Jakobson even notes that it is the only function that birds share with humans and is the first mastered by babies, who are "prone to communicate before being able to send or receive informative communication."[17]

The phatic communication of intelligent adults, unlike birds and babies, normally comes in preparation for passing a message of a more informative type. The state, however, uses phatic communication as a means of keeping the recipient rooted in a place of confinement. The policeman's writing need only fill this phatic function to accomplish its purpose—ensuring the physical presence of the intended recipient, in this case, the place assigned him by the state. Meanwhile, the state-run media fills a similarly phatic communication function, reminding the public that it controls the channels of communication, thus establishing both its place and the public's. While the policeman's ritual keeps this former activist quiet and controlled, the media's daily rituals of publication keep public discourse free of any messages other than those written by the state. In both cases, phatic communication serves to prevent, rather than facilitate, the passing of information. It would be decades before the Internet would change this situation forever, and for Ibrahim's alter ego, such a concept would have been pure fantasy. In 1966 Cairo, it is little wonder, then, that this protagonist has trouble writing in the face of daily reminders of the coercive power and media monopoly of the state.

If the protagonist, like his extratextual counterpart, quickly learns exactly where he stands in relation to the state, then discovering his relationship to the public requires a longer and more involved process. Upon his arrival to the local jail, after being released from prison and waiting for someone to pick him up, he ironically finds that he doesn't even fit in with the inmates. As the prisoners try to determine his crime, they run through a laundry list of known offenses. To each, he can only answer "no," leaving his fellow prisoners with no explanation for his presence there.[18] The embarrassing technicality that landed him in a local jail is not the kind of crime that would engender respect among the fraternity of inmates, so he is left in limbo—technically free, but belonging neither among the prisoners nor the people outside.

Once sprung from the jail, the protagonist's days involve dead-end visits to former friends he can no longer understand, interspersed with completely unsuccessful attempts at writing. Reticent and detached, he experiences failures to connect with formerly passionate lovers and old friends. He fails to perform with a prostitute, his sexual impotence matching a physical, emotional, and artistic loss of efficacy. Even a simple attempt to make himself useful by taking the daughter of an old friend to the public pool ends with the young girl being attacked and nearly drowned. Unable to swim, the protagonist must watch helplessly.

On the romantic front, many friends urge him to get married and suggest prospective brides, but the protagonist finds life around him moving too fast for him to be able to communicate with any of these women. One of his more promising social visits leads to a briefly blossoming interest in an attractive friend from his old days named Nihad, who takes an encouraging interest in his writing.

> She said: "Do you write stories?" I said, yes. She said: "From books?" I said: "No, from my head." Nihad said: "Then you are a personality."[19]

Rather than inquire as to what he is writing, Nihad immediately proclaims him a *shakhsiya*—a pop-culture buzzword for a 'personality,' or a 'public figure,' as if he has entered the ranks of her celebrity favorites, irrespective, apparently, of whether he earned his title playing football, singing pop songs, or writing stories. She does not characterize him as an artist, nor make any comment about the social value of his work—all the better since the protagonist secretly knows that he is not really writing anything, and therefore, the celebrity status Nihad has granted him is misplaced. In truth, he is a nobody in her world, despite his prison term and his artistic aspirations. Unfortunately, the protagonist's difficulties in relating to Nihad and her family get worse as the meeting goes on, as he cannot handle their Western foods nor deal with declarations like, "America is great. Don't you think so?"[20] After the awkward get-together ends, the protagonist has no further contact with Nihad until he later receives passing news that she has gotten engaged to a promising social climber.[21] Most of his relationships in this fast-moving society will be as perfunctorily terminated as the aborted courtship with Nihad.

If social interaction proves difficult, then politics presents a minefield the protagonist wisely avoids. Several of his friends offer openings for his commentary in their discussions of political and economic events with remarks like: "Our conditions are not bearable," but the protagonist lacks the words and the will to answer them. He declines to address Nihad's comments about the advantages of capitalism or her father's condemnation of Soviet economics as flatly as he passes up the chance to talk about his writing. In an exchange censored from the original Egyptian printing, the protagonist's sister's fiancé complains of having waited two hours in a government food line to buy meat. The man then theorizes that the government "wants poverty to spread," lamenting, "I have no opportunity to prosper. If I accumulate anything, the government takes it."[22] The conversation, however, stalls as the protagonist goes silent, passing on an opportunity tailor-made for an activist writer.

The professional world offers no better arena for expression. Visiting "the magazine," where he is evidently well known, he looks for a job opening, but finds only a friendly façade masking pure rejection. One writer explains that he would like to help, but "circumstances did not permit," and nonetheless goes on to trumpet his own work, insensitive to his visitor's plight. "Did you read my articles?" he boasts. "I'm the only one who writes this way now."[23] Sami, another friend at the magazine, only comments, "I don't have any idea what you have written," and then becomes annoyed when the protagonist remains in the office, needing a polite nudge out the door.[24] Neither the content of the protagonist's work nor of that of any other writer is ever mentioned in these discussions. The staff at the magazine forms a large, well-established clique, one that is by necessity of the political conditions allied with the government. The protagonist stands as an outsider, still under suspicion by the state, making hiring him a risk that they are not willing to take. In any case, the protagonist has little to offer as a writer. Stuck in a writer's block, unable to follow any of the public discourse around him, he cannot produce anything to offer the magazine.

Finding no place in the present, the protagonist pays a visit to his past. He finds an old acquaintance, a café ideologue and former prisoner named Majdi, now exiled to a corner of a coffeehouse with no audience but himself. Majdi rails rather incoherently against unnamed oppressors: "They are all sons of dogs . . . you are strong with the people . . . whereas on your own, you are weak." While the protagonist does not respond to Majdi, he notes that Majdi has indeed now become "on his own."[25] Behind the protagonist's impassive façade during Majdi's ranting, however, we receive a rare glimpse into his thoughts as he silently contemplates the broken revolutionary:

> The whole thing was noble at the beginning but has become now a curse. The fount that once suffered for others has gone dry. . . . When he stood and his back dripped blood, he was brave, not wavering, taking joy in his ability to stand firm. But today, the people no longer gave any weight to this, as the spirit of the time had definitely changed. It was not by chance that the words that he used had changed over time, and some of them had become nearly devoid of significance. . . . He was defeated at a game that doesn't recognize mercy.[26]

Instead of Majdi, this tragic picture could describe 'Umar, Isma'il, Shawqi, or any number of the broken and resigned activists that have filled the pages of Mahfouz or Idris's work. In this concise summary, Ibrahim addresses the mutation of nearly every component of *al-adab al-multazim*, showing a state that tortures those who fight for justice, a public that no longer cares about noble causes, and an activist who can survive the former, but not the latter. Of course, the protagonist sees a reflection of himself in the broken man. Like Majdi, he has neither an audience nor words with which to reach the public.

Insightful critics recognized the central role that the force of disillusion played in the protagonist's silence. Idris noted that the true "protagonist" or "hero" of this story was a "general feeling" with no name, a feeling that goes beyond bitterness, loss, alienation, or revolt, to be entirely Ibrahim's own creation. This nameless feeling captures the spirit of Ibrahim's generation so potently that Idris would claim of the novel "this is not a story . . . it is a slap, or a scream."[27] Ibrahim's accomplishment in giving voice to this spirit had particular interest for Idris, who was himself desperately searching to find expression for the anguish gripping his own cohort. Appreciating how well Ibrahim had expressed the spirit of a generation, Ahmad Hamrush titled one of the first reviews of the novel "The Language of the Age," although that article would be deleted from its parent publication upon news of the novel's confiscation.[28]

The "spirit" that Idris identified in the novel is embodied in the curious "smell" in the novel's title. Al-'Alim devotes considerable attention to identifying the "smell," finding the most likely candidate to be the smell of excrement, mentioned in different forms—such as flatulence or raw sewage—that pervades the text and, by extension, Cairo society. Yet as al-'Alim notes, the physical smell certainly symbolizes a general sense of corruption or disappointment.[29] The message of the novel, then, rests on something deeper than the censored paragraph of prison sex that has garnered so much attention. As Marina Stagh, in her detailed study of the novel's censorship, points out, the deletions cannot hide "that putrid odor."[30] Ibrahim realized this as well. Asked about the novel's confiscation, allegedly for its sexual references, the author asserted that this was merely an excuse to remove a work of political criticism.[31]

Ibrahim was surprised that so many readers, including "progressive critics," did not appreciate the novel. Many considered it merely another expression of the isolation of the intellectual, but Ibrahim felt that their skewed critical perspectives caused them to misinterpret his message. Ibrahim displayed an approach uniquely his own, and those accustomed to previously set formulae were likely to be disappointed. He freely admitted that the novel had a certain "pallor" of style, but asserted this was part of his overall textual strategy. Certainly, how one approached the novel's emotionless narration determined whether its protagonist seemed to be surrendering to the conditions of society or actively resisting them. Ibrahim, in his response to critics, condemned any attitude of submission to authoritarian regimes and felt his novel stood in strong opposition to such submission.[32] Much of the controversy surrounding the novel, therefore, revolved around Ibrahim's choice of a style that jarred expectations for stories of social and political criticism—expectations conditioned by decades of *al-adab al-multazim*. Writing in *al-Adab*, Ibrahim noted, "This short novel faced a complete rejection from the beginning, whether from the state that confiscated it or the critics that attacked it. As for those readers who were able to penetrate it, they were shocked by its frankness."[33] A novel disowned by the state and the literary establishment and only appreciated by the few who "penetrated it," rather than the masses, stood far apart from the model envisioned by *al-adab al-multazim*. The author's own description of the reaction to the novel shows that he well appreciated this wholesale rejection from all the players in the *iltizam* relationship. *That Smell* captured the disorientation and confusion that a committed writer like Ibrahim felt after his abrupt immersion into 1960s Cairo society. His second novel, continuing the semi-autobiographical 'trilogy,' reveals a writer still struggling with doubts about his place in the new society.

August Star

The second novel in Ibrahim's trilogy—far less renowned than the other two—continued the fictional protagonist's exploration of his role as a writer, following the same path that Ibrahim followed in the 1960s, as he traveled to Upper Egypt to investigate the construction of the Aswan High Dam, touted as the "new pyramid."[34] The political and economic significance of the dam for Ibrahim's generation could hardly be overstated. Financed by Nasser's boldest move, the seizure of the Suez Canal in 1956, the building project asserted Egyptian independence from the Americans who had withdrawn their financial support for the project as a punishment for Nasser's refusal to join a US-led military alliance. The dam itself promised to transform the Egyptian economy by providing water, fertile land, and electricity, while controlling the powerful Nile floods. Its most enduring effect was the appropriately named 'Lake Nasser,' an oasis in a parched land. Ceza Kassem Draz's insightful study of *August Star* notes: "Ibrahim belongs to the generation of the High Dam builders. They set all their hopes on it; it stood as the personification of what they believed in. They were truly fascinated by it. The High Dam provided that generation with the feeling of fulfillment and of 'building' as well as a sense of direction leading toward social and economic transformation."[35] Yet Ibrahim's interest lay beyond the promised economic transformation. He felt drawn to the region to find out how the High Dam project was changing the lives of Egyptians directly involved in its construction.[36]

By the time of Nasser's death, public perception of the High Dam project had shifted radically. The dam was generally recognized as a poorly planned engineering nightmare that had devastated much of the land around it. Draz points out that Sadat's active campaign of criticism of the old regime found the High Dam a fitting "nucleus" around which the "de-Nasserization" effort could center.[37] Ibrahim's *August Star*, published in 1974, the same year as *Karnak Café*, Mahfouz's scathing retrospective of the Nasser era, came as part of this wave of criticism. Its bleak picture stands in sharp contrast to the journalistic work that Ibrahim wrote in 1967 detailing his High Dam experience—*Man of the High Dam (Insan al-sadd al-ali)*, a state-sponsored glorification of the High Dam project. *August Star* mocks that earlier work by casting its protagonist in the same journalistic role that Ibrahim filled, allowing him to discover the horrors that Ibrahim could not print at the time. Draz claims that the two works jointly disturb the established notions of fiction and truth that had become so inverted in the Nasser period. In other words, the ostensibly truthful, journalistic reporting of *Man of the High Dam* comes across as deliberately fabricated, while the fictional novel *August Star* exposes harsh reality.[38] At issue between the two texts are the bedrock claims of the High Dam project: that it was first an engineering marvel that tamed nature, but also that it did so without widespread damage to the established culture and natural environment of Upper Egypt or the workers who constructed it. Ibrahim's 1967 text supports these claims, while his 1974 novel, as well as public discourse by that time, rejected them. Al-'Alim finds Ibrahim taking on two very different personae in the two works, the upbeat one necessarily associated with a work like *Man of the High Dam* undone by the troubled, alienated writer-protagonist of *August Star*.[39]

Like *That Smell*, *August Star* sketches the writer-protagonist's journey to find his place in a changed society, examining his position in relation to the public and the state. Yet rather than searching Cairo society, he goes to the frontlines of the workers' battle for national independence and dignity. Despite embarking on a very proletarian writing project, he follows few tenets of a *multazim* writer. He acknowledges having gone to Aswan without a definite journalistic agenda but rather with a curiosity to see how the dam was actually changing the lives of Egyptians. Nor does he have a definite plan for research or style of writing. Unlike his counterparts who took up writing in the 1940s or early 1950s, this writer does not turn to the critics and theorists of *al-adab al-multazim* for guidance, instead drawing his inspiration from a much further removed source—his study and contemplation of Michelangelo's sculptures, which provides a running commentary to the events he witnesses. Yet Michelangelo does not appear as an inspiration among the pages of either *That Smell* or *The Committee*, the other two novels in the trilogy. Far from adhering to a single school or artistic role model, then, Ibrahim's wandering protagonist(s) feel free to pick and choose in each novel from influences across the centuries.

As this writer begins his own education at the hands of his public, his conceptual flexibility will prove helpful. Almost immediately he finds that his role as a writer—with the accumulated baggage of associations that being a writer invokes in Nasser's Egypt—forms a barrier between him and the people. While he develops personal bonds of admiration and respect with the workers suffering under difficult conditions, he finds that the distortions of the official government press have undermined his credibility in their eyes. Unsure at first why he encounters this barrier, the protagonist receives a rude education in his attempt to speak to disillusioned workers Hilmi and Rif'at, men involved in the difficult project of saving the pharaonic Abu Simbel temple from the flooding caused by the dam. Hilmi launches his hostile opening salvo:

> "I have a complaint against journalists."
>
> I said: "What is it?"
>
> He said: "You don't respect the person who works in dignity and silence."
>
> Rif'at wanted to lighten the effect of his words and said: "Some journalists, not all of them."
>
> I said: "Maybe."[40]

Far from *iltizam*'s assumption of a bond between the writer and the proletariat, this exchange shows a perception of the writer as inherently opposed to the worker, separating the two sides and forcing the writer to begin from a disadvantage. Neither side quite knows how to position itself in this relationship. The worker feels forced to caveat his strong personal feelings against a systemic problem, while the writer shrouds his stance in ambiguity. From this tight-lipped protagonist, who prefers to divulge few of his own opinions, the rejoinder "maybe" sounds doubly inconclusive. Does he acknowledge that "maybe" some journalists are as bad as the man thinks, or does he lament that only "maybe" is Rif'at's polite but obviously insincere concession justified? Given the internal doubts that plague the narrator throughout his journey, it is unlikely he knows which meaning his word holds.

These men can only establish the personal trust needed to continue a fruitful discussion by dissociating themselves from the corrupted, official writing process. In doing so, Hilmi and his friend teach the protagonist about the failures of the media system in Egypt, explaining the real story behind the production of a news feature. They relate how a journalist from a popular Egyptian magazine visited the construction site at Abu Simbel yet concentrated only on photographing a German swimsuit model lounging around the area.

> "Didn't he write about any of you, or the heroic role you perform in preserving our history?"
>
> He said: "Not a word."
>
> I said: "He's wrong. . . . But that doesn't mean that all journalists are of his type."
>
> Hilmi distanced himself, saying: "Of course not. However, events like that cause us to lose confidence in all journalism."[41]

The protagonist follows this exchange by a rare declaration of journalistic intent, saying that he has come to give the workers an opportunity to show the public the true nature of the work at Abu Simbel, but the workers' only response is an awkward silence. Unlike his earlier, noncommittal "maybe," the protagonist has obviously erred in making a rash promise that both parties realize he has no power to fulfill. Learning his lesson, the writer returns to his role as a student under the tutelage of a disgruntled public and refrains from further promises.

Despite a strong concern for the worker, the protagonist does not know how to surmount the government hold on the media nor how to reach a public that prefers to read about models lounging in the sand rather than the "heroic" construction efforts. Even his use of recognizably socialist terminology—recalling the "worker heroes" of Soviet literature—sounds flat and outdated. Unable to relate directly to the workers, he turns to some of the other professionals around him for advice, instead encountering only a strong sense of disappointment. A veteran doctor serving on the construction project compares his former enthusiasm with the protagonist's and notes: "We dreamed of graduation day, we dreamed of going to the countryside and curing the peasants who lived like animals. . . . I am here now only because I want to accumulate some money to open a private clinic. For that's the only language spoken in our country today."[42] The term he uses to describe his desired clinic, *khassa*, is the same word that was used for 'the elite,' in contrast to 'the masses,' in the titles of the two sides in the Husayn–Khuri debate. This wise veteran, who sought to do in the medical field largely what the *multazim* writer sought in the literary arena, acknowledges that the only effective language now belongs to the elite.

Although still quite unsure of his role, the protagonist's commitment eventually faces a test when a mysterious epidemic begins taking the lives of workers. A brief investigation at the local hospital reveals a dangerous and uncertain threat that contradicts the rosy reports in the newspapers. Even the temperature, a major contributing factor to the epidemic that could be measured objectively, becomes subject to distortion. The newspapers report a hot 44 degrees Celsius, which comes nowhere close to the life-threatening 60 degrees the doctor reports.[43] Even the forces of nature, it seems, have been subjected to press censorship.

The narrator and his fellow reporters face the difficult choice of staying in personal danger to uncover the truth about working on the High Dam or leaving to avoid the disease, tempered by the knowledge that the truth may never see publication in any case. When his colleague, Sa'id, announces he would return to Cairo rather than face death from the disease, the protagonist's simple question turns into an ambiguous exploration of the writer's commitment: "What if they said you were a martyr for your journalistic duty?" he asks, only to have Sa'id reply mockingly, "Then make me a national hero." The parody of socialist terminology in their flippant conversation masks a genuine concern for their mission. The protagonist himself cannot answer the same question, however, concluding, "Neither am I ready to give my life, but

I'm going to stay," although he rejects the suggestion he wants to stay "with the masses until the end," offering rather, "I want to see what happens."[44] Despite his public denials, the protagonist does seem rooted in the same spirit of commitment that motivated the earlier writers of *iltizam*, but he feels the need to dissociate himself from the discredited platitudes of such high-minded doctrine and conceal his concern as an individual curiosity.

In *August Star*, an impulse to write in hopes of revealing the true condition of the workers—an aim in harmony with that motivating the pioneers of *al-adab al-multazim*—leads the writer to conclusions fundamentally opposed to that model. The extratextual actors in the writing process have now become the regular and acceptable focus of the text, while the suffering workers appear only where needed to facilitate the examination of the weaknesses in the system of writing and publishing. Indeed, in an inversion of the fundamental principles of *iltizam*, the suffering worker, far from being a mere subject, turns his voice to critique the system of writing and publishing. The mass public no longer fits the type assumed by *iltizam*, instead being fascinated with commercialism, rather than social justice. Tragically, there is genuine suffering among the laboring class that deserves to be addressed, but the writer has no confidence that he can get this message past a censoring government to reach an uncaring public.

The state has chosen to feed this distracted public with the cheery disinformation that keeps it from dealing with the social reality. Al-'Alim focused on the novel's critique of the corrupted version of Soviet-style control that characterized the building of the dam. Acknowledging the noble goals of Nasser's project, the critic lamented the oppressive means used to reach the goal. However, he felt that the novel went beyond "a specific historical period, or a particular historical project, that is the period of 'Abd al-Nasser's rule or the High Dam building project, rather giving its verdict for past, present, and future."[45] Ultimately, he believed, the novel describes the "crisis of the absence of democracy in a society attempting to build a new, progressive, humanistic life."[46] The same forces, however, exact a toll on the writer as well as the worker. In al-'Alim's eyes, state oppression eroded the narrator's confidence and sense of identity. Indeed, the protagonist's alienation from the rest of society, which al-'Alim finds pervading the entire text, mounts as he encounters frustration in this environment of oppression and fear instilled by the regime.[47]

Despite the hard blows that Ibrahim's wandering protagonist experiences in his voyage of self-discovery, al-'Alim praised the hero's determination to find a place for himself in a changed Egyptian society. Al-'Alim stressed the continuity of Ibrahim's three novels, asserting at the end of his critique of *August Star* that the protagonist headed off from the High Dam for a "nine o'clock appointment with *The Committee.*"[48] Yet over five years would pass before that appointment, and fifteen years over the course of this trilogy of personal discovery.[49] As the leader of a literary movement that once expressed such a clear vision for the writer and a strong sense of urgency, this critic—like the author—now seems willing to accept a long, meandering journey of examination to find the writer's proper role in his ambiguous relations to the people and the state. The next stop on this journey, however, would prove the most trying and disappointing.

The Committee

In a 1980 *al-Adab* feature detailing his experience as a writer, Ibrahim announced that he had begun work on a new novel with a style unlike any of his previous works or, truly, unlike any other established form. Yet he also cautioned that this upcoming work would not represent a "new model," holding rather that every novel would be a distinct, free experiment.[50] Unquestionably, *The Committee*, published in 1981, marked a major stylistic departure from the previous two novels, although its subject remains remarkably similar—an activist writer released from prison to face an intrusive authority and a callous public. While the story's central preoccupation, as with its two predecessors, is the scrutiny of the relationships essential to activist writing—relationships that formed the framework of *iltizam*—it moves even further from the realist mode that had once been the mainstay of *al-adab al-multazim*.

The Committee is truly the unique stylistic experiment that Ibrahim promised. The psychological effect of its ingenious narrative technique defies a simple description. Critics most often compare the novel to the works of Kafka,[51] but this is much like describing only the trunk of the proverbial elephant. Ibrahim's novel presents two distinct narrative worlds, one occupied by the eponymous "Committee," the intrusive state apparatus that controls the freedom of the writer, while the other is occupied by the people of Cairo, as firmly surrendered to Western commercialism as in *That Smell*.

The protagonist's dilemma springs from his belonging in neither realm, while his duty as a writer forces him to negotiate his way through both. He aspires throughout the novel to eventually link the two worlds through his writing. The stark contrast of the two environments, however, with their drastically differing views on the essential components of a writer's art—language, perception, and methods of representation—conveys the depth of the chasm separating the state and the public. While the narrator understands the languages of each world, as a writer, he feels that he can and should try to establish some type of mutually intelligible communication between the two. The novel, then, details a search to understand both domains and to link them, in this case through a writing project.

The "Committee" that plays such a central role in the protagonist's life remains perpetually shrouded in mystery. Ibrahim never indicates whether it is an Egyptian government organization, some type of supranational body, or something otherworldly. The group members are a hybrid civilian–military type, alternately appearing as either. They speak some unidentified language other than Arabic and most people prefer to pretend that the organization doesn't exist. The size of this body remains maddeningly ambiguous, as the protagonist laments that he had three opportunities to count the number of members but failed to do so so each time. While this might suggest a large group, the same people are able to fit into the narrator's small apartment during a totally implausible surprise visit.

While critics have struggled to piece the clues together to determine the identity of this committee—reaching conclusions ranging from a United States mission in Egypt to a mindless bureaucracy or a multinational corporation—Ibrahim has constructed his foggy picture in such a way as to preclude one-to-one identification with any extratextual entity.

There are, for example, numerous clues to suggest the Committee's mysterious language might be English, yet this in itself says nothing, given the ubiquity of English as the language of global commerce. Al-'Alim, while finding support for the secret US–Israeli junta theory, allows for other readings, including perhaps the most useful—that the Committee represents raw "power" itself.[52]

Whatever its ultimate identity, the Committee definitely exerts a coercive influence over the protagonist strong enough to make him sick with nervousness at his appearance before the board, despite having practiced for a year in frightened anticipation. The Committee desires his services as a writer and the protagonist realizes he has no other avenue to publish his work, ultimately choosing to die if the Committee will not approve his writing project.

The Committee appears both omnipresent and formless. It flaunts its intrusiveness by assigning a guard to accompany the narrator twenty-four hours a day—even into the bathroom and into his bed. Yet it remains amorphous enough that its members cannot be counted or identified. If the "true protagonist" of Ibrahim's first novel was a "general feeling" of disillusion, then the Committee may represent, more than any particular agency, the general sensation of an intrusive, controlling, coercive authority that hampers the intellectual's activity. The narrator's final spoken words of the novel, given in address to the Committee, support this interpretation. For he confesses that even if the Committee were destroyed, "by the nature of things, a new Committee would assume your place. Regardless of how good its intentions or sound its goals, corruption would not take long to pervade it."[53]

The Committee's oppression, however distressing to its victims, seems largely self-serving and counterproductive. The group revels in the trappings of power and secrecy in a kitschy style of Orwellian omnipotence, while it delights in its ability to strike fear in the protagonist. All the while, it enjoys its appropriation of the language of liberation and social justice for its coercive purposes, never issuing direct threats or commands, instead veiling everything in a language of voluntarism and camaraderie. "The Committee has placed itself from the beginning in the service of revolutionary goals, moral foundations, and religious values. Its members have aided all that supports basic values and the deepening of freedom," the chairman boasts.[54] This outwardly friendly discourse clashes with the protagonist's inner turmoil, as he is reduced to a nervous wreck during his Committee appearance, which begins with a reminder that his presence there is totally voluntary. His totally voluntary appearance involves belly dancing for the Committee and a rectal exam to check for homosexuality conducted in front of men and women. Every move strikes him with fear and doubt, such as closing a door with one hand instead of two, leading him to despair of the conclusions the Committee will draw from his error. Eventually, the Committee insists on hounding him in his apartment, watching him use the bathroom, and finally assigning him the task of eating himself, which he will placidly execute.

All the while, however, Ibrahim gives no indication that the Committee succeeds in doing anything more than harassing individuals for its own amusement. Possessed by fear, rather than respect for the organization, the protagonist notes, "Some people, and I am among them, consider membership in it [the Committee] to be an indicator of diminishing talent and total failure."[55] When presented with the threat of torture—expressed in the Committee's ironically benign discourse—the protagonist tries to explain why such treatment, although harmful to him, would ultimately prove counterproductive. "I know the techniques you allude to," he boldly asserts. "Surely they would compel me to confess anything. But what I would confess—in that case—would not be true. As for you, you would remain forever uncertain of the facts."[56] Moreover, the protagonist needs only a kitchen knife to easily dispatch the symbol of the Committee's omniscience, the annoying twenty-four-hour guard assigned to watch him. Yet the strongest indictment of the Committee's overall failure arises from the streets of Cairo, the other 'world' of this novel. There, society moves at a fast pace in pursuit of the fruits of Western consumerism, constantly seizing upon the latest trends and fads that dominate public attention. The protagonist tries in vain to convince the Committee that "by means of this activity itself—the activity of change and continuous replacement—your organization will lose gradually the power it now has."[57]

Ibrahim paints his scenes of Cairo life in a vastly different narrative style than the misty, surreal world of the Committee. The differences are so pronounced, in fact, that the novel would be a very uneven and inconsistent reading experience were its unity not achieved in the stark contrast of the two worlds. On the one hand, descriptions of the Committee's world remain shrouded in a physical and contextual ambiguity which confounds the protagonist's natural curiosity as a writer:

> I tried to have a clear idea of the work of the Committee, searching for those who had previously stood before it. Despite my confidence in the abundance of such people, I gained access to only a few of them, the majority denying going to the Committee on any occasion, rather disclaiming any knowledge of its existence. The others gave the pretext that they forgot the details of what happened to them, therefore their statements came out unclear, conflicting. The other fragments I gathered from different sources didn't help me to produce anything useful. The sole fact that emerged from this was that the work of the Committee had no defined formula.
>
> When I attempted to find information about its members—perhaps I would be able to form an idea of their orientations and inclinations—I found a solid curtain of secrecy had shrouded their names and occupations. Everyone that I asked about them looked at me with anxiety and apprehension.[58]

The narrative style used for the world outside the Committee chambers, however, is full of clear detail, as evidenced in this typical paragraph:

> The friend who supplied me with the cards was the one who recommended I pursue my goal in the library at the American Embassy. I went to the new location, the one it had moved to after the furious crowds burned the old site in the year 1965, protesting the United States' support of Mubutu, the president of Zaire, known at that time as the Congo-Kinshasa, and its role, prior to that, in the assassination of the nationalist leader, Lumumba.[59]

The novel's heteroglossia highlights the communication gap that separates the two worlds. While the Committee never uses names to refer to anything or anybody, the street scenes feature a constant bombardment of titles of foreign products, politicians, and celebrities. On one page alone, twelve Western brand names are cited. Narrative time slows down considerably when the Committee is involved, as the protagonist must give verbose presentations and arguments that have no effect on the group; meanwhile, the Cairo street scenes progress rapidly. While the Committee treasures its secrecy, the Western companies seize public space, exemplified by the succession of billboards along the road to the airport, as well as the psychological associations of status symbols, like the protagonist's oft-mentioned "Samsonite briefcase."[60]

The narrator understands the outside world, at least on an analytic, intellectual level. As a writer, he faces the challenge of relating that world to his patron, the Committee, hoping to convince the group of the value of his realistic, documentary writing in the service of its stated aims of liberation. In this quest, he struggles to translate the reality of the outside world into the language of the Committee, uniformly failing despite his extensively researched and logically presented expositions. Failing to explain the influence of Marilyn Monroe, Belgian detective stories, or automobile manufacturing, the protagonist pours his intellectual prowess into an exhaustive lecture on the most "significant" name of the century: Coca-Cola.

Upon this most banal of household names, the protagonist weaves a verbal exposition—taking up a large part of the text—that will demonstrate his faculty and usefulness as a writer, yet which also highlights the predicament of this artist trapped between the authority and the public. He offers a masterful piece of systematic analysis, linking political, economic, natural, psychological, and social factors in orderly fashion to explain the dominance of Coca-Cola on the world market. Showcasing his extensive research, he delves into the links between US Senator Walter Mondale, the Brooklyn Museum, migrant fruit pickers, Zbigniew Brzezinski's Trilateral Commission, and the Korean War, to cite a few bits from his endless stream of facts. The barrage of recognizably authentic names contrasts with the titles of the Committee's members, whom the protagonist can only designate as "The Blond One" or "The Short One," not knowing their real names. In his Coca-Cola speech, the narrator elaborates the tremendous social, cultural, and political impact of the beverage company's economic success and warns of the severe implications for the Arab world of missing the wide-scale social and economic transformation it heralds. While he demonstrates the makings of a stellar *multazim* artist, with his eye for systematic social analysis, it remains unclear whether contemporary Egypt holds a place for such work.

The message in the protagonist's exposition on Coca-Cola, calling for a different type of communication to reach this changed society, eludes the members of the Committee. The protagonist argues that Coca-Cola achieved dominance in the world market, and popular culture, through its "elegant" appearance—the distinct shape of its bottle and ubiquitous brand name. The public outside does not need this elaborate explanation, for they see the message everywhere, as boxes of Coca-Cola appear constantly in the narrator's description of the Cairo streets where countless vendors peddle the drink. Dozens of other brand names have followed suit, infiltrating their catchy product names into the rapid-paced street slang of city residents. The foreign names, transliterated into Arabic by the familiar process of adding a large number of long vowels, break the normally rhythmic pattern of Arabic speech, just as their profusion of printed *alif*s and *waw*s break up the normally continuous flow of the cursive script much more than in words with genuine Arabic roots.

A walk down any Cairo street would explain the situation better than a long exposition, yet the protagonist understands that the Committee is not attuned to what transpires on Cairo streets. Instead, he struggles to relate in the verbose discourse of the Committee how a new, compact language has taken over communication with the public, but his attempt fails to bridge the gap. While he has imitated the style of speech the Committee prefers, he naively believes they will accept a strong, specific, and transformational message wrapped up in that language. He discovers, unfortunately, that the Committee wants long-winded expositions, but it wants them free of any real meaning, like their own ambiguous, cliché-ridden speeches extolling freedom.

Nonetheless, despite all he knows about the nefarious Committee, the protagonist insists until the end on pursuing a writing project under Committee auspices that he believes will change the Arab world. The Committee, after much delay and unseen deliberation, has assigned him the vague task of writing about the "most luminous" Arab personality.[61] The superlative adjective presents a very strange task, and a particularly ambiguous one, like most of the Committee's speech. They ask for not 'the greatest,' 'most important,' or 'most noble,' but rather 'the most shining, lustrous' personality—that is, the person with the most dazzling exterior. The same Arabic spelling *(alma)*, however, could also mean 'clever' or 'shrewd.' Too frightened to ask for clarification, the protagonist takes the command with the most naively straightforward interpretation, assuming the Committee wants to hear about a genuinely influential person who deserves to shine. Yet one could easily read a second voice behind the Committee's guidance—ordering him to give the public some clever, exciting propaganda to distract people from seeking the truth.

Lacking any further clarification as to the genre, length, purpose, or even deadline of the task, and fearing to ask such practical questions of the Committee, the protagonist launches on his project. In a scene of bitter irony, the protagonist runs through a list of potential candidates—Arab military, political, artistic, and scientific figures—and finds them all undeserving. "I searched fruitlessly to find a single judge whose name was associated with a sincere stand on behalf of truth. In this regard, I was also able to eliminate the journalists, the labor leaders, and, in no time, those so-called representatives of the people were discarded with them."[62]

The protagonist's choice for the honor turns out to be an influential Arab entrepreneur known only as "the Doctor." Unlike the Committee, the Doctor operates in the real world, his success solidly anchored in the political and economic events of his day. The protagonist recalls his one glimpse of the powerful figure:

> The only time that I saw him with my own eyes, it was maybe five years ago, when the taxi I was in stopped in front of a traffic signal in Ramses Square. I saw all eyes directed at a luxurious Mercedes, of the most recent style, our friend was settled in the back, holding

> the receiver of a telephone. That was a strange thing at that time, because we were still not long after the October War, prior to our *infitah*. Not only that, but most of the non-mobile phones in the country didn't work. How could a mobile phone work?[63]

Not surprisingly, the narrator's research into Arabic sources produces nothing. Yet while the official Arab media have labored to keep the Doctor a secret, the protagonist finds abundant information in *Time* and *Newsweek*. Like the Committee's outdated coercive measures, the state clings tenaciously to an outdated policy of censorship that has been negated by the penetration of Western culture into the country. Ibrahim's warning of the growing power of global media is but a precursor of the tide that will come with electronic media little more than a decade later.

The narrator's research quickly explains the key to the Doctor's success: he has grasped the secrets of the Western commercial domination of the Arab world and established himself as an important middleman. Yet the protagonist argues that the new rules of the world offer an opportunity, rather than a threat. The Doctor, he explains, is one of the leading advocates of Arab unity, and while that goal has largely died out as a political movement, the Doctor has struck upon a more subtle and influential type of unity through commercial influence. In other words, the Doctor knows how to compete with the West at its own game.

The Committee warns the protagonist several times that he treads on dangerous ground and advises him to change his project. "I engaged in research guided by pure objectivity. I noted only confirmed truths and scientific explanations," he pleads, only to be told: "That is exactly what led us to offer you some advice."[64] The cause of the Committee's concern—whether the Doctor is an ally they wish to protect, an enemy they wish to avoid, or merely a figure they cannot understand—remains ambiguous, like the Committee's ultimate identity. What emerges clearly, however, is that this monolingual, coercive authority objects to the writer's production of a text with a real, socially transforming message and will not allow the writer to pursue the task his conscience dictates to be in the best interests of society. By leaving the identity and motivations of the Committee ambiguous, Ibrahim forces the reader's attention to the clear breakdown of the expected roles of writer and authority and the predicament of the committed writer in a society like 1980s Egypt.

While the Committee affirms its intent to stop the intended biography of the Doctor, the protagonist has since shed his paralyzing fear and replaced it with an unquenchable enthusiasm for his project, vowing to continue despite their objections and threats. Here, Ibrahim, like Mahfouz and Idris before him, having examined the harsh and oppressive control of the political authority on the writer, eventually shows his protagonist making a decision to continue, despite the risks. Ultimately, however, it is the public reaction, not the hostility of the state that breaks the committed writer's spirit.

In his final appearance before the Committee, the narrator receives the "most extreme punishment," that is, being ordered to eat himself,[65] without further clarification as to how this will actually occur. Having passed the sentence, however, the Committee does not stop him from walking out the door and going back into the flow of Cairo life. There, he tries unsuccessfully to mingle with the crowds of people on a bus and on the street. Bypassing the Committee, and not deterred by the death sentence they have imposed on him, he attempts to confront directly the systemic injustices he sees on the streets, but meets only hostility.

Once again, Ibrahim firmly anchors the scenes outside the Committee chambers in the real world of contemporary Egypt. Boarding a bus, the protagonist notes not only the make of the bus, which like everything else outside, carries a catchy, American brand name—the "Carter" bus, after the American president—but he also describes the history of the political, economic, and social impact of the Egyptian acquisition of these American-donated vehicles, beginning:

> As for the reason for attaching the name of the American president to this type of bus, it doesn't relate to its distinctive shape, which resembles a large caterpillar with a morose appearance, or its unusual length, or to the loud noise that occurs when it passes, or the increase in the fare (five times the usual), or its manufacture in the United States. Instead, it relates to the symbol affixed on its side, right next to the front door. It shows an American flag and two hands shaking, and expression of friendship.

> This, for the most part, is the secret behind the people's happiness at its appearance on the streets two or more years ago. For they considered it the first sign of the promised abundance for which they all waited. They seemed ready to disregard the noise that it produced on the basis that noise is a familiar thing in a backward country like our country, and the increase in fares on the basis of the worldwide increase in prices, and the heavy exhaust smoke it produced on the basis that pollution of the environment is a problem in advanced countries alone.[66]

From the outset, this style of description contrasts with the amorphous pictures of the Committee. Precise in its sensory details, it aims to bring together, in a systematic fashion, all the causes and effects associated with the buses' particular name, realizing, unlike the secret Committee, that name recognition confers real power. The protagonist will go on to discuss minute details, such as mechanical problems with gaskets and rivets, safety deficiencies, and the reaction of the Egyptian press to the defects in the buses. He uses the bus as a particular example of the general problem of dependency on American aid in Egyptian society, a major controversy at a time when Egypt had just begun to receive large doses of US aid in return for its peace settlement with Israel. Yet this protagonist suspects, as many dissenters did, that US generosity was a really means of dumping inferior American products on an Egyptian market and, in the process, closing down domestic factories. His analysis upholds the finest traditions of *al-adab al-multazim*, yet he has already concluded that the Committee wants no part of his type of political commentary. Will the public outside the Committee chambers be any more receptive?

As he looks at his fellow passengers to see what they think of the buses, he notes, "It seemed they were busy with other things, as they were looking earnestly at the advertisements that decorated the streets."[67] Finally, the protagonist's ire erupts at what he considers an outrage, a man groping and slapping a female passenger on the bus. Taking action, he springs to his feet to confront the offender, noting: "I envisioned that all the passengers—those who knew well what had happened, having followed the matter from the beginning—would stand beside me."[68] Instead, the passengers who had been watching the harassment turn away as the lecher proceeds to beat up the quixotic protagonist, then the group collectively shoves him out the door of the bus, leaving him with a broken arm.

His ideas about chivalry and social decency shattered, the narrator searches for medical care, finding only a callous, corrupt, and greedy medical establishment. Here, the narrator exposes a very real and well-known scam in the ostensibly free public health system as the protagonist waits for hours in agony at the public hospital only to be told the doctor cannot see him, but that for a fee he will examine him in his "private clinic"—the same term used by the doctor in *August Star*, and once again synonymous with 'elite.' Charged twice for the same exam, the protagonist complains that "this is nothing more than exploitation," only to be rebuffed with "this is our system and you're a free person,"[69] proffering the façade that the protagonist's choice of the private clinic is a personal one, rather than a systemic necessity. Once again, the protagonist tries an analytic elaboration of the corruption in the system to sway the doctor and the waiting room full of passive onlookers. "You and those like you profit from a number of inherited advantages that were taken from me and others. . . ."[70] begins his long speech, linking the educational system to the competition of private and public healthcare. Realizing he has failed to persuade anyone in the doctor's office, the protagonist storms out, threatening that he will find justice in the law. Silently, he adds, "I didn't mean it, of course."[71] Only then, after having found the public and the civil servants to be greedy, selfish, uncaring, and totally averse to messages of social justice, does the protagonist return to his apartment, listen to the music of his favorite composers, and begin eating himself. He prefaces his self-consumption with a contemplation of the fallen Soviet writer Vladimir Mayakovsky, whose disillusionment with his place as a propagandist in the Communist production system led to his 1930 suicide, concluding, "Remembering the end that he met spoke to my tragedy."[72] With no Committee members anywhere in sight, indeed, not having seen any sign of the group since he freely walked out their door, the protagonist voluntarily enters their world. One can hardly miss the shift in narrative environments that occurs as he sits calmly at his desk, consuming his arm to pleasant music—an arm that in the real world of the Cairo streets caused him unbearable pain at merely being broken. In common with nearly all the tormented activists considered in this study, Ibrahim's protagonist endures the cruelty of the controlling authority to defend his beliefs, yet when confronted with a public that no longer cares about those beliefs, finally resigns himself to become what that authority demands.

The protagonist of *The Committee*, like his counterparts in the previous two novels, explores the question that Ibrahim himself asked at the beginning of his writing—What does the writer do in this new society? As writing in Egypt had been for so long defined by the writer's relation to his or her two partners—the state and the public—this protagonist boldly searches through both sectors, risking everything in the process of bringing a message he believes will transform society. The controlling authority—which in 1980s Egypt may truly have been as amorphous a conglomeration of political, military, economic, and police forces from within and without the country as critics have variously seen the Committee to be—stands adamantly opposed to such writing, despite its avowed support for liberation movements. Meanwhile, it has lost 'the language of the people' and persists in a self-defeating style of oppression that cannot lessen its rapidly eroding hold on the public psyche. The writer, despite his suffering at the hands of that authority, nonetheless braves a death sentence in order to bring forth his message. Only the public, now addicted to Western consumerism and scorning any social commitment, has the power to finally destroy the writer's spirit, here, as in *That Smell*. In the meantime, this writer who seemed so skilled at the kind of research and writing that *al-adab al-multazim* once cherished, finds that type of writing unwelcome by either the state or the public. The former objects to the meaningful truth his writing contains, the latter disregards anything more engaging than a billboard slogan.

For all its pessimism, *The Committee* offers a message of hope, as the protagonist prefaces his auto-cannibalism with an assurance that the power of the Committee will eventually be broken by the rapid change in society. As in many of the texts previously addressed, the novel's conclusions about the writing of the future lie in a project deferred outside the text. The aborted study of the Doctor, which the Committee will not allow to reach the public, contains a message for the Arab world so strong that the protagonist willingly dies for it. While he laments not living to see his mission come to fruition, he believes that the message it contains will eventually transform Egyptian society. The focus in this novel, however, rests not on the Doctor and his methods but rather on the disconnect between the state and public and the inability of the writer to bridge it with any common language. The counterproductive censorship that exorcises from Egyptian newspapers the secrets of a global conquest openly touted in *Time* and *Newsweek* must end, allowing the Egyptian writer to discuss what everyone can plainly see happening on the streets around them. Perhaps this insightful writer, with his genius for analysis of real-world problems, could have leveraged his research on the Doctor to give Egypt a means of communication to reach the public as effectively on social issues as Western companies reach it with messages of commercialism. This would certainly be a fitting *multazim* text for his current age. In any case, however, that text will never take shape. The Committee has forbidden such writing for the moment.

Eventually, the Internet revolution would circumvent the censorship of the political authority, as the protagonist warned. If Coca-Cola was the most pervasive Western import of the time, this protagonist would be truly amazed to see the influence that communications services like Google and YouTube would exert. Ibrahim sounded a warning in this novel that the Mubarak government—like the Committee—ignored for too long, until Facebook replaced Coca-Cola in the public psyche. The popularity of Ibrahim's banned first novel, which circulated in bootleg copies, was but a precursor to what blogs could accomplish for an activist writer. Commenting in *al-Adab* while he was still at work on *The Committee*, Ibrahim spoke of the challenge of reaching a mass public, rather than just a small, intellectual elite, with something more significant than entertainment literature. While he could not see the form that such a change would take, even his doomed protagonist predicted a massive transformation that would bring down the regime.

Yet *The Committee* was prescient in other ways as well. Ibrahim's defiant protagonist had indeed walked out on the controlling body, but found no antidote for the apathy and commercialism of the public. While he had sounded the death knell of the nefarious organization, he had also predicted that a new one would emerge to take its place. Unlike his predecessors Mahfouz and Idris, Ibrahim would live to see a new revolution, powered by unstoppable communications media, sweep away the controlling old order. Although the author would celebrate that moment, it would be but a short time before he would be forced to confront once again the same disappointments that had confounded his protagonist.

Conclusion: From Literary Disillusion to Electronic Revolution

As the preceding study has shown, the path of activist writing in twentieth-century Egypt was marked by extreme highs and lows. From the bold pronouncements of *al-adab al-multazim*'s 'dominance' in the 1950s, to Yusuf Idris's bitter declaration of defeat in the 1980s, activist writing has at times seemed confident in its power to change the world and painfully impotent at others. The digital age, despite the profound changes it has brought to the writer's media, has not resolved this tension between optimism and disappointment. If anything, the rapid pace of the electronic era has brought with it an even more rapid succession of highs and lows. The prominent role of twenty-first-century Egyptian authors in leading thousands on Facebook or blogs during the 2011 revolution seemed to prove the potency of the modern writer as surely as the helpless plea in 2013 of leading writers for the army to restore order spoke to their impotence. Both the highs of *al-adab al-multazim*'s glory days and the lows of disillusion have relevance to the situation of the writer today.

This study, therefore, has focused on the common bonds of those seemingly very different periods. It has argued that over the course of a century, the paradigm of *al-adab al-multazim*, a distinct form of activist writing, has remained central to the work of Egyptian authors, whether at times of confidence or despair. Even the pained expressions of Idris of "the total lack of value of writing . . . all the writing since man learned to write,"[1] did not mark an escape to the detached Author-Observer model of writing. Truly, as much as Idris may have sought such a role to ease his pain, even he rose reluctantly from his deathbed to acknowledge that he was destined to remain an activist author. From the analysis of texts of the most profound authorial disillusion in the preceding chapters, we have seen not an escape to the author-as-observer paradigm but rather a continuous reinterpretation and renegotiating of the activist author's role. Whether in the era of Nasser or the digital age, the central debate for Egypt's public intellectuals has not been a rehash of the battle between aesthetics and engagement, as was the case with Sartre or Baudelaire. Instead, the debate revolves around the relationships of the writer, political authority, and public, no matter how strained or weak those relationships may be.

While the high point of the 2011 revolution bore strong parallels to the zenith of *al-adab al-multazim*, with digital-age authors bringing unvarnished social and political writing to audiences of millions, seemingly unhindered by any interference, the climate in the years that followed better suits a comparison with the years of disillusion after 1952. After all, one can hardly imagine that it was with great joy that Sonallah Ibrahim called for a military intervention. Thus, both the traditional model of *al-adab al-multazim*, and the inversion of that model which has underlain the works of disillusion profiled in this study, will be valuable in understanding the role of the activist author today and in the future. In chapter 2, I offered a detailed look at the model of *al-adab al-multazim* in its purest form. Here, after having considered works of disillusion that invert this model, I would like to offer a summary of the inversion of *al-adab al-multazim*. Having considered the common elements that underlie both paradigms, I will conclude with a brief look at the position of activist writers in current-day Egypt.

An Inversion of *al-Adab al-Multazim*

In their works of the late twentieth century, the three authors in this study have engaged in a dialogue with the numerous satiric voices coming from the caricatures populating their texts. At times, this dialogue has been sympathetic, at times condescending or condemning, at other times humorous and light, while at still other times very painful. Yet the extended dialogue with characters like Samara Bahjat, 'Umar al-Hamzawi, 'Abbas Yunis, Shawqi the doctor, Idris the VCR technician, and all of Ibrahim's nameless protagonists has addressed the problems besetting a once-cherished vision of *iltizam* from many sides, in many different ways. Taken as a whole, this collective dialogue provides an inversion of the established model of *al-adab al-multazim*. This inversion constitutes a negative vision that captures all that has gone wrong with the expectations of committed writing, and which shows by implication what must change for the vision of *iltizam* to become valid again. In the 1940s, the central challenge of the activist writer in motivating the masses was assumed to be public ignorance; if the public could be enlightened to the injustices around it, so the belief ran, that public could be motivated to fix those injustices. In a rather Lukácsian approach, clear, realistic analysis was seen as the key to illuminating the injustices of Egyptian society. By the 1960s, neither the corrupted revolutionary state nor the commercialized public could claim ignorance as an excuse for turning their backs on social justice. The challenge, then, was to shock them back into pursuing the noble course they had abandoned. This challenge called for a more Brechtian approach. The inverted picture of *al-adab al-multazim* was the device for inducing this 'wake-up' call, in the spirit of Brecht's alienation effect.

I return now to the model of *al-adab al-multazim* described in chapter 2 in order to examine how the inverted picture engages it on a point-by-point basis. I offer this model to show how every component of the *al-adab al-multazim* paradigm came in for satire during the period of the 1960s to 1980s, yet remained central to the consciousness of the activist writer even in that period of disillusion.

As in the original model, the inversion of *al-adab al-multazim* features a mutual relationship between the writer, the public, and the state. In this case, however, all three actors in that relationship exhibit characteristics opposed to those demanded by *iltizam*, while their mutual relationships serve to hinder, rather than promote, communication and enlightenment. These negative examples run a wide gamut from the comical to the despicable and the tragic, with grievances and vices as varied. The public can be as rapacious as in "The Aorta," or as uncaring as that in "The Alif in al-Ahrar," or as corrupted by commercialism as in *The Committee* or *The Beggar*. The writer can be as deluded as playwright 'Abbas Yunis, as self-serving as Samara Bahjat, as tired as 'Umar al-Hamzawi, or as terrified as Doctor Shawqi. Lastly, the political power can be a brutal state apparatus like that seen in *Karnak Café* or *The Black Policeman*, a mind-numbing bureaucracy as in "The Alif in al-Ahrar," or a deceitful propaganda machine like in *August Star*.

Furthermore, these three actors often collude to keep meaningful communication out of the public sphere. The story of struggling workers on the Aswan Dam featured in *August Star* remained untold because the state, public, and writers had tacitly agreed to produce and consume flimsy journalism for public diversion instead. Meanwhile, 'Umar al-Hamzawi and his friend Mustafa put their writing talents in the service of state-run industries to placate a commercialistic public and for their own profit. The greedy public of "The Aorta" finished the state's work of neutralizing poor 'Abduh, while tacit police tolerance of the illegal drug habits of the houseboat clique in *Gossip on the Nile* facilitated the pacification of a group of former activists. Countless examples serve as evidence that, far from being innocent victims, these partners worked together to silence a pesky concept like *iltizam*.

Those rare exceptions who tried to defy this unspoken order usually ended in disaster: shot down like Buthayna and 'Uthman, condemned to death like the protagonist of *The Committee*, or selling out their ideals like Samara Bahjat. The misguided playwright 'Abbas Yunis stands as the one character in all these works to believe himself a success as a committed artist, yet who, in a thickly satiric picture, feeds a selfish public with the material to assist in whitewashing the real problems in his little society.

Another of the foundational principles of *al-adab al-multazim* violated in the works of disillusion is the separation of the intra and extratextual realms.

Advocates of *al-adab al-multazim* recognized and devoted great attention to the role of the writer, state, and public in the writing process, yet insisted that the overt stamp of these actors be kept outside the text. The textual space belonged to stories of the working class, told in realist fashion and generally without irony. The works of disillusion, by contrast, place the writer, state, and public, as well as their mutual relations, at the heart of the story. Writer-protagonists feature in a large number of the texts, including three of the four Mahfouz novels examined in detail in chapter 3, three of the Idris stories in chapter 4, and all of Ibrahim's novels in chapter 5. The obstacles they encounter from the public and state in their attempts to write figure prominently in all of those works. When working-class heroes do appear, they are left on the sidelines waiting for writer-protagonists to work out their numerous problems with the state and the public, as seen in Ibrahim's *August Star*. That novel's image of a construction worker offering a struggling writer advice on the world of publishing may be the clearest indication that the paradigm of *al-adab al-multazim* had been turned inside out.

In this inverted picture of *iltizam*, traditional works of *al-adab al-multazim* must be deferred outside the text. For a period in which *al-adab al-multazim* had fallen out of fashion, it is striking how many of these works feature references to *multazim* texts that are kept out of public reach due to the lack of an environment conducive to *iltizam*. *Multazim* writing projects are aborted, like Samara Bahjat's play, Hilmi Hamada's biography, and the thesis on "the Doctor," or are locked away, like 'Umar's poems or Mustafa's plays. In the rare exception where the intended work actually comes to the public—that being 'Abbas Yunis's play—Mahfouz chooses to keep the work unseen by the reading audience and focus instead on the reactions of his fictional writer, public, and power holders.

Considering the sum of the deferred texts, the reading public has been denied a wealth of valuable *multazim* writing in the works of disillusion. Shawqi set out to convince oppressors of the futility of torture, *August Star*'s protagonist had seen inspiring examples of "heroic" workers, and "the Doctor's" life held the secrets for achieving Arab unity in the modern age. Yet in all cases, the dysfunction of the writing relationship was so overwhelming as to ensure these stories would never come to the reading public.

A final, essential component of *al-adab al-multazim*, the elusive 'language of the people,' has disappeared from the works of disillusion, replaced by a heteroglossia of negative mutations, or by a yawning void. The faith in 'the language of the people,' however an author chose to define it, undergirded efforts at committed writing by assuming the capacity for unambiguous communication with the audience. In the works of disillusion, the recurring theme of the inability of writers or the state to communicate with the public takes many forms, but always pervades the text. The protagonist of *The Committee* finds himself unable to communicate with either of his partners in *iltizam*, as society speaks a language of Western commercialism, while the Committee has appropriated the discourse of liberation and recoded it into a language of intimidation, much as Khalid Safwan had done in *Karnak Café*. The protagonist Ahmad Rashwan of "The Alif in al-Ahrar" believed he had discovered a message so powerful that he willingly gave up everything in order to bring it to the public, but it merely struck his audience as the ravings of one on hashish. Pure greed made the crowd in "The Aorta" deaf to the victim's entreaties, and a tired doctor in *August Star* noted that "the only language" Egyptians understood was money.

What does the inversion of *al-adab al-multazim* look like when viewed as a whole? In chapter 2, I offered a schematic model of *al-adab al-multazim* based on the common threads in critical discussions of the 1940s and 1950s. Below, I sketch a similar schematic of the inversion of that model.

The extratextual actors now occupy center stage, while the bonds linking them are broken. Meanwhile, a text—finished or projected—written in the manner of classic *iltizam* remains of interest, but is deferred outside the bounds of the fictional text, awaiting resolution of the problems in the writing process. This inverted vision demonstrates the inadequacy of the model of *al-adab al-multazim* in describing the writing process in Egypt in the latter part of the twentieth century. It negates, inverts, breaks, and turns the old model inside out, yet does not provide a new model for the future. Rather, it calls attention to the fact that all the components for socially committed communication exist, waiting to be put back into their proper relation.

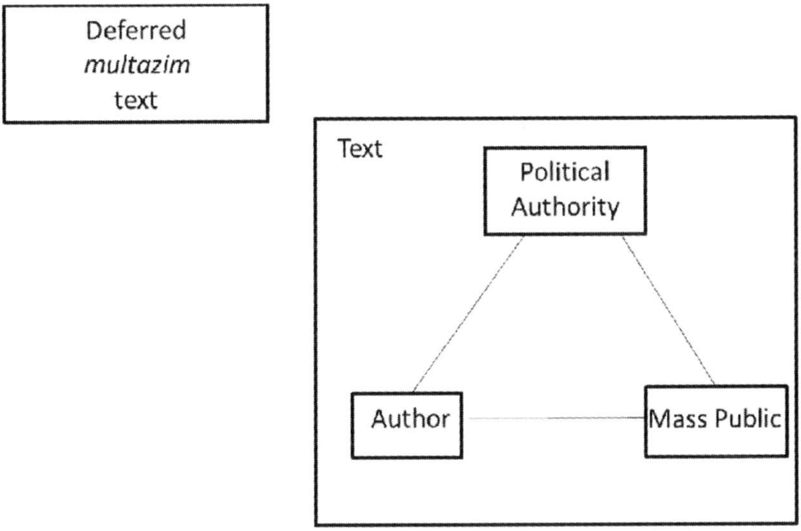

Figure 4: Inverted Model of *al-adab al-multazim*

Activist Writing after *al-Adab al-Multazim*

The inversion of *al-adab al-multazim* that runs through the works of disillusion from the 1960s on remains firmly engaged with the activist model of writing, however bitter that relationship may be. The central roles of writer, public, political authority, and their shared responsibilities in these texts mark not a retreat to the detached author-observer of the Bohemian style but rather a renegotiation of the activist view of writing. Yet the conflicting emotions of this strained relationship between the author and his or her partners created a fair degree of ambiguity about the writer's view of his or her role. How could writers so disillusioned with activist art remain so attached to it? The answer lies in the way in which the ideology of so many fields was being re-envisioned in the late twentieth century.

The latter part of the twentieth century might well be dubbed the 'post' era—witnessing the rise of poststructuralism, postcolonialism, and postmodernism in the post–World War II world. The leading exponent of *al-adab al-hadif* in the 1950s, Mahmud Amin al-'Alim, captured this spirit when he described the close of the century as an era of "what afters?"

(ma ba'diyat?), the Arabic counterpart of the 'post'-terminology, such as "what after socialism?" *(ma ba'd al-ishtirakiya?)*, or "what after colonialism?" *(ma ba'd al-kuluniyaliya?)*. The Arabic idiom carries a much clearer sense of questioning than the more ambiguous English equivalent. Al-'Alim captures this sense in his explanation: "The *ma ba'diya* is a descriptor denying, contradicting, and surpassing what went before it, not merely the chronological successor to the era that preceded it." He goes further to note that it implies "the removal, the death, or end of what went before it."[2]

Postcolonialism relies on colonialism for its meaning and orientation. Similarly, post-*iltizam* writing is in dialogue with *iltizam* but both contradicts and surpasses it. Unlike the assertive declarations of Anwar al-Ma'addawi that *al-adab al-multazim*'s definition was universally understood, ambiguity, disagreement, and polysemy became the advertised hallmarks of any post-*iltizam* view of writing. It is, therefore, no surprise that the writers in this study chose to critique an old model of writing, rather than propose a new one. At the height of *iltizam*'s influence, following established models of writing was a virtue. Mahfouz had proudly announced the model for his magnum opus *The Cairo Trilogy* to be Tolstoy's *War and Peace*, an admission that only enhanced the stature of the work. By the 1980s, however, such imitation was passé. Ibrahim, chronologically the last of the authors in this study, openly confessed that he had considered and rejected adoption of the writing styles of earlier Arab and European authors. After penning his innovative novel *The Committee*, he quickly cautioned a public eager for more of the same that the novel would not mark a "new model" or "new style." Indeed, Ibrahim's further works—like *Dhat*, or *Amrikanli: Amri Kana Li*—bear out the author's refusal to repeat himself.

While a few voices in the waning decades of the twentieth century, like Ahmad Muhammad 'Atiya, were still calling for a return to the old model of *al-adab al-multazim*—with provocative declarations like "Where to, Yusuf Idris?"—leading authors of committed fiction had already moved beyond the old paradigm. By 1979, Halim Barakat, the author of some of the most politically daring works of the time, had relegated the term *multazim* to the ranks of the inadequate and proposed a new type of writer for the contemporary age. A quantitative glimpse at the critical debate over the period in this study speaks clearly to the change in attitude toward models of writing. *Al-Adab*, the avowed flagship journal of *al-adab al-multazim*, served as a leading platform for debate among politically engaged writers. In the first three years of the journal (1953–55), the terms *multazim* and *iltizam* alone appear in the titles of articles eleven times. This is to say nothing of related terms like revolutionary or socialist literature (*al-adab al-thawri* or *al-ishtiraki*), nor the preponderance of these terms in the texts of articles and editorials. The inaugural issue plainly declared that the journal would be dedicated to the mission of *al-adab al-multazim*. In the entire decade of the 1980s, however, there is only one title with any of the terminology of *al-adab al-multazim*, and that is a 1980 reprint of al-Ma'addawi's 1953 article "*al-Adab al-multazim*" in the Sartre memorial issue published upon Sartre's death in 1980. Moreover, that edition of the journal, dedicated to the spiritual father of committed literature—indeed, the man who inspired the term *iltizam*—included only one article dealing with committed literature, that being al-Ma'addawi's piece. The rest of the issue was given over to discussion of existentialism, Sartre's position on Algeria and Israel, and other issues removed from *la littérature engagée*.[3]

Despite the absence of the terminology of *al-adab al-multazim* from the pages of *al-Adab* in the late twentieth century, the journal continued to be filled with discussions germane to the concept of socially engaged writing. One 1981 issue alone contained articles dedicated to "The Arab Intellectual and Democracy,"[4] "The Intellectual and the State,"[5] and even the very pointed, "Position of the Intellectuals and Their Role in Treating the Crisis of Democracy."[6] Socially and politically concerned writing, less the distinctive terminology of *iltizam*, still had substantial reach, even before the advent of electronic media. Activist writing, which had been kept alive through constant re-negotiation and re-imagining even in the darkest years of the latter twentieth century, was about to enjoy a boom in the electronic era. Activist writers had struggled for decades to find safe media to convey their ideas; in the twenty-first century, they would be overwhelmed by a profusion of media that grew and diversified almost daily.

The Activist Writer in the Electronic Age

From the print issues of *al-Adab* with their limited circulation, the rise of electronic media ushered in a dramatic transformation of the scope and impact of the author's communication with the public. The question for the 2010s, quite unlike the 1980s, was not whether socially engaged writers could reach their audience, but rather whether the advent of electronic media had finally solved the problems that had vexed Idris, Ibrahim, and their colleagues. While the prevalence of electronic media, so central to the 2011 revolution, undoubtedly changed the relationship of the writer and the mass public, there was much that technological development could not change. Fiction writers played a very active role in the public dialogue before, during, and after the 2011 revolution, very often on blogs, Facebook, or Twitter. Ibrahim Abdel Meguid, Radwa Ashour, Ezzedine Choukri Fishere, and Khaled al-Berry were among the many names frequently offering comments on the Internet. The state had lost its power to confiscate unfavorable texts, but this alone did not mean that all the writer's challenges were over. The ability of the writer to impact society and the political power through those texts is no more certain in the Internet age than it was in the 1950s.

Ibrahim's protagonist noted in closing *The Committee* that the nature of society and communications was changing, and that the old order, with its state suppression of writing, was about to pass. When the Mubarak era ended, the prophecy appeared fulfilled. Thus, it seems particularly ironic that Ibrahim would emerge as the most prominent of the intellectuals signing a 2013 "urgent plea" for intervention against the Muslim Brotherhood that was widely seen as an invitation for a military takeover. At the time, Elliot Colla opined that "among all the defections, Sonallah Ibrahim's was the most serious, precisely because he is arguably the most politically and aesthetically *autonomous* writer working in Egypt."[7] Perhaps Ibrahim's switch was not so surprising, though. His protagonist in *The Committee* endured endless persecution from the political authority without losing his resolve to fight on; the hostile reaction he received from the public for his noble efforts, however, drove him to his death. Similarly, the ubiquitous political authority fell in 2011, but what emerged from street demonstrations and open elections truly frightened Ibrahim, such that he was soon applauding the military intervention with the assertion that the Egyptian army was the only actor with Egypt's best interests at heart. But Ibrahim was hardly the only intellectual celebrating this step backward. Salwa Bakr, a writer whose works focus on the oppressed and marginalized and who, like Ibrahim, served time in prison for her activism, marched in support of then-Defense Minister Abdel-Fattah al-Sisi and the July 2013 military intervention.[8]

Yet no artist's statement of support for the military action was more of a surprise than that of the writer who had come to seem like the voice of revolution in the Western media: Alaa Al Aswany. Al Aswany, more than any other figure, became the face of the committed writer of the new revolution. American novelist and literary scholar Jay Parini sounded a very familiar tone when he declared Al Aswany "a suitable heir to the mantle worn by Naguib Mahfouz, his great predecessor," noting that Mahfouz's "influence is felt on every page" of Al Aswany's work.[9] Indeed, comparisons between the two seem almost obligatory, as hardly an article published in the Western media on Al Aswany lacks a reference to Mahfouz.

Al Aswany learned his craft from his father, 'Abbas al-Aswany, a writer of Idris's generation who wrote a weekly opposition column in the periodical *Rose al-Yusuf*. He received the State Prize for Literature in 1972, an award Mahfouz won twice. Al Aswany followed a somewhat similar path to writing as Idris, beginning as a dentist working for a large industrial complex. Although his book sales earn him more than enough to live comfortably, he continues his dental practice in order to stay in touch with the people.[10] Al Aswany even credits a meeting with Mahfouz for inspiring his choice of styles.[11] Like Mahfouz, Al Aswany has long organized weekly gatherings of aspiring writers in Cairo cafés, often risking threats by the government. Modern technology, however, gave Al Aswany access to communications media that Idris or Mahfouz never imagined. The great writer Mahfouz, who never tired of meeting people at Cairo street cafés, would have doubtlessly made a superb blogger had he been born into a different generation. Prior to the revolution, Al Aswany and Ibrahim were leading members of the opposition group 'Movement for Change,' better known by the Arabic name *Kefaya* (Enough), which also relied on electronic communication to organize frequent public protests.

The Internet not only increased the size of the writer's audience, however. At a much deeper level, electronic media gave the writer a freedom that his or her predecessors never experienced. Indeed, one of the most profound turning points in the 2011 revolution came in the Mubarak regime's unsuccessful attempt to shut off the Internet on January 26. When the state effectively lost the battle over cyberspace, censorship became moot. Al Aswany always took full advantage of this freedom. His 2002 novel *The Yacoubian Building*, a scathing indictment of the Mubarak regime on multiple fronts, saw publication in large part because suppressing it completely would have proved ineffective. The novel, translated into twenty-one languages, made Al Aswany an international star primarily because of its popularity in the West. The author, educated in the United States, noted that he could have easily relocated to the US and enjoyed a prosperous career there during the Mubarak era.[12] By implication, he would have launched an even more biting and direct campaign of anti-Mubarak writing, both in fiction and nonfiction in America, which would not only have reached an international audience but millions of Egyptians as well. Al Aswany himself noted that his celebrity status protected him: "Before doing something to me, the regime must calculate the repercussions. . . . I don't need them—and they do need me."[13]

The immediacy and currency of electronic media also affected print media. When Al Aswany's collection of essays entitled *On the State of Egypt* was published on the eve of the revolution, he quickly wrote an introduction to the English translation to address the unfolding uprising.[14] In a bit of irony, the new, post-revolution version of the book carried the subtitle "What Made the Revolution Inevitable."[15] A last-minute rush to add mention of something that was "inevitable" spoke to the information-age demand for even historical perspectives to be constantly updated to match the latest events.

Electronic media changed the nature of the author's communication with his or her audience as well. Al-Aswany's blog, very popular since 2004, provides an important link between the world of literature and daily reportage. While Egypt's countless bloggers were an unquestionable driving force in the revolution, one could turn to a literary blogger like Al Aswany for a wider historical and philosophical perspective. 'Abbas al-Aswany reached an audience weekly; his son can now reach millions instantly. The effect goes beyond timeliness. The older al-Aswany was still in a class distinct from his readership—he wrote in a print journal and they were mere consumers. The younger Al Aswany is a participant in the same conversation as his readers, with the only difference between writer and reader being the quality of their ideas and not their access to outlets of communication. Abdel Meguid, for example, posts his email address for all readers to see and al-Berry maintains a very active Facebook page.

Ironically, the commercialism that earlier writers decried had been transformed from a tool of suppression to one of subversion. While Idris talked of becoming a VCR repairman, fixing electronic devices that kept Egyptians distracted from reality, the most sought-after Western technologies of the twenty-first century brought uncensored news as well as cheap entertainment. By 2011, the same young people who watched comedy videos on YouTube also watched video captures of interrogations in Egyptian jails. The same cell phone that could download American pop music could instantly turn into a covert camera to capture police brutality. The government could no longer encourage the infiltration of Western luxury goods to divert the public from political criticism, as the most sought-after consumer goods were virtual portals to the outside world. This dramatic shift was prefigured, to some extent, in Ibrahim's lengthy analysis about the power of the Coca-Cola brand name in *The Committee*, but even "The Doctor" would have been hard pressed to envision Facebook or Google. Breaking down the walls between 'literature' and 'reportage' had reached a level that would have exceeded Salama Musa's dreams. User-posted videos and pictures may technically belong in a different category from the 'art' of Al Aswany's novel, but YouTube videos of torture taken on cell phones were remarkably similar to the descriptions of torture in the novel. Their easy availability on the Internet gave Al Aswany's 'fiction' a greater sense of realism.

In this environment, it is hardly surprising that Al Aswany achieved his greatest success with a literary style hewing closer to the realism of *al-adab al-multazim* than modernist expressionism. In fact, Arabic author Elias Khuri claimed no less than that Al Aswany "reinvented the popular Egyptian novel, which had died."[16] Khuri referred to the fact that

Al Aswany rejected the stylistic experimentation of the gloomy post-1952 period, returning to pure storytelling, a style that Al Aswany calls "easy to read, but very difficult to write."[17] Al Aswany's career-making novel *The Yacoubian Building* stylistically recalls the realism of Mahfouz's earlier days. Depicting a teeming Cairo apartment building hosting a microcosm of all classes of Egyptian society, the novel traces their battles with systemic corruption in a manner not unlike *A Beginning and an End* or *Midaq Alley*. While Al Aswany's stark depiction of subjects like rape, homosexuality, prostitution, and drug use may have pushed the boundaries of the taboo, *Midaq Alley* was no less shocking for its time.

As in the glory days of *al-adab al-multazim*, the modern writer's intra and extratextual expressions worked together to address issues of social justice. Al Aswany's style, by his own admission, is "storytelling," that is, populating a text with realistic narratives of credible Egyptian characters, with little overt social analysis or commentary. His characters, like Mahfouz's, include the sympathetic and the offensive; most often they are three-dimensional human beings who display a mix of those qualities. Their individual struggles take center stage while the systemic injustices of Egyptian society form the background, the structure that facilitates rather than dictates their choices. In his extratextual role, however, Al Aswany prefers to be very direct in making the attributions and conclusions that emerge by implication in his fictional work. In a 2006 interview with the American magazine *National Geographic*, quite typical of the type Al Aswany gives to Western reporters, and conducted at a time when the Mubarak regime seemed firmly entrenched, the author spoke freely about the problems of Egyptian society, openly blaming the government. He attributed the rise of fanaticism to "poor areas, because the poor are desperate." He then leveled responsibility for their conduct directly at the government: "The current regime here is dealing with them in an inhuman way, arresting and torturing them." He further identified the only solution as "Western-style democracy, with a free press and the rule of law, where all people can choose their elected officials," going further to talk about the rights of women and the need for religious tolerance.[18] Just as Mahfouz would name the villain of his novel *A Beginning and an*

End as the unmentioned Prime Minister Sidqi, Al Aswany frequently leveled direct criticism at the Mubarak regime which reinforced the conclusions implied in his fictional stories.

Thus, it was all the more surprising when Al Aswany came out with unabashed approval of the July 2013 military intervention. In an opinion piece in the Lebanese newspaper *al-Safir*, Al Aswany firmly declared the intervention "a completely democratic procedure." He firmly stated that "the army did not carry out a military coup," asserting rather that Defense Minister al-Sisi "had no choice but to implement the rule of the people and save Egypt," ensuring readers that the prospect of the military leader retaining power was strictly "out of the question." Alternately assuring his audience that both the army and the police had new leadership with only the purest of intentions, the homage sounds nothing like the biting commentary that made Al Aswany famous.[19] While praising the virtue of the army, Egyptian writers were quick to indict formerly popular liberals as nefarious conspirators behind Egypt's troubles, with Al Aswany naming US President Barack Obama and Ibrahim accusing Mohamed ElBaradei, the international diplomat and favorite for president in the aftermath of Mubarak's fall. Ibrahim exhorted, "It is not useful to the cause to criticize Sisi now because of the imminent danger the country faces. Now everybody should be with Sisi—not behind him, with him, as I said. The danger is coming from the West, from the USA, from the Muslim Brothers."[20]

Defection of the Artists

Al Aswany's panegyrics aside, the support of liberal artists for the military was a sincere, if reluctant, expression of concern with the direction of post-revolutionary politics. It also marked a grudging acknowledgment of the limits of the change that the electronic era heralded. In the euphoria of what was often dubbed the "Facebook revolution" in the media, it was easy to overlook the fact that it was the Egyptian army that actually deposed President Mubarak. The massive crowds in Tahrir Square created the impression that everyone in Egypt was on social media. In reality, Internet penetration of Egyptian society was less than half, and a mere 16 percent of those over thirteen years of age had access to Facebook.[21]

These are impressive numbers, no doubt, but their limitations became very obvious in the first round of Egypt's post-revolution elections, which produced a runoff between a military general and the Muslim Brotherhood, rather than a liberal blogger. Electronic media provided new means of communication between the writer and the public, but those means had yet to reach most of the public.

Despite Al Aswany's assurances that democracy was running like clockwork, the protesting artists were not naive about the dangers of inviting military control. Yet the painful reality was that they saw the trajectory of the popularly elected government of Muhammad Morsi as a greater danger to freedom. Provoked by the minister of culture's replacement of key officials in the ministry, such as the director of the Cairo Opera House and National Book Organization with Brotherhood allies, they protested the "Brotherhoodization" of culture.[22] Particularly vexing was Article 44 of the new constitution which prohibited "insulting the prophets." Prosecutions for blasphemy increased under the Morsi government, targeted at non-Islamist writers and bloggers. The international organization Freedom House downgraded Egypt from "partly free" to "not free" on its scale of freedom of the press, due to "officially tolerated campaigns to intimidate journalists, increased efforts to prosecute reporters and commentators for insulting the political leadership or defaming religion, and intensified polarization of the pro- and anti-Muslim Brotherhood press."[23]

The authors discussed in this book have perennially been able to accept disappointment with the political authority much easier than with the public. The characters in Mahfouz's *The Beggar*, for example, could brave the threat of prison but not the rejection of the public. The protagonist of *The Committee* stood up to the threat of torture and death from the political authority, but collapsed before a self-absorbed public. Thus, to the artists who had previously decried the military command council, the direct military intervention of 2013, with its attendant curbs on freedom, was a lesser threat than a mass public that could produce only a choice between the "disgrace" of the old regime and the "fire" of the Islamists, in the words of 'Abd al-Halim Qandil.[24] To the artists who formed the Front for Creativity, the Muslim Brotherhood's "fire" represented the greater danger. This was certainly understandable given that the Islamist agenda aimed at a deeper level of cultural transformation than the simple public order of military control. Yet the stark choice between two such alternatives was once again a source of disappointment with the mass public. Truly, much had changed, but there was still more change needed.

Artists were accordingly reframing the public debate away from the idealism of 2011 to deal with the tough choices of 2013 and beyond. Little wonder that they found inspiration in those years of disillusion that had followed 1952. Amid fears that the military action would mark a return to Nasser-style control, Ibrahim responded that "the period of the 1960s is the most glorious period in the modern history of Egypt, in spite of certain things: despotism, military or security control."[25] The "certain things" that once dominated scornful works like *That Smell* and *The Committee* were to be relegated to secondary concerns in the face of a war on terrorism—that is, the Muslim Brotherhood. "The priority now is to stop terrorism! How can you plan for anything, if the trains aren't running, if people are being shot in front of police stations? The main thing now is security. It is to stop terrorism," Ibrahim warned, exhorting Egyptians to defer criticism of the military and security forces. "It is not useful to the cause to criticize Sisi now because of the imminent danger the country faces. Now everybody should be with Sisi." Even police excesses should be forgiven: "The fundamental thing now is, if the police officer who used to insult me and kick me and beat me under Mubarak, if now he is fighting against terrorism, I am with him."[26]

When questioned about writing fiction to address the current situation, Ibrahim deferred: "I have no desire to work seriously. . . . It's not wrong, it's not impossible, to write directly about what's happening. But in my case I need some distance."[27]

Nonetheless, even the strong supporters of the army retained their optimism that the rise of electronic media provided some guarantee against a return to the era of Nasser with its unpleasant "certain things": "When you see everything in chaos," Ibrahim opined, "the first thing that comes to your mind may be: We need a strong man. But this is not practical now any more. Thanks to many things—a growing awareness, the existence of the media."[28] Even Al Aswany's glowing elegy for the military intervention contained some admonitions: "The fact that we are pleased that good relations have been restored between the police and the people does not prevent us from demanding vengeance for the martyrs who were killed by police officers," as did his caveat that the public would support the actions of the army only "when the latter aligns with the will of the people."[29] Artists may have retreated from pure optimism in 2013, but they were not ready for a wholesale embrace of the 1960s again.

Predictions about Egypt's social and political direction in the coming decades are bound to prove as inaccurate as those made in the previous decades. The brief period of the 2010s so far best resembles the meeting of two old clichés: "the only constant is change" and "the more things change, the more they look the same." In a blindingly short period of time, Egypt came under a greater variety of political authorities than in the previous century. The rapid development of communications media promises to continue unabated, far from the control of any national authority. At the same time, the effect that these changes will have on the public can only be imagined. The role of the author is bound to change as communications become increasingly horizontal and immediate.

The central relationship of the writer, public, and political authority will likely remain in play, as it has for over a century. The paradigm of the activist author, tying these three players together, has been inverted, turned inside out, stretched, and re-envisioned throughout periods of optimism and disillusion, but it has always remained essential to the modern author's concept of his or her role in Egypt. As Egyptian writers find echoes of 1952, 1964, or other ups and downs in the history of their nation, both the models of *al-adab al-multazim* and its disillusioned inversion will have their moments of applicability. Whomever the popular media chooses to bestow the 'mantle of Mahfouz' upon at any given moment will have to negotiate specific opportunities and challenges that the late Nobel laureate never encountered. Yet the path of activist writers through the peaks of dominance and valleys of disillusion will continue to offer lessons for future generations.

Notes

Introduction

1 Jay Parini, "Between Two Worlds," *The Guardian*, October 3, 2008.
2 Robyn Creswell, "Sonallah Ibrahim: Egypt's Oracular Novelist," *The New Yorker*, August 20, 2013.
3 Ursula Lindsey, "Et Tu Sonallah?," *The Arabist*, August 25, 2013.
4 Samia Mehrez, *Egyptian Writers between History and Fiction* (Cairo: American University in Cairo Press, 1994), 125.
5 M. Lynx Qualey, "Sonallah Ibrahim: 'The Only Role of the Writer is to Entertain,'" *Arablit*, May 8, 2015.
6 Ursula Lindsey, "A Voice of Dissent Joins the Nationalist Chorus," *Mada Masr*, October 6, 2013.
7 Mehrez, *Egyptian Writers*, 125.

Chapter 1

1 Ra'if Khuri, "al-Adib yaktub li-l-kaffa," *al-Adab* 3.5 (1955): 2–8.
2 Taha Hussein, "al-Adib yaktub li-l-khassa," *al-Adab* 3:5 (1955): 9.
3 Hussein, "al-Adib," 9.
4 Theodor Adorno, "Commitment," Ernst Bloch, et al., *Aesthetics and Politics*, trans. Francis McDonagh (London: Verso, 1980), 188.
5 Hussein, "al-Adib," 9.
6 Mark Twain, "Adventures of Huckleberry Finn," in *Anthology of American Literature II: Realism to the Present*, ed. George McMichael, et al., (New York: MacMillan, 1974), 297.

7 Asit K. Biswas, "Aswan Dam Revisited: The Benefits of a Much-Maligned Dam," *D+C Magazine for Development and Cooperation* (November/December 2002): 25–27.

8 Herman Ermolaev, *Soviet Literary Theories 1917–1934: The Genesis of Soviet Socialist Realism*, University of California Publications in Modern Philology, vol. 69, (Berkeley: University of California Press, 1963), 2-3, 16-17.

9 Lynn Mally, *Culture of the Future: The Proletkult Movement in Revolutionary Russia* (Berkeley: University of California Press, 1990), 52.

10 Mally, *Culture of the Future*, 37–39.

11 Joseph Schull, "The Ideological Origins of 'Stalinism' in Soviet Literature," *Slavic Review* 51.3 (1992): 472–73.

12 Ermolaev, *Soviet Literary Theories*, 11–12, 15–16.

13 Edward J. Brown, *The Proletarian Episode in Russian Literature, 1928–1932* (New York: Columbia University Press, 1953), 10–12.

14 J. A. Cuddon, *A Dictionary of Literary Terms and Literary Theory*, (Oxford: Blackwell, 1990).

15 The best description of the Soviet production novel, as well as Gladkov's role as an exemplar and the criticisms of his accuracy, is given by Katerina Clark in *The Soviet Novel: History as Ritual* (Chicago: University of Chicago, 1981).

16 Ermolaev, *Soviet Literary Theories*, 174–76, 201.

17 Ermolaev, *Soviet Literary Theories*, 36–37.

18 C. Vaughan James, *Soviet Socialist Realism: Origins and Theory* (New York: St. Martin's Press, 1973), 12–14.

19 Ermolaev, *Soviet Literary Theories*, 56–57, 59–60.

20 Ermolaev, *Soviet Literary Theories*, 108–109, 119–20.

21 Edward J. Brown, *Russian Literature Since the Revolution* (Cambridge, MA: Harvard University Press, 1982), 172–74.

22 Katerina Clark, *The Soviet Novel: History as Ritual* (Chicago: University of Chicago, 1981), 46–47, 136–37.

23 Clark, *The Soviet Novel*, 69–70.

24 Schull, "The Ideological Origins of 'Stalinism,'" 483–84.

25 Abram Tertz, (Andrei Sinyavsky), *On Socialist Realism*, trans. George Dennis (New York: Pantheon, 1960), 49–50; David Pike, *German Writers in Soviet Exile, 1933–1945* (Chapel Hill: University of North Carolina Press, 1982), 259–60, 265.

26 Andrei Zhdanov, et al., *Problems of Soviet Literature: Reports and Speeches at the First Soviet Writers' Congress* (New York: International Publishers, 1935), 21–23.

27 Taha Hussein, "Mulahazat," *al-Katib al-Misri* 6.21, (1947): 9–21.
28 Jean-Paul Sartre, *What Is Literature?*, trans. Bernard Frechtman (New York: Harper Colophon, 1965), 17.
29 Sartre, *What Is Literature?*, 142–43.
30 Sartre, *What Is Literature?*, xvii–xviii.
31 Sartre, *What Is Literature?*, 122.
32 Sartre, *What Is Literature?*, 21.
33 Sartre, *What Is Literature?*, 110–11.
34 Sartre, *What Is Literature?*, 115.
35 Sartre, *What Is Literature?*, 119.
36 Sartre, *What Is Literature?*, 109.
37 Sartre, *What Is Literature?*, 77–83, 93–100.
38 Sartre, *What Is Literature?*, 64–67.
39 Sartre, *What Is Literature?*, 116–17.
40 Sartre, *What Is Literature?*, 126–27.
41 Charles Baudelaire, *Paris Spleen*, trans. Louise Varese (New York: New Editions, 1970), 11.
42 Salama Musa, *al-Adab lil-Sha'b* (Cairo: Maktabat al-Anjilu al-Misriyya, 1956), 28–30.
43 Sartre, *What Is Literature?*, 1.
44 Sartre, *What Is Literature?*, 5–6.
45 Sartre, *What Is Literature?*, 10–13.
46 Jean-Paul Sartre, "Orphee Noir," in *Anthologie de la Nouvelle Poesie Negre et Malgache*, ed. Leopold Sedar Senghor (Paris: Presses Universitaires de France, 1969), xii–xv.
47 Sartre, *What Is Literature?*, 250–51.
48 Albert Camus, *Resistance, Rebellion and Death*, trans. Justin O'Brien (New York: Modern Library, 1960), 190.
49 Brian Masters, *Camus: A Study* (London: Heinemann, 1974), 108.
50 György Lukács, *Writer and Critic and Other Essays*, trans. Arthur D. Kahn (New York: Grosset and Dunlap, 1970), 83.
51 Bertolt Brecht, "Popularity and Realism," in *Aesthetics and Politics*, ed. Ernst Bloch, et al., trans. Stuart Hood (London: Verso, 1980), 85.
52 György Lukács, *Realism in Our Time: Literature and the Class Struggle*, trans. John and Necke Mander (New York: Harper & Row, 1971), 76–77.
53 Fielding's *Tom Jones* and Smollett's *The Expedition of Humphrey Clinker* are two of many examples.
54 Lukács, *Writer and Critic*, 75.
55 Lukács, *Realism in Our Time*, 47.

56 Lukács, *Writer and Critic*, 110–11.
57 Lukács, *Realism in Our Time*, 33.
58 Lukács, *Realism in Our Time*, 76.
59 Lukács, *Realism in Our Time*, 79.
60 Pike, *German Writers*, 295.
61 Pike, *German Writers*, 286.
62 Lukács, *Realism in Our Time*, 18, 44–45.
63 Lukács, *Realism in Our Time*, 20–21, 33–34.
64 Bertolt Brecht, *Brecht on Theatre: The Development of an Aesthetic*, ed. and trans. John Willet (New York: Hill and Wang, 1964), 109.
65 Brecht, *Brecht on Theatre*, 91.
66 Brecht, *Brecht on Theatre*, 87, 91.
67 Reinhold Grimm, "Alienation in Context: On the Theory and Practice of Brechtian Theatre," in *A Bertolt Brecht Reference Companion*, ed. Siegfried Mews (Westport, CT: Greenwood, 1997), 38.
68 Brecht, *Brecht on Theatre*, 101.
69 *Zaynab* by Muhammad Husayn Haykal, published in 1913, is most often cited, but even this was a highly romanticized narrative and not the type of realism that Lukács advocated.

Chapter 2

1 Salama Musa, *The Education of Salama Musa*, 126–27, 130–31.
2 Salama Musa, *The Education of Salama Musa*, 126–27.
3 Salama Musa, *The Education of Salama Musa*, 126–27.
4 Mahmud al-Sharqawi, *Salama Musa: al-mufakkir wa-l-insan* (Beirut: Dar al-'Ilm li-l-Millayin, 1965), 154.
5 al-Sharqawi, *Salama Musa*, 156–58, 160–61.
6 Salama Musa, *The Education of Salama Musa*, 231.
7 Salama Musa, *The Education of Salama Musa*, 126–27.
8 Salama Musa, *The Education of Salama Musa*, 240–42
9 Salama Musa, *The Education of Salama Musa*, 141.
10 Salama Musa, *The Education of Salama Musa*, 117.
11 Salama Musa, *The Education of Salama Musa*, 241.
12 Salma Khadra al-Jayyusi, *Trends and Movements in Modern Arabic Poetry*, vol. 2 (Leiden: Brill, 1977), 574–76.
13 Albert Camus, *Resistance, Rebellion and Death*, trans. Justin O'Brien (New York: Modern Library, 1960), 190.
14 M.M. Badawi, "Commitment in Contemporary Arabic Literature," in *Critical Perspectives on Modern Arabic Literature*, ed. Issa J. Boulatta (Washington, DC: Three Continents, 1980), 35.

15 Anwar al-Ma'addawi, "Zawaya wa laqatat," *al-Adab* 3.2 (1955): 9.
16 Taha Hussein, "al-Adab bayn al-itisal wa-l-infisal," *al-Katib al-Misri* 3.11 (1946): 373–88; "Fi-l-Adab al-Faransi: Jan Pul Satra wa-l-sinama," *al-Katib al-Misri* 7.26 (1947): 179–202; "Mulahazat," *al-Katib al-Misri* 6.21 (1947): 9–21.
17 Muhammad Wahbi, "Adabuna al-multazim," *al-Adab* 2.8 (1954): 24.
18 Tawfiq al-Hakim, *Yawmiyat naib fi-l-aryaf* (Cairo: Maktabat al-Adab, 1965).
19 Tawfiq al-Hakim, *'Usfur min al-sharq* (Cairo: Dar al-Ma'arif, 1974).
20 Jayyusi, *Trends and Movements*, 574–75.
21 Badawi, "Commitment in Contemporary Arabic Literature," 29.
22 Suhayl Idris, "Risalat al-Adab," *al-Adab* 1.1 (1953): 1–2.
23 Idris, "Risalat al-Adab," 1.
24 Anwar al-Ma'addawi, "al-Adab al-multazim," *al-Adab* 1.2 (1953): 12–15.
25 al-Ma'addawi, "al-Adab al-multazim," 12–15.
26 Badawi, "Commitment in Contemporary Arabic Literature," 35.
27 Verena Klemm, "Different Notions of Commitment (Iltizam) and Committed Literature (al-adab al-multazim) in the Literary Circles of the Mashriq," *Arabic and Middle Eastern Literatures* 3.1 (2000): 55–57.
28 Mahmud Amin al-'Alim, *al-Thaqafa wa-l-thawra* (Beirut: Dar al-Adab, 1970), 54, 81.
29 Klemm, "Different Notions of Commitment," 54–56.
30 Klemm, "Different Notions of Commitment," 53.
31 Badawi, "Commitment in Contemporary Arabic Literature," 36.
32 I gratefully borrow the concept of a tripartite relationship of the actors in *al-adab al-multazim* from Dr. William Granara of Harvard University, who first suggested this paradigm in his excellent seminar on Modern Arabic Literature. Over the ensuing decade, I have been privileged to work with him in refining and applying this concept to the works discussed in this book.
33 Badawi, "Commitment in Contemporary Arabic Literature," 24.
34 Anwar al-Ma'addawi, "Bidaya wa nihaya li-Naguib Mahfouz," *al-Risala* 19.939 (1951): 757–58.
35 Roland Barthes, *S/Z*, trans. Richard Miller (New York: Hill and Wang, 1974), 4.
36 Naguib Mahfouz, *Amam al-'arsh* (Cairo: Maktabat Misr, n.d.), 192–200.
37 Sonia Dabbous, "Nasser and the Egyptian Press," in *Contemporary Egypt through Egyptian Eyes*, ed. Charles Tripp (London: Routledge, 1993), 100.
38 Dabbous, "Nasser and the Egyptian Press," 100–101.
39 Dabbous, "Nasser and the Egyptian Press," 104–107

40 Dabbous, "Nasser and the Egyptian Press," 100, 110–111.
41 Anthony McDermott, *Egypt from Nasser to Mubarak: A Flawed Revolution* (London: Croom Helm, 1988), 235.
42 Abdul-Nabi Isstaif, "Forging a New Self, Embracing the Other: Modern Arabic Critical Theory and the West—Louis 'Awad," *Arabic and Middle Eastern Literatures* 5.2 (2002): 162.
43 Isstaif, "Forging a New Self," 165–68.
44 al-'Alim, *al-Thaqafa wa-l-thawra*, 71–74.
45 Yusuf Idris, *al-'Usfur wa-l-silk*. See discussion of the presence or absence of literary commitment in the story in Mahmud Amin al-'Alim, "'Alam Yusuf Idris al-qisasi," *Ibda'* 9 (1991): 34–35.
46 Naguib Mahfouz, *al-Liss wa-l-kilab* (Cairo: Maktabat Misr, n.d.). See also the discussion in chapter 3.
47 Kirk Beattie, *Egypt During the Sadat Years* (New York: Palgrave, 2000), 121.
48 Suhayr al-Qalamawi, "al-Adib al-'arabi wa mushkilat al-iltizam," *al-Adab* 20.1 (1972): 4–6.
49 Abdallah Abd al-Da'im, "al-Adib al-'arabi bayn al-hurriya wa-l-iltizam," *al-Adab* 20.2 (1972): 4–5.
50 Halim Barakat, "Arabic Novels and Social Transformation," in *Studies in Modern Arabic Literature*, ed. R.C. Ostle (Warminster, UK: Aris and Phillips LTD, 1975), 128–30, 135–37.
51 Halim Barakat, "al-Katib al-'arabi wa-l-sulta," *Mawaqif* 10 (1970): 36.
52 Barakat, "al-Katib al-'arabi," 31–34.
53 Barakat, "al-Katib al-'arabi," 39–42.
54 Based on a survey of the annual indices of the journal; see the conclusion.

Chapter 3

1 Naguib Mahfouz, *Atahaddathu Ilaykum* (Beirut: Dar al-'Awda, 1977), 45.
2 Mahfouz, *Atahaddathu Ilaykum*, 45.
3 Mahfouz, *Atahaddathu Ilaykum*, 45.
4 Ahmad Muhammad 'Atiya, *Ma'a Naguib Mahfouz* (Damascus: Manshurat Wizarat al-Thaqafa, 1971), 145. The actual publication date of *Hams al-junun* has been long disputed, but Mahfouz himself had given the date of 1938, which 'Atiya cites here. See also Rasheed El-Enany, *Naguib Mahfouz: The Pursuit of Meaning* (London: Routledge, 1993), 196.
5 Menahem Milson, *Naguib Mahfouz: The Novelist–Philosopher of Cairo* (New York: St. Martin's Press, 1998), 32–33.
6 Mahfouz, *Atahaddathu Ilaykum*, 94.
7 Mahfouz, *Atahaddathu Ilaykum*, 48.

8 Milson, *Naguib Mahfouz*, 36, 40.
9 Mahfouz, *Atahaddathu Ilaykum*, 94–95.
10 The term "alley" as used here refers to a small, residential side street of the old section of Cairo, rather than an area used for trash disposal as in US culture.
11 Anwar al-Ma'addawi, "Bidaya wa nihaya li-Naguib Mahfouz," *al-Risala* 19.939 (1951): 757.
12 Milson, *Naguib Mahfouz*, 40.
13 Roger Allen, *Modern Arabic Literature* (New York: Ungar, 1987), 193.
14 al-Ma'addawi, "Bidaya wa nihaya," 757.
15 Mahmud Amin al-'Alim, *Ta'ammulat fi 'alam Naguib Mahfouz* (Cairo: al-Hay'a al-Misriya al-'Amma li-l-Ta'lif wa-l-Nashr, 1970), 46–48, 50–52, 56.
16 Naguib Mahfouz, *Bidaya wa Nihaya*, 14th edition (Cairo: Maktabat Misr, 1984), 30.
17 Mahfouz, *Bidaya wa Nihaya*, 26.
18 Mahfouz, *Bidaya wa Nihaya*, 23–24.
19 Mahfouz, *Bidaya wa Nihaya*, 289.
20 Mahfouz, *Bidaya wa Nihaya*, 288.
21 Mahfouz, *Bidaya wa Nihaya*, 180.
22 Mahfouz, *Bidaya wa Nihaya*, 183.
23 Mahfouz, *Bidaya wa Nihaya*, 189.
24 Mahfouz, *Bidaya wa Nihaya*, 164.
25 Mahfouz, *Bidaya wa Nihaya*, 183.
26 Mahfouz, *Bidaya wa Nihaya*, 287.
27 Mahfouz, *Bidaya wa Nihaya*, 310.
28 Mahfouz, *Bidaya wa Nihaya*, 289.
29 Mahfouz, *Bidaya wa Nihaya*, 338.
30 al-'Alim, *Ta'ammulat*, 55.
31 Mahfouz, *Atahaddathu Ilaykum*, 153.
32 Mahfouz, *Bidaya wa Nihaya*, 182.
33 Mahmud 'Abd al-Zahir, "al-Nihaya fi 'bidaya wa nihaya'," *al-Adab* 8.11 (1960): 45–47.
34 Mahfouz, *Bidaya wa Nihaya*, 28–29.
35 Matti Moosa, *The Early Novels of Naguib Mahfouz: Images of Modern Egypt* (Gainesville: University Press of Florida, 1984), 6.
36 'Abd al-Zahir, "al-Nihaya," 45.
37 'Abd al-Zahir, "al-Nihaya," 47.
38 al-'Alim, *Ta'ammulat*, 47, 51, 55.
39 al-Ma'addawi, "Bidaya wa nihaya," 757–59.

40 Milson, *Naguib Mahfouz*, 43.
41 Mahfouz, *Atahaddathu Ilaykum*, 98–99.
42 Milson, *Naguib Mahfouz*, 154–55.
43 Stefan G. Meyer, *The Experimental Arabic Novel: Postcolonial Literary Modernism in the Levant* (Albany: State University of New York, 2001), 21.
44 Mahfouz, *Bidaya wa Nihaya*, 3.
45 Mahfouz, *Bidaya wa Nihaya*, 4–5.
46 Mahfouz, *Bidaya wa Nihaya*, 201.
47 Naguib Mahfouz, *al-Liss wa-l-kilab* (Cairo: Maktabat Misr, n.d.), 7–8.
48 Mahfouz, *al-Liss wa-l-kilab*, 9.
49 Mahfouz, *al-Liss wa-l-kilab*, 12–13.
50 Mahfouz, *Bidaya wa Nihaya*, 144–45.
51 Mahfouz, *Bidaya wa Nihaya*, 144–45.
52 Mahfouz, *al-Liss wa-l-kilab*, 59.
53 Mahfouz, *al-Liss wa-l-kilab*, 60–61.
54 Mahfouz, *al-Liss wa-l-kilab*, 69.
55 ʻAtiya, *Maʻa Naguib Mahfouz*, 7.
56 ʻAtiya, *Maʻa Naguib Mahfouz*, 55.
57 Naguib Mahfouz, *al-Shahhadh* (Cairo: Maktabat Misr, 1982), 13.
58 Anwar al-Maʻaddawi, "Zawaya wa laqatat," *al-Adab* 3.2 (1955): 9.
59 Mahfouz, *al-Shahhadh*, 136
60 Mahfouz, *al-Shahhadh*, 9
61 Mahfouz, *al-Shahhadh*, 39
62 Mahfouz, *al-Shahhadh*, 42
63 Mahfouz, *al-Shahhadh*, 20.
64 Mahfouz, *al-Shahhadh*, 40.
65 ʻAtiya, *Maʻa Naguib Mahfouz*, 54–55.
66 Mahfouz, *al-Shahhadh*, 148.
67 Mahfouz, *al-Shahhadh*, 148.
68 Mahfouz, *al-Shahhadh*, 40.
69 Mahfouz, *al-Shahhadh*, 173.
70 Naguib Mahfouz, *Tharthara fawq al-Nil* (Cairo: Maktabat Misr, n.d.), 84.
71 Mahfouz, *Tharthara fawq al-Nil*, 59.
72 Mahfouz, *Tharthara fawq al-Nil*, 77–78.
73 Mahfouz, *Tharthara fawq al-Nil*, 60.
74 Mahfouz, *Tharthara fawq al-Nil*, 124.
75 Mahfouz, *Tharthara fawq al-Nil*, 108.
76 ʻAtiya, *Maʻa Naguib Mahfouz*, 137.
77 Mahfouz, *Tharthara fawq al-Nil*, 160.
78 Mahfouz, *Tharthara fawq al-Nil*, 180.

79 Mahfouz, *Tharthara fawq al-Nil*, 116.
80 Mahfouz, *Tharthara fawq al-Nil*, 113–114.
81 Mahfouz, *Tharthara fawq al-Nil*, 145.
82 Mahfouz, *Tharthara fawq al-Nil*, 53.
83 Mahfouz, *Tharthara fawq al-Nil*, 76.
84 Mahfouz, *Tharthara fawq al-Nil*, 112–113.
85 Mahfouz, *Tharthara fawq al-Nil*, 113.
86 Mahfouz, *Tharthara fawq al-Nil*, 114.
87 Mahfouz, *Tharthara fawq al-Nil*, 129.
88 Mahfouz, *Tharthara fawq al-Nil*, 129.
89 ʻAtiya, *Maʻa Naguib Mahfouz*, 139.
90 Allen, *Modern Arabic Literature*, 203.
91 Naguib Mahfouz, *al-Karnak* (Cairo: Maktabat Misr, 1986), 24.
92 Mahfouz, *al-Karnak*, 11.
93 Mahfouz, *al-Karnak*, 11.
94 Mahfouz, *al-Karnak*, 48.
95 Mahfouz, *al-Karnak*, 66.
96 Mahfouz, *al-Karnak*, 59–60.
97 Milson, *Naguib Mahfouz*, 242–43.
98 Mahfouz, *al-Karnak*, 16.
99 Mahfouz, *al-Karnak*, 16–17.
100 Mahfouz, *al-Karnak*, 34.
101 Mahfouz, *al-Karnak*, 107.
102 Mahfouz, *al-Karnak*, 111.
103 El-Enany, *Naguib Mahfouz*, 118–19.
104 El-Enany, *Naguib Mahfouz*, 116.
105 Naguib Mahfouz, *Afrah al-qubba* (Cairo: Maktabat Misr, 1987), 6.
106 Mahfouz, *Afrah al-qubba*, 75.
107 Mahfouz, *Afrah al-qubba*, 146.
108 Mahfouz, *Afrah al-qubba*, 163.
109 Mahfouz, *Afrah al-qubba*, 135–36.
110 Mahfouz, *Afrah al-qubba*, 26–27.
111 Mahfouz, *Afrah al-qubba*, 7.
112 Mahfouz, *Afrah al-qubba*, 18.
113 Mahfouz, *Afrah al-qubba*, 9.

Chapter 4

1 Rajaa' al-Naqash, *Fi hubb Naguib Mahfouz* (Cairo: Dar El Shorouk, 2006), 41.
2 P.M. Kurpershoek, *The Short Stories of Yusuf Idris: A Modern Egyptian Author* (Leiden: Brill, 1981), 55.

3 'Abd al-Rahman Abu 'Auf, *Yusuf Idris wa 'alimuhu fi-l-qissa al-qasira wa-l-riwaya* (Cairo: Maktabat al-Usra, 2001), 264.
4 Kurpershoek, *The Short Stories of Yusuf Idris*, 51–52.
5 Mahmud Amin al-'Alim, "'Alam Yusuf Idris al-qisasi," *Ibda'* 9 (1991): 32.
6 al-'Alim, "'Alam Yusuf Idris," 37, 39.
7 al-'Alim, "'Alam Yusuf Idris," 36.
8 Ahmad Muhammad Atiya, *al-Iltizam wa-l-thawra fi-l-adab al-'arabi al-hadith* (Beirut: Dar al-'Awda, 1974), 119.
9 Sabry Hafez, "The Egyptian Novel in the Sixties," *Journal of Arabic Literature* VII (1976): 70.
10 Yusuf Idris, "Mishwar," in *Arkhas layali* by Yusuf Idris (Cairo: Dar al-Katib al-'Arabi li-l-Tiba'a wa-l-Nashr, 1967), 160
11 Idris, "Mishwar," 161.
12 Idris, "Mishwar," 170, 173–74.
13 Idris, "Mishwar," 170.
14 Idris, "Mishwar," 175.
15 Idris, "Mishwar," 175.
16 Abu 'Auf, *Yusuf Idris*, 194.
17 Ahmad Muhammad 'Atiya, *Ma'a Naguib Mahfouz* (Damascus: Manshurat Wizarat al-Thaqafa, 1971), 145.
18 Tawfiq Hanna, Review of *Jumhuriyat Farahat*, *al-Adab* 4.3 (1956): 40
19 al-'Alim, "'Alam Yusuf Idris," 40.
20 Idris, "Jumhuriyat Farahat," in *Jumhuriyat Farahat*, by Yusuf Idris, (Cairo: Maktabat Misr, 1981), 28–29.
21 Hanna, *Jumhuriyat Farahat*, 40.
22 Muhammad Fawzi al-'Antil, Review of *Arkhas Layali*, *al-Adab* 2.12 (1954): 34–35.
23 Yusuf Idris, "Al-Shaykh Shaykha," in *al-Mu'allafat al-kamila* by Yusuf Idris (Cairo: 'Alam al-Kutub, 1971), 390–91.
24 Idris, "Mishwar," 160.
25 Ahmad Muhammad 'Atiya, "Yusuf Idris . . . ila ayna?" *al-Adab* 19.5 (1971): 53–56.
26 Roger Allen, *Modern Arabic Literature* (New York: Ungar, 1987), 155.
27 Allen, *Modern Arabic Literature*, 155.
28 Mahmud Amin al-'Alim, *al-Thaqafa wa-l-thawra* (Beirut: Dar al-Adab, 1970), 80–81.
29 Yusuf Idris, "Alif al-ahrar," in *al-Mu'allafat al-kamila*, by Yusuf Idris, vol. I (Cairo: 'Alam al-Kutub, 1971), 409.
30 Idris, "Alif al-ahrar," 408–409.
31 Idris, "Alif al-ahrar," 409.

32 Idris, "Alif al-ahrar," 407–408.
33 Idris, "Alif al-ahrar," 410.
34 Idris, "Alif al-ahrar," 420.
35 Idris, "Alif al-ahrar," 420.
36 Idris, "Alif al-ahrar," 427–28.
37 Idris, "Alif al-ahrar," 414–15.
38 Idris, "Alif al-ahrar," 415–16.
39 Idris, "Alif al-ahrar," 414–15.
40 Idris, "Alif al-ahrar," 430.
41 Idris, "Alif al-ahrar," 430–31.
42 Idris, "Alif al-ahrar," 431.
43 Dayla Cohen-Mor, *Yusuf Idris: Changing Visions* (Potomac, MD: Sheba, 1992), 116.
44 Abu 'Auf, *Yusuf Idris*, 252.
45 Albert Camus, *Resistance, Rebellion and Death*, trans. Justin O'Brien (New York: Modern Library, 1960), 204.
46 Yusuf Idris, *al-'Askari al-aswad* (Cairo: Maktabat Misr, 1982), 11.
47 Idris, *al-'Askari al-aswad*, 13.
48 Idris, *al-'Askari al-aswad*, 11.
49 Idris, *al-'Askari al-aswad*, 13.
50 Idris, *al-'Askari al-aswad*, 14.
51 Idris, *al-'Askari al-aswad*, 5.
52 Idris, *al-'Askari al-aswad*, 18.
53 Idris, *al-'Askari al-aswad*, 20.
54 Idris, *al-'Askari al-aswad*, 37.
55 Idris, *al-'Askari al-aswad*, 5.
56 Idris, *al-'Askari al-aswad*, 6.
57 Idris, *al-'Askari al-aswad*, 35.
58 Kurpershoek, *The Short Stories of Yusuf Idris*, 53.
59 Idris, *al-'Askari al-aswad*, 10.
60 Idris, *al-'Askari al-aswad*, 11.
61 Idris, *al-'Askari al-aswad*, 11.
62 Idris, *al-'Askari al-aswad*, 17.
63 Idris, *al-'Askari al-aswad*, 18.
64 Idris, *al-'Askari al-aswad*, 34–35.
65 Idris, *al-'Askari al-aswad*, 50.
66 Idris, *al-'Askari al-aswad*, 47.
67 Idris, *al-'Askari al-aswad*, 28.
68 Idris, *al-'Askari al-aswad*, 42–43.
69 Idris, *al-'Askari al-aswad*, 78.

70 Idris, *al-'Askari al-aswad*, 76–77.
71 Idris, *al-'Askari al-aswad*, 86.
72 Idris, *al-'Askari al-aswad*, 86.
73 Idris, *al-'Askari al-aswad*, 86.
74 al-'Alim, "'Alam Yusuf Idris," 32.
75 Yusuf Idris, "al-Aurta," in *Lughat al-ay ay* (Cairo: Mu'assat Rose al-Yusuf, 1965), 127.
76 Idris, "al-Aurta," 127–28.
77 Idris, "al-Aurta," 127.
78 Idris, "al-Aurta," 129.
79 Idris, "al-Aurta," 132–33.
80 Idris, "al-Aurta," 130.
81 Yusuf Idris, "al-Martaba al-Muq'ara," in *al-Naddaha* by Yusuf Idris (Cairo: Dar al-Hilal, 1969), 70–71.
82 Idris, "al-Martaba al-Muq'ara," 71.
83 Idris, "al-Martaba al-Muq'ara," 71.
84 'Atiya, *al-Iltizam wa-l-thawra*, 135.
85 Yusuf Idris, "Yamut al-zammar," in *Uqtulha* by Yusuf Idris (Cairo: Maktabat Misr, 1982), 19.
86 Idris, "Yamut al-zammar," 22.
87 Idris, "Yamut al-zammar," 20.
88 Idris, "Yamut al-zammar," 21.
89 Idris, "Yamut al-zammar," 20.
90 Idris, "Yamut al-zammar," 29.
91 Idris, "Yamut al-zammar," 24–25.
92 Idris, "Yamut al-zammar," 24.
93 Idris, "Yamut al-zammar," 33.
94 Idris, "Yamut al-zammar," 43.
95 Idris, "Yamut al-zammar," 50.
96 Quoted in Allen, "Introduction," in Yusuf Idris's *In the Eye of the Beholder: Tales of Egyptian Life from the Writings of Yusuf Idris*, ed. Roger Allen (Minneapolis: Bibliotheca Islamica, 1978): xxxv–xxxvi.

Chapter 5

1 Yusuf Idris, "Laysat mujarrad qissa," introduction to *Tilka al-ra'iha* by Sonallah Ibrahim (al-Minya, Egypt: Dar al-Huda li-l-Nashr wa-l-Tawzi', 2003), 25, 28.
2 Idris, "Laysat mujarrad qissa," 27.
3 Abdalla F. Hassan, "Black Humor in Dark Times," *World Press Review*, June 19, 2003.

4 Sonallah Ibrahim, "Tajribati al-riwa'iya," *al-Adab* 28.2–3 (1980): 101.
5 Ibrahim, "Tajribati al-riwa'iya," 100–101.
6 Ibrahim, "Tajribati al-riwa'iya," 100–101.
7 Hassan, "Black Humor."
8 Charles P. Freund, "Sonallah Ibrahim's Nostalgia for Failure," *The Daily Star Online*, November 20, 2003.
9 *Egypt Independent*, "Q&A with Sonallah Ibrahim," August 27, 2011.
10 Freund, "Sonallah Ibrahim's Nostalgia."
11 Mahmud Amin al-'Alim, *Thulathiyat al-rafd wa-l-hazima* (Cairo: Dar al-Mustaqbal al-'Arabi, 1985), 30, 63–65.
12 Marina Stagh, *The Limits of Freedom of Speech: Prose Literature and Prose Writers in Egypt under Nasser and Sadat* (Stockholm: Almqvist & Wiksell, 1993), 184–86, 210.
13 Ibrahim, "Tajribati al-riwa'iya," 101.
14 Ibrahim, "Tajribati al-riwa'iya," 101.
15 Sonallah Ibrahim, *Tilka al-ra'iha* (al-Minya, Egypt: Dar al-Huda li-l-Nashr wa-l-Tawzi', 2003), 29.
16 Ibrahim, *Tilka al-ra'iha*, 29.
17 Roman Jakobson, *On Language*, ed. Linda R. Waugh and Monique Monville-Burston (Cambridge, MA: Harvard University, 1990), 71–74.
18 Ibrahim, *Tilka al-ra'iha*, 30.
19 Ibrahim, *Tilka al-ra'iha*, 44.
20 Ibrahim, *Tilka al-ra'iha*, 44.
21 Ibrahim, *Tilka al-ra'iha*, 58.
22 Ibrahim, *Tilka al-ra'iha*, 46.
23 Ibrahim, *Tilka al-ra'iha*, 52.
24 Ibrahim, *Tilka al-ra'iha*, 52.
25 Ibrahim, *Tilka al-ra'iha*, 47.
26 Ibrahim, *Tilka al-ra'iha*, 48.
27 Idris, "Laysat mujarrad qissa," 27.
28 Stagh, *The Limits of Freedom of Speech*, 185
29 al-'Alim, *Thulathiyat*, 31–35.
30 Stagh, *The Limits of Freedom of Speech*, 210.
31 Hassan, "Black Humor."
32 Ibrahim, "Tajribati al-riwa'iya," 101–102.
33 Ibrahim, "Tajribati al-riwa'iya," 101–102.
34 The statement is attributed to Muhammad Haykal; see Asit K. Biswas, "Aswan Dam Revisited: The Benefits of a Much-Maligned Dam," *D+C Development and Cooperation* No. 6 (November/December 2002): 25–27.

35 Ceza Kassem Draz, "Opaque and Transparent Discourse in Sonallah Ibrahim's Works," in *The View from Within: Writers and Critics on Contemporary Arabic Literature*, eds. Ferial J. Ghazoul and Barbara Harlow (Cairo: The American University in Cairo Press, 1994), 137.

36 Ibrahim, "Tajribati al-riwa'iya," 101.

37 Draz, "Opaque and Transparent Discourse," 137.

38 Draz, "Opaque and Transparent Discourse," 136–39.

39 al-'Alim, *Thulathiyat*, 136–37.

40 Sonallah Ibrahim, *Najmat Aghustus* (al-Minya, Egypt: Dar al-Huda li-l-Nashr wa-l-Tawzi', 2003), 237.

41 Ibrahim, *Najmat Aghustus*, 237.

42 Ibrahim, *Najmat Aghustus*, 256.

43 Ibrahim, *Najmat Aghustus*, 132.

44 Ibrahim, *Najmat Aghustus*, 131

45 al-'Alim, *Thulathiyat*, 136.

46 al-'Alim, *Thulathiyat*, 126.

47 al-'Alim, *Thulathiyat*, 126, 136–37.

48 al-'Alim, *Thulathiyat*, 141.

49 The first chapter of *The Committee* was published before the rest of the novel.

50 Ibrahim, "Tajribati al-riwa'iya," 103.

51 al-'Alim, *Thulathiyat*, 147; Roger Allen, "Afterword," in *The Committee* by Sonallah Ibrahim, trans. Mary St. Germain and Charlene Constable (Syracuse: Syracuse University Press, 2001), 160.

52 al-'Alim, *Thulathiyat*, 147–48, 176.

53 Sonallah Ibrahim, *al-Lajna* (Cairo: Dar al-Mustaqbal al-'Arabi, 2004), 120.

54 Ibrahim, *al-Lajna*, 89.

55 Ibrahim, *al-Lajna*, 15.

56 Ibrahim, *al-Lajna*, 102.

57 Ibrahim, *al-Lajna*, 120.

58 Ibrahim, *al-Lajna*, 11.

59 Ibrahim, *al-Lajna*, 48–49.

60 Ibrahim, *al-Lajna*, 7.

61 Ibrahim, *al-Lajna*, 30.

62 Ibrahim, *al-Lajna*, 32.

63 Ibrahim, *al-Lajna*, 35.

64 Ibrahim, *al-Lajna*, 57.

65 Ibrahim, *al-Lajna*, 105.

66 Ibrahim, *al-Lajna*, 107.

67 Ibrahim, *al-Lajna*, 110.

68 Ibrahim, *al-Lajna*, 113.
69 Ibrahim, *al-Lajna*, 115.
70 Ibrahim, *al-Lajna*, 116.
71 Ibrahim, *al-Lajna*, 117.
72 Ibrahim, *al-Lajna*, 119.

Conclusion

1 Yusuf Idris, "Yamut al-zammar," in *Uqtulha* by Yusuf Idris (Cairo: Maktabat Misr, 1982), 20.
2 Mahmud Amin al-'Alim, *Min naqd al-hadir ila ibda' al-mustaqbal: musahama fi bina' al-mashru' al-nahdawi al-'Arabi* (Cairo: Dar al-Mustaqbal al-'Arabi, 2000), 32.
3 Anwar al-Ma'addawi, "al-Adab al-multazim," *al-Adab* 28.4–5 (1980): 41-44; *al-Adab*, "Ghiyab Sartre," 28.4–5 (1980).
4 Antun al-Muqdisi, "al-Muthaqaf al-'arabi wa-l-dimuqratiya," *al-Adab* 29.11–12 (1981): 12–29.
5 Muhammad Sabila, "al-Muthaqaf wa-l-Sulta," *al-Adab* 29.11–12 (1981): 29–34.
6 'Amr BinSalim, "Mawqa' al-muthaqafin wa-dawruhum fi mu'alajat azmat al-dimuqratiya fi-l-watan al-'arabi," *al-Adab* 29.11–12 (1981): 35–41.
7 Elliot Colla, "Revolution on Ice," *Jadaliyya*, January 6, 2014.
8 *Ahram Online*, "Culture Minister Leads Artist Pro-Army March to Tahrir," July 27, 2013.
9 Jay Parini, "Between Two Worlds," *The Guardian*, October 3, 2008.
10 Karen Kostyal, "Alaa Al Aswany: Voice of Reason," *National Geographic*, September 2006.
11 Maya Jaggi, "Cairo Calling," *The Guardian*, August 22, 2008.
12 Jaggi, "Cairo Calling."
13 Kostyal, "Alaa Al Aswany."
14 Wendell Steavenson, "Writing the Revolution," *The New Yorker* 87.44 (2012): 38–45.
15 Alaa Al Aswany, *On the State of Egypt: What Made the Revolution Inevitable*, trans. Jonathan Wright (New York: Vintage, 2011).
16 Jaggi, "Cairo Calling."
17 Jaggi, "Cairo Calling."
18 Kostyal, "Alaa Al Aswany."
19 Alaa Al Aswany, "Morsi's Ouster a Triumph for Democracy," trans. Tyler Huffman, *al-Monitor*, July 10, 2013
20 Ursula Lindsey, "A Voice of Dissent Joins the Nationalist Chorus," *Mada Masr*, October 6, 2013.

21 *The Economist*, "Arab Media: A Guttering Flame," February 14, 2015.
22 Maha al-Nabawi, "Inside the Culture Ministry," *Mada Masr*, June 29, 2013.
23 Freedom House, "Freedom of the Press: Egypt, 2013," n.d.
24 al-Aswany, "Morsi's Ouster."
25 Lindsey, "A Voice of Dissent."
26 Lindsey, "A Voice of Dissent."
27 Lindsey, "A Voice of Dissent."
28 Lindsey, "A Voice of Dissent."
29 al-Aswany, "Morsi's Ouster."

Bibliography

'Abd al-Da'im, 'Abdallah. "al-Adib al-'Arabi bayn al-hurriya wa-l-iltizam." *al-Adab* 20.2 (1972).

'Abd al-Zahir, Mahmud. "al-Nihaya fi 'bidaya wa nihaya'." *al-Adab* 8.11 (1960): 43–47.

Abu 'Auf, 'Abd al-Rahman. *Yusuf Idris wa 'alimuhu fi-l-qissa al-qasira wa-l-riwaya*. Cairo: Maktabat al-Usra, 2001.

al-Adab. "Ghiyab Sartre." 28.4–5 (1980).

Adorno, Theodor. "Commitment." Bloch, Ernst, et al. *Aesthetics and Politics*. Translated by Francis McDonagh. London: Verso, 1980.

Ahram Online. "Culture Minister Leads Artist Pro-Army March to Tahrir." July 27, 2013.

———. "General Prosecutor Investigates 31 Artists for Culture Ministry Occupation." June 12, 2013.

al-'Alim, Mahmud Amin. "'Alam Yusuf Idris al-qissasi." *Ibda'* 9 (1991): 32–44.

———. *al-Thaqafa wa-l-thawra*. Beirut: Dar al-Adab, 1970.

———. *Min naqd al-hadir ila ibda' al-mustaqbal: musahama fi bina' al-mashru' al-nahdawi al-'Arabi*. Cairo: Dar al-Mustaqbal al-'Arabi, 2000.

———. *Ta'ammulat fi 'alam Naguib Mahfouz*. Cairo: al-Hay'a al-Misriya al-'Amma li-l-Ta'lif wa-l-Nashr, 1970.

———. *Thulathiyat al-rafd wa-l-hazima*. Cairo: Dar al-Mustaqbal al-'Arabi, 1985.

Allen, Roger. "Afterword." Sonallah Ibrahim. *The Committee*. Translated by Mary St. Germain and Charlene Constable. Syracuse: Syracuse University Press, 2001.

———. *Modern Arabic Literature*. New York: Ungar, 1987.

al-'Antil, Muhammad Fawzi. Review of *Arkhas Layali. al-Adab* 2.12 (1954): 34–35.

Al Aswany, Alaa. "Morsi's Ouster a Triumph for Democracy." Translated by Tyler Huffman. *Al-Monitor*. July 10, 2013.

———. "Mulahazhat sariha 'ala mashad ra'i'." *al-Safir*. July 9, 2013.

———. *On the State of Egypt: What Made the Revolution Inevitable*. Translated by Jonathan Wright. New York: Vintage, 2011.

'Atiya, Ahmad Muhammad. *al-Iltizam wa-l-thawra fi-l-adab al-'arabi al-hadith*. Beirut: Dar al-'Awda, 1974.

———. *Ma'a Naguib Mahfouz*. Damascus: Manshurat Wizarat al-Thaqafa, 1971.

———. "Yusuf Idris . . . ila ayna?" *al-Adab* 19.5 (1971): 53–56.

Badawi, M.M. "Commitment in Contemporary Arabic Literature." In *Critical Perspectives on Modern Arabic Literature*, edited by Issa J. Boulatta, 23–44. Washington, DC: Three Continents, 1980.

Barakat, Halim. "al-Katib al-'arabi wa-l-sulta." *Mawaqif* 10 (1970).

———. "Arabic Novels and Social Transformation." In *Studies in Modern Arabic Literature*, edited by R.C. Ostle, 126–37. Warminster, UK: Aris and Phillips LTD, 1975.

Barthes, Roland. *S/Z*. Translated by Richard Miller. New York: Hill and Wang, 1974.

Baudelaire, Charles. *Paris Spleen*. Translated by Louise Varese. New York: New Editions, 1970.

Beattie, Kirk. *Egypt During the Sadat Years*. New York: Palgrave, 2000.

BinSalim, 'Amr. "Mawqa' al-muthaqafin wa-dawruhum fi mu'alajat azmat al-dimuqratiya fi-l-watan al-'Arabi." *al-Adab* 29.11–12 (1981): 35–41.

Biswas, Asit K. "Aswan Dam Revisited: The Benefits of a Much-Maligned Dam." D+C Magazine for Development and Cooperation. November/December (2002): 25-27.

Brecht, Bertolt. "A Little Organum for the Theatre." Translated by Beatrice Gottleib. *Accent* XI.1 (1951): 13–40.

———. *Brecht on Theatre: The Development of an Aesthetic*. Edited and translated by John Willet. New York: Hill and Wang, 1964.

———. "Popularity and Realism." In *Aesthetics and Politics*, edited by Ernst Bloch, et al., translated by Stuart Hood, 68–86. London: Verso, 1980.

Brée, Germaine. *Camus and Sartre: Crisis and Commitment*. New York: Delacorte Press, 1972.

Brown, Edward J. *Russian Literature Since the Revolution*. Cambridge, MA: Harvard University Press, 1982.

———. *The Proletarian Episode in Russian Literature, 1928–1932*. New York: Columbia University Press, 1953.

Camus, Albert. *Resistance, Rebellion and Death*. Translated by Justin O'Brien. New York: Modern Library, 1960.

Carbone, Nick. "Top 10 Everything of 2012." *Time*. December 4, 2012.

Clark, Katerina. *The Soviet Novel: History as Ritual*. Chicago: University of Chicago, 1981.

Cohen-Mor, Dalya. *Yusuf Idris: Changing Visions*. Potomac, MD: Sheba, 1992.

Colla, Elliot. "Revolution on Ice." *Jadaliyya*. January 6, 2014.

Creswell, Robyn. "Sonallah Ibrahim: Egypt's Oracular Novelist." *The New Yorker*. August 20, 2013.

Cuddon, J. A. *A Dictionary of Literary Terms and Literary Theory*. Oxford: Blackwell, 1998.

Dabbous, Sonia. "Nasser and the Egyptian Press." In *Contemporary Egypt through Egyptian Eyes*, edited by Charles Tripp, 100–121. London: Routledge, 1993.

Draz, Ceza Kassem. "Opaque and Transparent Discourse in Sonallah Ibrahim's Works." In *The View from Within: Writers and Critics on Contemporary Arabic Literature*, edited by Ferial J. Ghazoul and Barbara Harlow, 134–48. Cairo: The American University in Cairo Press, 1994.

The Economist. "Arab Media: A Guttering Flame." February 14, 2015.

Egypt Independent. "Q&A with Sonallah Ibrahim." August 27, 2011.

El-Enany, Rasheed. *Naguib Mahfouz: The Pursuit of Meaning*. London: Routledge, 1993.

Ermolaev, Herman. *Soviet Literary Theories 1917–1934: The Genesis of Soviet Socialist Realism*. University of California Publications in Modern Philology, vol. 69. Berkeley, CA: University of California Press, 1963.

Freedom House. "Freedom of the Press: Egypt, 2013." n.d.

Freund, Charles P. "Sonallah Ibrahim's Nostalgia for Failure." *The Daily Star Online*. November 20, 2003.

Friedman, Thomas L. "The Arab Quarter Century." *The New York Times*. April 10, 2013.

Grimm, Reinhold. "Alienation in Context: On the Theory and Practice of Brechtian Theatre." In *A Bertolt Brecht Reference Companion*, edited by Siegfried Mews. Westport, CT: Greenwood, 1997.

Hafez, Sabry. "The Egyptian Novel in the Sixties." *Journal of Arabic Literature* VII (1976): 68–84.

al-Hakim, Tawfiq. *'Usfur min al-sharq*. Cairo: Dar al-Ma'arif, 1974.

———. *Yawmiyat na ib fi-l-aryaf*. Cairo: Maktabat al-Adab, 1965.

Hanna, Tawfiq. Review of *Jumhuriyat Farahat*. *al-Adab* 4.3 (1956): 40.

Hassan, Abdalla F. "Black Humor in Dark Times." *World Press Review*. June 19, 2003.

Hussein, Taha. "al-Adab bayn al-itisal wa-l-infisal." *al-Katib al-Misri* 3.11 (1946): 373–88.

———. "al-Adib yaktub li-l-khassa." *al-Adab 3:5* (1955): 9–16.

———. *al-Ayyam*. Cairo: Dar al-Ma'arifa, 1945–47. Microfilm.

———. *al-Mu'adhdhabuna fi-l-ard*. Cairo: Dar al-Ma'arif, 1952.

———. "Fi-l-Adab al-Faransi: Jan Pul Satra wa-l-sinama." *al-Katib al-Misri* 7.26 (1947): 179–202.

———. "Mulahazat." *al-Katib al-Misri* 6.21 (1947): 9–21.

Ibrahim, Sonallah. *al-Lajna*. Cairo: Dar al-Mustaqbal al-'Arabi, 2004.

———. *Najmat Aghustus*. al-Minya, Egypt: Dar al-Huda li-l-Nashr wa-l-Tawzi', 2003.

———. "Tajribati al-riwa'iya." *al-Adab* 28.2–3 (1980): 100–103.

———. *Tilka al-ra'iha*. al-Minya, Egypt: Dar al-Huda li-l-Nashr wa-l-Tawzi', 2003.

Ibrahim, Sonallah, Kamal al-Qilsh, and Ra'uf Mus'ad. *Insan al-sadd al-'ali*. Cairo: Dar al-Kitab al-'Arabi li-l-Tiba'a wa-l-Nashr, 1967.

Idris, Suhayl. "Risalat al-Adab." *al-Adab* 1.1 (1953): 1–2.

Idris, Yusuf. "19502." *Uqtulha*. Cairo: Maktabat Misr, 1982. 55–62.

———. *al-'Askari al-aswad*. Cairo: Maktabat Misr, 1982.

———. "al-Aurta." In *Lughat al-ay ay*. Cairo: Mu'assat Roseal-Yusuf, 1965. 127–33.

———. "Alif al-ahrar." In *al-Mu'allafat al-kamila*, by Yusuf Idris, 407–31. Vol I. Cairo: 'Alam al-Kutub, 1971

———. "al-Khuda'." In *Bayt min lahm*, by Yusuf Idris, 91–97. Cairo: 'Alam al-Kutub, 1971.

———. "al-Martaba al-Muq'ara." In *al-Naddaha*, by Yusuf Idris, 70–71. Cairo: Dar al-Hilal, 1969.

———. "Al-Shaykh Shaykha." In *al-Mu'allafat al-kamila*, by Yusuf Idris, 390–405. Cairo: 'Alam al-Kutub, 1971.

———. "Jumhuriyat Farahat." In *Jumhuriyat Farahat*, by Yusuf Idris, 8–29. Cairo: Maktabat Misr, 1981.

———. "Laysat mujarrad qissa." Introduction to *Tilka al-ra'iha*, by Sonallah Ibrahim, 25–28. al-Minya, Egypt: Dar al-Huda li-l-Nashr wa-l-Tawzi', 2003.

———. "Mishwar." In *Arkhas layali*, by Yusuf Idris, 160–75. Cairo: Dar al-Katib al-'Arabi li-l-Tiba'a wa-l-Nashr, 1967.

———. "Yamut al-zammar." In *Uqtulha*, by Yusuf Idris, 19–51. Cairo: Maktabat Misr, 1982.

Isstaif, Abdul-Nabi. "Forging a New Self, Embracing the Other: Modern Arabic Critical Theory and the West—Louis 'Awad." *Arabic and Middle Eastern Literatures* 5.2 (2002): 161–80.

Jaggi, Maya. "Cairo Calling: Interview with Alaa Al Aswany." *The Guardian*. August 22, 2008.

Jakobson, Roman. *On Language*. Edited by Linda R. Waugh and Monique Monville-Burston. Cambridge, MA: Harvard University, 1990.

James, C. Vaughan. *Soviet Socialist Realism: Origins and Theory*. New York: St. Martin's Press, 1973.

Jayyusi, Salma al-Khadra. *Trends and Movements in Modern Arabic Poetry*. Vol. 2. Leiden: Brill, 1977.

Khuri, Ra'if. "al-Adib yaktub li-l-kaffa." *al-Adab* 3.5 (1955): 2–8.

Klemm, Verena. "Different Notions of Commitment (Iltizam) and Committed Literature (al-adab al-multazim) in the Literary Circles of the Mashriq." *Arabic and Middle Eastern Literatures* 3.1 (2000): 51–62.

Kostyal, Karen. "Alaa Al Aswany: Voice of Reason." *National Geographic*. September 2006.

Kurpershoek, P.M. *The Short Stories of Yusuf Idris: A Modern Egyptian Author*. Leiden: Brill, 1981.

Lindsey, Ursula. "A Voice of Dissent Joins the Nationalist Chorus." *Mada Masr*. October 6, 2013.

———. "Et Tu Sonallah?" *The Arabist*. August 25, 2013.

Long, Richard. *Tawfiq al-Hakim: Playwright of Egypt*. London: Ithaca, 1979.

Lukács, György. *Realism in Our Time: Literature and the Class Struggle*. Translated by John and Necke Mander. New York: Harper & Row, 1971.

———. *Writer and Critic and Other Essays*. Translated by Arthur D. Kahn. New York: Grosset and Dunlap, 1970.

al-Ma'addawi, Anwar. "al-Adab al-multazim." *al-Adab* 28.4–5 (1980): 41–44.

———. "al-Adab al-multazim." *al-Adab* 1.2 (1953): 12–15.

———. "Bidaya wa nihaya li-Naguib Mahfouz." *al-Risala* 19.939 (1951): 757–58.

———. "Zawaya wa laqatat." *al-Adab* 3.2 (1955): 9–11.

Mahfouz, Naguib. *Afrah al-qubba*. Cairo: Maktabat Misr, 1987.

———. *al-Karnak*. Cairo: Maktabat Misr, 1986.

———. *al-Liss wa-l-kilab*. Cairo: Maktabat Misr, n.d.

———. *al-Shahhadh*. Cairo: Maktabat Misr, 1982.

———. *Amam al-'arsh*. Cairo: Maktabat Misr, n.d.

———. *Atahaddathu ilaykum*. Beirut: Dar al-'Awda, 1977.

———. *Bidaya wa nihaya*. 14th edition. Cairo: Maktabat Misr, 1984.

———. *Tharthara fawq al-Nil*. Cairo: Maktabat Misr, n.d.

Mally, Lynn. *Culture of the Future: The Proletkult Movement in Revolutionary Russia*. Berkeley: University of California Press, 1990.

Masters, Brian. *Camus: A Study*. London: Heinemann, 1974.

McDermott, Anthony. *Egypt from Nasser to Mubarak: A Flawed Revolution*. London: Croom Helm, 1988.

Mehrez, Samia. *Egyptian Writers between History and Fiction*. Cairo: American University in Cairo Press, 1994.

———. *Egypt's Culture Wars: Politics and Practice*. London: Routledge, 2008.

Metcalf, Amanda. "The Founding of the Federation of Soviet Writers: The Forgotten Factor in Soviet Literature of the Late Twenties." *The Slavonic and East European Review* 65.4 (1987): 609–16.

Meyer, Stefan G. *The Experimental Arabic Novel: Postcolonial Literary Modernism in the Levant*. Albany: State University of New York, 2001.

Milson, Menahem. *Naguib Mahfouz: The Novelist–Philosopher of Cairo*. New York: St. Martin's Press, 1998.

Moosa, Matti. *The Early Novels of Naguib Mahfouz: Images of Modern Egypt*. Gainesville: University Press of Florida, 1984.

al-Muqdisi, Antun. "al-Muthaqaf al-'arabi wa-l-dimuqratiya." *al-Adab* 29.11–12 (1981): 12–29.

Musa, Salama. *The Education of Salama Musa*. Translated by L.O. Schuman. Leiden: Brill, 1961.

———. al-Adab lil-Sha'b. Cairo: Maktabat al-Anjilu al-Misriyya, 1956.

al-Nabawi, Maha. "Inside the Culture Ministry." *Mada Masr*. June 29, 2013.

al-Naqash, Rajaa'. *Fi hubb Naguib Mahfouz*. Cairo: Dar El Shorouk, 2006.

Parini, Jay. "Between Two Worlds." *The Guardian*. October 3, 2008.

Pike, David. *German Writers in Soviet Exile, 1933–1945*. Chapel Hill: University of North Carolina Press, 1982.

Podeh, Elie and Onn Winckler, eds. *Rethinking Nasserism: Revolution and Historical Memory in Modern Egypt*. Gainesville: University Press of Florida, 2004.

al-Qalamawi, Suhayr. "al-Adib al-'arabi wa mushkilat al-iltizam." *al-Adab* 20.1 (1972).

Qualey, M. Lynx. "Sonallah Ibrahim on the Stages of Revolution." *Arablit*. June 1, 2011.

———. "Sonallah Ibrahim: 'The Only Role of the Writer is to Entertain.'" *Arablit*. May 8, 2015.

Sabila, Muhammad. "al-Muthaqaf wa-l-Sulta." *al-Adab* 29.11–12 (1981): 29–34.

Sartre, Jean-Paul. "Orphee Noir." In *Anthologie de la Nouvelle Poesie Negre et Malgache*, edited by Leopold Sedar Senghor, ix–xliv. Paris: Presses Universitaires de France, 1969.

———. *What Is Literature?* Translated by Bernard Frechtman. New York: Harper Colophon, 1965.

Schull, Joseph. "The Ideological Origins of 'Stalinism' in Soviet Literature." *Slavic Review* 51.3 (1992): 468–84.

al-Sharqawi, Mahmud. *Salama Musa: al-mufakkir wa-l-insan*. Beirut: Dar al-'Ilm li-l-Millayin, 1965.

Stagh, Marina. *The Limits of Freedom of Speech: Prose Literature and Prose Writers in Egypt under Nasser and Sadat*. Stockholm: Almqvist & Wiksell, 1993.

Starkey, Paul. *From the Ivory Tower: A Critical Study of Tawfiq al-Hakim*. London: Ithaca, 1987.

Steavenson, Wendell. "Writing the Revolution." *The New Yorker* 87.44 (2012): 38–45.

Terras, Victor, ed. *Handbook of Russian Literature*. New Haven, CT: Yale University Press, 1985.

Tertz, Abram (Andrei Sinyavsky). *On Socialist Realism*. Translated by George Dennis. New York: Pantheon, 1960.

Twain, Mark. "Adventures of Huckleberry Finn." In *Anthology of American Literature II: Realism to the Present*, edited by George McMichael, et al., 297–517. New York: MacMillan, 1974.

Wahbi, Muhammad. "Adabuna al-multazim." *al-Adab* 2.8 (1954): 24–26.

Zhdanov, Andrei, et al. *Problems of Soviet Literature: Reports and Speeches at the First Soviet Writers' Congress*. New York: International Publishers, 1935.

Index